The biggest challenge in creating value with analytics is rarely the math—more often it's ensuring leaders are actively identifying and framing problems in the right ways, so that mathematical insights can be developed and leveraged for decision-making. In this book the authors provide practical advice to business leaders as they seek to fulfill their responsibilities in leading with analytics.

—Eric Huls
Chief Data Officer, Allstate

This book is a must-read for any leader trying to accelerate AI and analytics progress. Zettelmeyer and Anderson have turned common thinking on its head, creating a compelling case for why we as leaders need to lean in and engage. Easy-to-digest stories bring AI and analytics to life in a way that any leader can start asking more relevant questions immediately.

—Barbara Hulit
SVP, Fortiv

Leading with AI and Analytics presents a critical road map for business transformation, scaling evidence-based decision-making to deliver value. Eric and Florian make this road map actionable, with steps for leaders to take that impact their company's culture—including how people partner and how decisions are made.

—Chris Perry
Chief Innovation Officer, Weber Shandwick

These days, analytics and AI seem to be everywhere, except where they need to be—deployed consistently to make companies work better and improve their performance. This book stands out as really getting into the nitty-gritty of how business leaders can make their organizations think and breathe analytics and AI as natural, effective elements at all levels of their business. This is a very important and timely book that will resonate with any business leader who has ever struggled to improve business performance with analytics and AI.

—Matthew Denesuk
SVP Data Analytics & AI, Royal Caribbean Cruise Lines

Leading with AI and Analytics is a must-read for any CXO trying to compete on AI and data. I have personally seen Florian and Eric lead a CEO and his Top 10 executives through this data-driven, AI-powered journey at a Fortune 500 Company.

—Ketan Awalegaonkar
Global Head of AI & Data Strategy, Accenture

The authors are two of the top professors at Northwestern's Kellogg School of Management because they have the ability to demystify complex AI and analytics methods and make them immediately applicable to solving real-world business issues. I'll be recommending their new book far and wide to my business partners.

—Carter Cast
Venture Partner at the Pritzker Group and
former CEO of Walmart.com

LEADING
WITH AI AND
ANALYTICS

BUILD YOUR DATA
SCIENCE IQ TO DRIVE
BUSINESS VALUE

ERIC ANDERSON
FLORIAN ZETTELMEYER

**Mc
Graw
Hill**

New York Chicago San Francisco Athens London Madrid
Mexico City Milan New Delhi Singapore Sydney Toronto

1 2 3 4 5 6 7 8 9   LCR   25 24 23 22 21 20

ISBN   978-1-260-45914-2
MHID   1-260-45914-4

e-ISBN   978-1-260-45915-9
e-MHID   1-260-45915-2

Library of Congress Cataloging-in-Publication Data

Names: Anderson, Eric T., author. | Zettelmeyer, Florian, author.
Title: Leading with AI and analytics: build your data science IQ to drive business
    value / Eric Anderson and Florian Zettelmeyer.
Description: New York : McGraw Hill Education, [2020] | Includes bibliographical
    references and index.
Identifiers: LCCN 2020032369 (print) | LCCN 2020032370 (ebook) |
    ISBN 9781260459142 (hardback) | ISBN 9781260459159 (ebook)
Subjects: LCSH: Management—Statistical methods. | Decision making—Statistical
    methods. | Artificial intelligence. | Big data.
Classification: LCC HD30.215 .A54 2020 (print) | LCC HD30.215 (ebook) |
    DDC 658.4/033—dc23
LC record available at https://lccn.loc.gov/2020032369
LC ebook record available at https://lccn.loc.gov/2020032370

McGraw Hill books are available at special quantity discounts to use as premiums and sales promotions or for use in corporate training programs. To contact a representative, please visit the Contact Us pages at www.mhprofessional.com.

CONTENTS

SECTION 1
Introduction

SECTION 2
Consuming AI and Analytics

SECTION 3
Actively Participating in AI and Analytics

PREDICTIVE ANALYTICS

CAUSAL ANALYTICS

SECTION 4

Executing on AI and Analytics

SECTION 5

Success Stories with AIA

PREFACE

We want to begin by sharing our inspiration for writing this book.

The past five years have been an exciting time to be a data scientist, to say the least! More than 20 years ago, when we were both working on our PhDs at MIT, neither of us could have anticipated the incredible advances that have been made in data science and the types of data that power AI and analytics have made.

That trend alone represents a sea change worth documenting and discussing in a book. But we are not just data scientists. We are also business school professors who regularly teach senior executives, consult with companies across sectors, and engage in other in-depth interactions with organizations and individuals navigating the business domain. As a result, we have had a front-row seat to the rapid evolution of data science, while also witnessing hundreds of real-life examples of applications of AI and analytics by firms and the executives who lead them.

That experience has been both inspiring and sobering for us. On one hand, it's exciting to see how many new analytics techniques and tools are at business leaders' disposal. On the other, we've observed that many firms we work with have struggled to consistently add business value using AI and analytics, often investing large resources in such efforts with little return. The reason, we've come to understand, is that the data science is way ahead of firms' business practices. For example, every executive gets that it's important to understand a balance sheet. Nonetheless, many executives punt on knowing even the basics of data science, believing this is an area reserved for technical experts alone. Similarly, planning—a daily activity in business—is often not extended to AI and analytics. Nor is there a systematic process for finding business problems where AI and analytics could add value. The list goes on.

We wrote this book to address that costly disconnect between data science and business—to close the gap in business practices needed to make AI and analytics (AIA) successful. This is not a book about data science. This is a book about what you, as a leader, need to do to make the data science work for your business, and to reap the many rewards of doing that successfully.

WHAT'S IN THE BOOK

The book is laid out so that each section builds on your understanding of AIA in an organizational context, to help you increase your data science intuition quotient (DSIQ). The sections presented are as follows:

- *Section 1: Introduction:* In Chapter 1 we explain why your role as a leader is critical for the success of AI and analytics. In Chapter 2 we present our go-to analytics framework for taking a comprehensive approach to AIA in your organization: the AIA Framework.
- *Section 2: Consuming AI and Analytics:* Before you are ready to take an active role in AI and analytics, we want to give you some pointers on how to be an educated consumer of AIA. In Chapter 3, we present a systematic way to understand what is going on with your data. In Chapter 4, we focus on how to distinguish good from bad analytics.
- *Section 3: Actively Participating in AI and Analytics:* This section includes three subsections. The first, "Predictive Analytics," contains two chapters (Chapters 5 and 6) that illuminate the inner workings of proven AIA predictive techniques—including regression and machine learning—and help you understand how to assess the quality of a predictive model and move from prediction to profit. The second subsection, "Causal Analytics" (Chapters 7, 8, and 9), covers how to design data using experimental and quasi-experimental approaches, and how to work with data that you have on hand or that you collect during business as

usual (opportunistic data). The third subsection, "Making Decisions" (Chapter 10), explains how to use AIA to optimize and scale your decisions.

- *Section 4: Executing on AI and Analytics:* In this section we turn to your role as a leader who wants to create business value. Chapter 11 helps you identify, prioritize, and plan for AIA opportunities in your business. Next, we turn to your role in transforming the organization to adapt and change so that these projects can succeed. Chapter 12 teaches you to identify barriers within your existing organization. Last, in Chapter 13 we provide our advice on how you can lead the organizational changes needed in people, data and systems, culture, and structure to support AIA.
- *Section 5: Success Stories with AIA:* We wrap up the book with real-life stories of five companies that have harnessed analytics effectively to create value.

A WORD ABOUT OUR EXAMPLES

Few things are as boring as reading about a data science technique without an example to illustrate it. Because of that, we make extensive use of examples and stories to bring the concepts to life.

We will use three kinds of examples. First are *real examples.* You will read some of these right off the bat in Chapter 1, including the Moneyball and Harrah's stories. In some cases we can reveal the names of the company and/or individuals involved; in others, we make the real example anonymous by omitting or changing the company name, the names of actors, or the industry setting, while staying as true as possible to the real story—the North American cable company in Chapter 1 is one such example.

Second are *narrative* examples, or what we think of as "historical fiction," where we combine several different businesses or characters into one and modify events to create a more streamlined and compelling narrative. These examples are inspired by real events but ultimately represent a composite of anecdotes from multiple sources woven into a narrative set in a fictitious business context. The car ad in Chapter 1 is an example of this. The meeting and presentation really happened, and one of us was really there, but we changed the exact numbers on the figure (while preserving their meaning) and paraphrased the comments of multiple participants by inventing the story's protagonist and putting the participants' comments into her voice.

Third are *hypothetical* examples. The ultrasound example in Chapter 1 is of this type. We constructed these examples fully from scratch to illustrate key concepts. Throughout the book we will call out narrative examples and hypothetical examples. For instance, if we start an example with "Imagine," "Suppose," "Say," or "Let's assume," it indicates that you're about to read a hypothetical example.

We know you're eager to boost your DSIQ, and we are looking forward to guiding you on that journey in the chapters ahead. Let's get started!

Introduction

n this first section of the book we'll discuss why AI and analytics are a leadership problem. They are not just a problem for leaders of AI and analytics groups, or data scientists, or the head of IT, or the CEO. AI and analytics are *your* problem; in fact, they are every business leader's problem. Chapter 1 illustrates the reason for this: the most difficult decisions your organization must make to create value with AI and analytics are those in the domain of business leaders, rather than of data scientists or technologists. But what makes you good at these decisions? A working knowledge of data science, or a high data science intuition quotient (DSIQ). In Chapter 2 we will help you increase your DSIQ by presenting our AIA Framework: a go-to framework for taking a comprehensive approach to AI and analytics in your organization.

CHAPTER 1

AI AND ANALYTICS ARE A LEADERSHIP PROBLEM

"What's the best AI and analytics strategy for us?"

"How do we start using data, analytics, and AI to drive business value like the industry leaders we read about?"

These are the kinds of questions C- and VP-level executives ask during our analytics workshops. Like most leaders across sectors, these executives are highly committed and capable. But they struggle with AI and analytics—which we will refer to as "AIA" throughout the book. Despite the wealth of data out there today, organizations of every type find it difficult to transform data-driven insights into profit. A recent survey of nearly 400 chief marketing officers conducted by the American Marketing Association and Fuqua School of Business showed that barely a third of available data is used to drive decision-making in businesses. Some of the barriers include a lack of processes or tools to measure success through analytics and an insufficient presence of talent to bridge analytics to marketing practices.[1] In fact, an estimated 85 percent of big data business initiatives fail.[2] Similarly, many if not most businesses are missing out on opportunities to drive greater value with AI.[3] This is even more alarming because AI and analytics are not just passing fads. The availability of unprecedented amounts of data and technology-enabled tools for analyzing it has fundamentally changed the way decisions are made in organizations across sectors. Data-driven decision-making is real, and here to stay.

We've written this book for every leader within any organization who wants to move from best-guess or even misinformed decision-making to truly evidence-based decisions. Specifically, we want to provide you with a road map to better decisions. This book is for CEOs or executive directors who want to make the right high-stakes decisions and invest in supporting AIA organization-wide; for business unit or division leaders who want to drive results through specific AIA initiatives; and for rising leaders who want to craft strategies and tactics to create real impact.

Fortunately, there is a path for any leader who wants to gain capability and confidence with AI and analytics. And the first step is to accept this book's most basic premise: AI and analytics are a leadership problem. That means AI and analytics are not just the domain of data scientists or specific departments, including those with "Data," "Analytics," or "AI" in their title, but also the responsibility of the highest-level leaders, those in C-suite and VP-level roles or their equivalent. Too many leaders still struggle with this idea. But if you agree with it—and hopefully you do, or are at least open to considering it, since you're reading this book—then the natural question becomes: "How can I understand and drive AI and analytics most effectively?" After all, most leaders aren't data analysis experts. You probably have solid analytical skills and capabilities that helped you advance to a leadership role in the first place, but no one's going to mistake you for a data scientist anytime soon.

The good news is that to use AIA effectively in your organization, you don't need deep expertise in data science. But you do need a *working knowledge* of data science, a capability that can be powered by something you likely already have in abundance: critical thinking skills. This working knowledge is called a data science intuition quotient, or DSIQ. Note that we purposely use "intuition" rather than "intelligence," to emphasize that it's about having a feel for what constitutes good AI and analytics, rather than some innate ability to create and recognize effective analytical approaches.

A high DSIQ enables you to do three critical things:

- Identify what good analytics looks like (and doesn't look like)
- Understand where AIA can add value in your organization
- Lead AIA-driven business initiatives with greater skill and confidence

Boosting your DSIQ is the first step. It will help you catalyze similar growth in your organization—namely, to take the specific steps and make the specific investments required to build more powerful AI and analytics muscle. Through our training and consultation sessions with business executives, we have seen firsthand how improved DSIQ can greatly benefit an organization.

MONEYBALL: THE REAL STORY

To illustrate the intimate relationship between leadership and AI and analytics, we're going to share our take on the well-known "Moneyball" narrative of a Major League Baseball team's analytics-driven turnaround.

"Moneyball," a concept popularized by Michael Lewis in his book of the same name, has become shorthand for applying statistical analytical techniques to data to develop sports strategy, especially to optimize scouting and recruiting new players or making trades. This is a major departure from the traditional reliance on scouts' and managers' intuition.

In his book Lewis shares the story of the data-fueled rise of the Oakland Athletics (A's) baseball team early in the new millennium.[4] But few people realize the real meaning of the Moneyball story. While the application of analytics has always taken center stage in this narrative and those like it, the real "star" and force for change is something much simpler.

We'll get there momentarily; but first let's take a look at the story's original context.

Billy Beane was the general manager of the Oakland A's at the turn of this past century. He'd started his professional baseball career as a player, traded among several teams (including the A's), spending stints in the minor league, never meeting scouts' original expectations. Things changed when he voluntarily transitioned from the A's players roster to the scouting organization in 1990. As a scout, Beane demonstrated talent for identifying high-potential players, ultimately rising in 1997 to the general manager role, a top leadership role in baseball organizations.

Unlike most sports, recruiting for baseball happens not at the college level but with focus on high school players. So most professional baseball organizations maintain extensive scouting arms, visiting high schools nationwide to recruit talent. Traditionally, players were recruited for their strengths with standard skills such as hitting, fielding, and baserunning.

Of course, money was a major factor in recruiting success. But in the late 1990s, when Beane took the reins, the A's had very little of it: a $40 million recruiting budget compared to American League rival New York Yankees, who spent about three times that amount. Beane had to think differently—and did. In 1999 he recruited a new assistant named Paul DePodesta, a young Harvard economics major who'd proven himself with the Cleveland Indians. DePodesta helped Beane overhaul the team's recruiting approach. Instead of seeking out traditional skills, they targeted recruits based on other factors: specifically, the statistics most likely to contribute to scoring runs, which drives baseball wins. Conventional wisdom was that metrics like batting average and runs batted in (RBIs) led to wins, and nearly every team in baseball paid attention to them. The big "aha!" from the analytics was that on-base percentage (OBP, the proportion of times a batter reaches base) and slugging percentage (number of total bases divided by number of at-bats) were also drivers of success. Because traditional recruiting didn't pay a premium for these metrics—focusing instead on overall batting average, for example—Beane was able to create an "arbitrage" opportunity by affordably recruiting players who struggled with sought-after stats but outpaced others on metrics uncovered by the analytics.

As the A's roster included more and more "analytically recruited" players, the team's win rate rose: the A's reached the playoffs every year from 2000 to 2003, winning 20 consecutive games in 2002. In 2006 the team advanced to the American League Championship Series, just one step short of the World Series. That season, the

A's were twenty-fourth of all 30 major league teams for payroll, but finished with the fifth-best regular-season record, highlighting the cost-effectiveness of Beane's analytical approach.

Not surprisingly, other baseball teams adopted a similar approach, seeking out players with off-the-radar stats that translated into more runs. Results came quickly. For example, Theo Epstein, who had worked with DePodesta, used a Moneyball approach as general manager of the Boston Red Sox and as president of baseball operations for the Chicago Cubs, leading both teams to win the World Series in 2004 and 2016, respectively. The Red Sox hadn't done that in 86 years (and they did it again three years later), the Cubs in a world-famous 108 years!

We can trace these headline-making successes back to the Oakland A's team Billy Beane helmed in 2002. The Moneyball story is baseball's *analytics moment*, a truly revolutionary development that quickly rippled out to other arenas, changing the strategies and tactics for other sports, leagues, and teams to be much more driven by data and analytics. All major sports teams today now use analytics for decision-making (at the time that this book was being written, Paul DePodesta was the chief strategy officer for the beleaguered Cleveland Browns football team, for example).

But why did this specific revolutionary moment for analytics in sports arrive around 2002? Why for the A's specifically? What was the catalyst for it, the driving engine?

The way most people think of the story, the most powerful pistons in that engine were data and analytics; Beane and his front-office team were able to apply the latter to the former to identify and recruit valuable players teams with much more money overlooked. That leads people to believe it was most likely some combination of new data, innovative statistical methods or computational capabilities, and more skilled talent that drove baseball's analytics moment.

Let's consider each of those explanations.

First, consider baseball data. Did the turn of the millennium mark a revolution in the availability of new, better data in the sport? Not by any stretch. Such numbers had been available since the late 1800s, in part because of managers' and fans' obsessions with sports data.[5] In fact, it's safe to say that data about batting and pitching in a Yankees–versus–Red Sox game goes just as far back as historical weather data about the East Coast.

So if it wasn't about new data, was it the case that Beane and his ilk took advantage of new statistical methods or higher-powered computing to coax new insights out of old data? No and no. Most of the analytical approaches in question were based on regression, a longstanding statistical approach used to predict one variable (such as runs scored) on the basis of others (OPB and slugging percentage). Similarly, the analyses didn't require particularly high-powered computing; a standard desktop computer would've sufficed.

Maybe, then, it was about statistical talent. Did the application of an analytical approach to the A's recruiting require new statistical talent—people with revolutionary approaches to recruiting analysis? You can probably guess the answer here. Nope. Bill James, a legend in baseball statistics, coined the term "sabermetrics" (from SABR, the Society for American Baseball Research) for the systematic application of analytics to baseball statistics as early as 1971. He had advocated for the importance of statistics like OBP long before Billy Beane became the A's GM.

If none of those factors could explain the timing of baseball's analytics moment, we have a puzzle. In fact, it's the same conundrum so many organizations face today. They have volumes of data, a wide range of powerful statistical methods (including those powered by machine learning) and computational capabilities (like those based in cloud computing), and ample statistical talent (data scientists).

But something still prevents them from using AI and analytics for effective decision-making.

That something is *leadership*.

The best explanation for why baseball's analytics moment came specifically in 2002 and specifically for the Oakland A's is Billy Beane himself—the general manager who'd gone from failed player to movie-worthy baseball executive by leading in a revolutionary way, one that staked the future of a floundering team on the unconventional application of analytics. Beane's appreciation for and belief in the power of analytics, combined with the need to do something drastic to improve his team, motivated him to create a management approach and structure rooted firmly in analytics. The data, techniques, and tools he used weren't new; but his leadership approach was.

Moneyball is an analytics moment that changed the course of a baseball team, a league, and an industry. But what makes this moment special isn't about data, statistics, or computing power. It's about leadership. As we've suggested, all the necessary ingredients for success with analytics were in place well before 2002. The same exact story could have emerged in 1997, or even 1992. But Moneyball happened in 2002 because that's the year a leader named Billy Beane decided to step up and fundamentally change how his organization made decisions.

That's the real story behind Moneyball, a narrative that demonstrates that analytics is ultimately a leadership problem—and shows how a single leader with the right mindset can drive an analytics revolution in a given organization or industry.

WHY ANALYTICS AND AI ARE EVERY LEADER'S PROBLEM

AI and analytics are not just C-suite issues. They are *every* leader's problem. Leaders are responsible for planning, budgeting, and accountability. Leaders create organizational culture and structure. And ultimately, leaders need to "make the call" on tough decisions. Leaders who want to succeed with AIA recognize that these decisions are the domain of managers, not data scientists. Below we consider several reasons why AI and analytics are every leader's problem.

Analytics and AI Require Managerial Judgment

Leaders are increasingly required to make high-stakes decisions and judgment calls based on data rather than just intuition. But making the right call can be difficult—even for seasoned senior executives.

To illustrate this point, here's an example from our experience at a thought leadership retreat held by a major company providing digital services to manufacturers in the automobile industry and other sectors (to preserve confidentiality we have disguised and modified details of this story). Each participant was asked to share thoughts about what might change the future of the digital ad industry. One senior executive was animated as he began a presentation on a recent analytics initiative. "We've finally been able to close the loop between digital ads and offline sales!" he said.

Finding definitive associations between digital ads and sales in the auto industry is no small feat, in part because most products in the sector are sold through independent dealers, which have little obligation to share data fully with manufacturers. By bringing some of both manufacturers and dealers on board, they were able to track when people viewed or clicked on car ads and then use cookie information from an online post-sale survey to determine whether someone who'd been exposed to the advertising actually bought a car.

Figure 1.1   Digital Car Ad Sales Conversion Rate

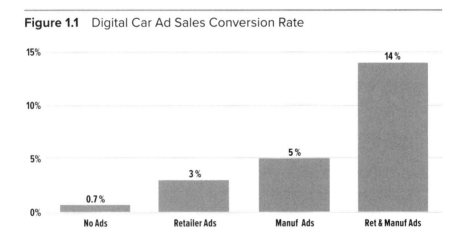

As the graph in Figure 1.1 shows, without exposure to digital ads, the conversion rate (the probability of purchasing a car) over a 90-day window was less than 1 percent. That proportion skyrocketed to 14 percent if a person saw both retailer and manufacturer ads online. The executive and his team concluded not only that the ads were extremely effective but also that retailer and manufacturer ads were complements instead of substitutes (14 percent is more than the sum of 3 percent and 5 percent). Most of the executive-level audience agreed. "We need to put out a press release about this ASAP!" one of the executives suggested.

The sales conversion figures the executive presented in the graph appeared to be evidence that advertisements helped car sales. For several minutes, the audience debated how best to monetize the firm's newfound capability to measure digital advertising effectiveness. Until one of the participants, let's call her Alice, spoke up: "Hold on," Alice said and pointed at the leftmost column, where consumers had received no ads. "Why would someone not see any product-related ads?" The answer, of course, is that these people did not search for a car on the search engine. Then, pointing to the rightmost column, Alice asked, "And why would someone see ads from both retailers and manufacturers in our industry?" Another executive replied, "I suppose because those consumers searched for a type of car and perhaps a location, which then triggered keywords that both manufacturers and dealers bid for."

Alice put the pieces together: "So what we have shown is that if you are not interested in a car you don't buy a car, and if you're very interested in buying a car you do buy one!" Slowly the team understood the implication: because retailer and manufacturer ads were targeted to people already more likely to buy a car, the relationship between ad exposure and purchase said nothing about ad effectiveness. Consumers may have purchased because of the ads, but it is also possible that they bought simply because they were already interested in buying a car. The data in hand cannot disentangle these two effects.

Most of the seasoned, high-level executives on the retreat failed to see how the data presented violated one of the most basic premises of a true experiment: random assignment to conditions. They could easily have gone down the path of launching a press release and touting their new finding, only to discover later that their interpretation of the results was deeply flawed. The executives in this example are far from alone. We see examples of flawed interpretation like this with nearly every group of managers we meet. When presented with convincing-looking data, our natural instinct is to believe it. It's human nature.

What's critical to remember is that the data in the advertising example above and in most other analytics cases is actually truthful.

In the ad example, the data does tell us what happened but doesn't tell managers what to do next. When things go amiss, it's not the fault of the data *per se*, but rather an error caused when a manager or group of managers offer or believe a (mis)interpretation of the data in question. That's what happened at that weekend retreat.

That's why working with AI and analytics requires *sound managerial judgment*; and that judgment must be based on a working knowledge of data science, or a strong DSIQ.

Data Can Create the Illusion of Insight

Imagine that you're the CFO of a major hospital, and your analytics dashboard has just lit up with key data you've been waiting for: real-time sensor data for a new ultrasound machine model you've agreed to pilot. The new machines came out earlier this year, and the legacy ones your hospital uses are approaching seven years of age—or near the end of their life expectancy.[6]

The new machines represent a sizable investment for your hospital. But, the manufacturer touts the machine's faster exam-completion times, which would justify the large capital outlay. Instead of just believing the sales pitch, you want confirmation of the new machines' performance benefits. So, you asked the manufacturer to place new ultrasound machines next to older machines and benchmark the decrease in exam times during one month.

The data comes in, and you're so glad you waited: contrary to expectations, technicians using the new, more expensive machines are actually taking *longer* to complete ultrasounds tests than techs working on the older machines (Figure 1.2). You quickly decide to hold off on the investment, confident you've saved the hospital from a significant loss.

It turns out you've just made the wrong call.

While the dashboard data for the ultrasounds was truthful—as in the earlier advertising example—it didn't tell the whole story, leading to a misguided decision with potentially greater long-term costs. The problem, again, isn't with the data but with the managers and others interpreting it. Executives routinely have data pushed their way,

Figure 1.2   Ultrasound Test Times: 2013 Versus 2020 Model

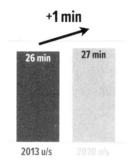

through dashboards and other means, and have to interpret what they see for decision-making; a high DSIQ is critical to do that effectively.

So why was the CFO's decision about the ultrasound machines a mistake? What was the whole story behind the data?

First, the data presented didn't lie: it was indeed true that the *overall* average time for ultrasound exams was longer on the new machines than on the old ones. But when the data was broken down by experience level of the technicians using the machines, both novice and experienced techs were faster with exams on the new machines than on the old ones: an average of nine minutes and six minutes faster, respectively, as shown in Figure 1.3. How could that be, when the overall average exam time was slower for the new machines?

Figure 1.3   Ultrasound Test Times by Technician Type

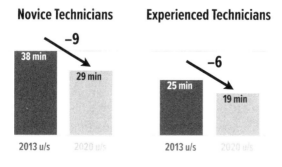

The explanation, as it turned out, was simple: the novice techs tended to use the newer machines, whereas their more senior counterparts favored the legacy equipment, as they had much more experience with it. Experienced technicians complete exams significantly faster than new ones, even when using older machines. So the speed comparison that had resulted in unfavorable times for the new ultrasounds was based on the difference in experience levels between types of technician (novice versus experienced), not types of machine (new versus old). After we hold experience constant, we clearly see the benefit of the new ultrasound machines. But the overall average masks this result.

Now, here's the interesting part of the story. An experienced data scientist looking at this data would have produced the correct result. But in today's market, managers are inundated with vast amounts of data in dashboards. Moreover, managers may not have the data science training or instinct to "drill into the data" and find the correct answer. Instrumentation-based data often creates the *illusion* of insight, as this ultrasound example suggests. For even simple tools like dashboards to be effectively deployed, managers need a high DSIQ.

Analytics and AI Require Structure, Process, and Incentive Changes

Imagine a 63-year-old grandmother named Evelyn. Evelyn is a retired schoolteacher from West Orange, New Jersey. She enjoys gardening, knitting, sudoku puzzles, and gambling—especially $5 slots and Keno. She gambles close to home in Atlantic City. She goes on gambling trips with a group of fellow retired teachers to places like Branson, Missouri. And she especially enjoys pulling the slot-machine handles while sipping mai tais in Las Vegas, where her husband often travels for trade shows. While careful not to overspend, Evelyn budgets a significant percentage of her entertainment dollars to gambling.

Evelyn is what would be considered a "cross-market gambler"—one who frequents multiple casinos in different regions of the country. In the late 1990s, Harrah's realized that was the exact type of customer the casino needed to target. The strategy management developed to do that, as described in the following real example, illustrates the high-stakes relationship among analytics, structure, process, and incentives—which leaders need to understand and harness for better results.

Harrah's was down on its luck in the late 1990s. The well-known casino chain held properties in destination markets like Las Vegas, but it also operated many properties in smaller cities throughout the United States. The business played on a competitive landscape that had grown increasingly grim. About 10 years earlier, rising casino mogul Steve Wynn had spent more than $600 million to build the Polynesian-themed Mirage Resort and Casino—including the hugely successful Siegfried & Roy spectacle with white lions and tigers. Other themed resorts catering to gamblers and families alike popped up quickly on the Strip in the early and mid-1990s, including the MGM Grand, Treasure Island, and Luxor, among others.

While gambling represented more than 50 percent of casino revenue at the time, this revenue stream had stalled by the late 1990s, and the real growth opportunity was in room revenue. But the investment required to compete on properties was massive, with no margin for bad bets. In this challenging environment, Harrah's had to find the right path to growth, taking advantage of its well-established national footprint.

Harrah's market research at the time—including extensive customer interviews—showed that the core Vegas gambling crowd wasn't really its target segment. Specifically, much of the gambling that happened in Sin City tended to stay there—the typical Vegas gambler didn't gamble much elsewhere. But those pulling the handles and placing poker bets at Harrah's were more likely to be cross-market players like Keno-crazy Evelyn, for whom gaming was part of a regular entertainment portfolio. Like Evelyn, they gambled in Vegas, other Nevada cities like Reno, casinos near their home cities, and other locations, enjoying such activities year-round. Even though Harrah's had good geographic coverage to attract cross-market players, the chain pulled in only 36 percent of this segment's spending in 1998.

Out of this preliminary analysis, Harrah's leadership developed a growth strategy with three key elements:

- Identify the segment of cross-market players
- Find the most profitable customers in this group—like Evelyn
- Provide effective incentives for high-value cross-market players to gamble at Harrah's

On paper, the strategy seemed like a good bet. Free stays, gambling chips, and lobster dinners could go a long way toward building loyalty. There was just one problem, and it was a big one: Each Harrah's casino was run as an autonomous business with its own P&L and reward program. As a result, property managers were territorial about their customers (considering them *my* customers, not the organization's), and rewards didn't transfer across casinos; the rewards earned in Reno, for example, had to be redeemed in Reno. Harrah's COO at the time characterized the setup as one of "feudal lords" running their own separate fiefdoms.[7]

Maintaining business as usual clearly wouldn't have driven the growth Harrah's needed. Nor would having the marketing organization simply roll out a new cross-market rewards program; it would have been an immediate failure due to structural and incentives issues. Instead, leadership shifted their overall strategy to focus on the *customer* as the key source of value, rather than the property. First they developed a new organizational structure in which property managers reported to the COO rather than the CEO, to emphasize that Harrah's customers belong to the company and not to each casino. Working closely with IT, business leaders created an integrated behavior-tracking system to generate key customer data to support a new "total rewards" loyalty program good across all properties with a single membership card; and they used predictive analytics to forecast customer value and test, refine, and implement reward-program incentives.

Now Harrah's was armed with the right structure, systems, and data to answer questions about what made the most valuable customers, whether related to win-loss patterns on the slot machines, time spent at poker tables, number of nights stayed, or many other factors. Leadership used the answers to design new loyalty incentives. For example, the business found that people who'd started their gaming career with Harrah's were much more likely to become customers with high lifetime value; so the casino offered such individuals large incentives, even if they hadn't spent much early on, to cement their loyalty.

The strategy helped Harrah's hit a business jackpot: that 36 percent share of cross-market spending in 1998 increased to 42 percent in 2001,[8] representing hundreds of millions of dollars in new profits. Today, the business uses even more sophisticated real-time, data-driven models to drive and maintain share, revenues, and profit. For example, the system can alert casino managers to dispatch their staff to offer drinks or other freebies to a high-potential customer frustrated by a losing spell. Such advancements made Harrah's a major success story in the gaming domain.

We have told this story to numerous audiences through the years, and the challenges Harrah's faced in 1998 still resonate with managers more than 20 years later. Siloed organizations with nonintegrated data and IT infrastructure are pervasive on the business landscape. Making the analytics-based strategy work at Harrah's required literally restructuring the company and overhauling its approach to attracting, developing, and retaining customers. In other words, the analytics itself was not the major hurdle—instead, it was organizing the company strategically so that analytics could succeed. As you will discover, data science has a nasty habit of not respecting organizational boundaries. For AIA to succeed, leaders need a working knowledge of data science so they can make the proper investments in organizational structure and integrated data and systems.

Analytics Must Be Problem-Driven— and Planned Up Front

"There's got to be *something* in the data to help us drive growth," the executives we train often say. They're talking about feeling optimistic but overwhelmed about the massive datasets their organizations have created, including sales and customer information, reporting figures, compliance data, and many others. "Not necessarily," we reply. In fact, they're thinking about the issue the wrong way: rather than seeing data as the source or starting point for strategic insights, they need to start with a *problem*. That approach will yield better insights while reducing stress.

Consider an anonymized real example. A major North American cable company recently brought in a new CEO to take a much more analytical approach to strategic issues, the largest of which is the trend toward "cord-cutting"—more and more consumers choosing streaming video through multiple available platforms over subscriptions to cable or satellite TV, eroding revenues. The CEO generated a list of 50 key questions the business had to be able to answer about customers to help formulate optimal strategy and tactics. An example query: What proportion of customers who bundled TV, phone, and Internet services tended to drop their subscriptions after the deeply discounted promotional price expired, converted to paying full price (the ideal outcome), negotiated an extension on the discount, moved to just one or two services, or quit altogether? Such information would help shape approaches to increasing profitability for key customer segments.

The problem was that the cable company's systems prevented answering the majority of these questions—only 14 of the 50 were initially answerable! Specifically, the business used a variety of different billing systems, so there was no easy, consistent way to track customer behavior across platforms and time. This despite the fact that the company had just invested $250 million overhauling IT to enable better analytics-based decision-making. However, integrating the billing systems had not made it into that investment. The leadership team knew they had to integrate the systems, but it didn't seem sufficiently important to include in that initial outlay. The problem illustrates the challenge of putting IT and data investments ahead of a strategic problem to solve, the proverbial buggy before the horse. The legacy billing systems generated a great deal of data, but not the type needed to answer key executive-level questions. If the business had started with cord-cutting as a strategic problem to solve, it could have made infrastructure and other investments to secure the right data to resolve it.

Again, executive leaders—not data scientists or technology specialists—need to frame and own the strategic problems that drive the direction and implementation of data analytics. So it follows that executives should be the ones to guide optimal *planning* of analytics as well. In this context, think about attention-getting ad campaigns, specifically the types showcased in *Mad Men*, the AMC TV series built around Sterling Cooper, a fictional advertising agency from the mid-twentieth century. While fans, and presumably consumers, loved the advertising campaigns the firm delivered—especially the Kodak, Lucky Strike, and other pitches that emerged from the creative mind of central character Don Draper (played by Jon Hamm)—where were the analytics to show the ads actually worked?

In many real-world cases, with advertising as a prime example, analytics is a literal afterthought: unplanned and implemented after the fact. Digital ads are seen as the holy grail of advertising data, with exposure, clicks, and purchase data all linked at the individual level. But having lots of detailed data still doesn't enable us to determine easily whether a given advertisement on Google, Bing, or other platforms actually worked.

So, what's new here? Isn't every business already engaged in some form of planning?

Yes, every company plans for business execution. This includes crafting a detailed plan with business goals and financial targets. Even Don Draper clearly created such plans back in the 1960s. But what's missing is an *AIA business plan* to prove, using data and models, that the new initiative worked. The challenge is that the AIA business plan must be defined *before* a new idea is launched. When this happens, analytics suddenly becomes both much more feasible and easier.

In summary, in 1960, success was declared with a handshake in the boardroom, and there was a minimal analytics plan, if any. Today, the best companies plan for AI and analytics with the same rigor they apply to business execution. Leaders need to step forward to make this transformation, so that AIA is seen as a ground-floor priority.

YOU NEED A WORKING KNOWLEDGE OF DATA SCIENCE (HIGH DSIQ)

So how can you take on these interrelated roles most effectively?

By gaining a working knowledge of data science, or high DSIQ, as we discussed at the beginning of this chapter. It's not about becoming a data science expert, but about having sufficient understanding of this domain to know what's going on at a very basic level. When you achieve that level of DSIQ, if you don't know what's going on, it won't be your fault but that of your analytics or technology experts.

As we noted earlier in the chapter, having a working knowledge of data science enables you to:

- *Judge what good analytics look like*, so you can "analyze" analytics presented to you more effectively and guide the AI and analytics elements of strategies better.
- *Identify where AIA adds value*, bridging the often-large gulf between the businesspeople who own executive-level problems and the data/technology people who are expected to provide information and tools to resolve those challenges but lack deep industry experience; this will enable you to make the right investments in analytics organization-wide, placing the best bets.
- *Lead with greater overall confidence* because you know how to do the two things above.

The good news is that you don't need a PhD in data science or mathematics to have a strong working knowledge of data analytics. In fact, the leaders we admire most are able to look at key charts or other analytical output for just a few minutes and ask the exact right questions to understand whether the relationships presented are valid—without knowing anything about the actual math behind the analyses!

So ultimately it's about applying the *critical thinking* skills you already have to a new domain: AI and analytics. We'll help you gain a high DSIQ, like the many leaders we've trained, by offering a framework, tools, tips, and encouragement throughout this book.

Our goal, in fact, is to position you to have your own "Billy Beane moment"—harnessing AI and analytics much more effectively to help your organization drive unprecedented results.

CHAPTER 2

A FRAMEWORK FOR AI AND ANALYTICS SUCCESS

To succeed with AI and analytics (AIA), organizations need to adapt. Of course, analytics requires integrated data, data scientists, and IT systems. But that's not enough. You also need a shared understanding of AIA and a formal process for tackling projects. Without these, large investments are unlikely to pay off. To help you overcome this challenge, this chapter introduces our AIA Framework.

HOW AI AND ANALYTICS ARE RELATED

AI, or artificial intelligence, is a field that has been around for decades. Today AI is an extremely hot topic. But this has not always been the case. In fact, for years many considered AI a somewhat dormant field, isolated to the hallowed halls of academia. Boy, has that changed!

So what is AI? In 1956 John McCarthy, a mathematician at Dartmouth College, coined the term "artificial intelligence" based on the "conjecture that every aspect of learning or any other feature of intelligence can in principle be so precisely described that a machine can be made to simulate it."[1] Or as our colleague Kris Hammond, a Northwestern University computer science professor, likes to say, "AI are systems that perform actions that, if performed by humans, would be considered intelligent." Notice that this definition is very much rooted in time: suppose you handed someone a modern iPhone in 1956. Would they think that the calendaring functions on the iPhone are actions that, if performed by humans, would be considered intelligent? They might very well think that, although today we simply consider those functions as "things that phones do." In contrast, the face-recognition function in the iPhone passes as AI today. In some sense, once a system is no longer "magical," we stop thinking of it as AI![2]

So what is AI trying to imitate? What do we consider to be "intelligent" in humans? We think it all boils down to *knowledge*. For example, consider two pieces of knowledge: (1) "rain makes things wet" and (2) "umbrellas block rain." These allow you to make an inference—"If I go out into the rain, my clothes will get wet." Once you have made inferences, you can solve problems—"How do I prevent myself from getting wet? By using an umbrella!" This process enables you to make decisions such as "I will buy an umbrella." Finally, we also think of planning as a sign of intelligence—"When the weather forecast suggests rain, I should walk out with my umbrella." But how do you get the knowledge in the first place? This is the role of learning, and to learn we need to interface with the world. We learn from understanding language, from reading, and from sensing and observing reactions to what we say, do, write, or control.

We present these ideas here in detail because the ambition of AI is to be intelligent in exactly the same way: to take in the world with what we tell machines or what they sense; to learn in order to create knowledge and then make inferences that enable the machine to solve problems, make decisions, and plan ahead; and finally, to either tell us what to do, or to directly control other machines or robots. The only difference is that we explicitly think about the interaction of machines with the world as creating data. Data, in turn, is the fuel that allows AI to learn and create knowledge!

So this is the general idea of AI. Now remember that AI has been around for 60 or 70 years. If it's such an old field, why the buzz now? To appreciate the craze today, you need to know that the original idea of AI was to *directly encode* knowledge. Think of this as crafting rules, like if-then-else statements, and a protocol for using these rules that would be specified by AI researchers. For example, suppose you wanted an AI system to help someone named Arvind book a flight.

ARVIND: "I would like to fly to Chicago tomorrow."
AI: "Where are you flying from?"
ARVIND: "From Boston."
AI: "At what time would you like to go?"
ARVIND: "Around noon."
AI: "Do you have a preference for an airline?"

You can tell from this conversation that the process of crafting rules for this AI is reasonably straightforward. There is a small set of information that is needed to book a flight. The AI can work with rules that say "IF the customer has not yet specified their preferred airline, THEN ask for their preferred airline." The rules can also include a suggested sequence of questions, as reflected in the example above.

This type of AI is referred to as "symbolic AI" or sometimes "classical AI," and often the rules involved were part of what were called expert systems, which became popular in the late eighties and early nineties. The approach of directly encoding knowledge by manually crafting rules breaks down when decisions become more complex. For example, let's take a look at a rule for driving an autonomous vehicle based on a sequence of images and radar signals of what is in front of the car. Can you imagine how hard it would be to write a rule that associates the intensity of different pixels in an image, and their movement over time, with whether the car should stop (and if so, how quickly), accelerate, go straight, turn left or turn right? Now imagine that these decisions have to work for all situations a car might encounter. The task would be impossible! This is why symbolic AI never entirely succeeded beyond deep but narrow domains of knowledge.

So what changed? The rise of incredible new data sources combined with machine learning! Modern AI learns *knowledge from data*, instead of directly encoding knowledge. This means inferring rules using many examples—and this requires huge quantities of data and also enormous computing power to process the data using machine learning algorithms. This type of AI is referred to as "statistical (or machine learning–based) AI." The challenge of translating between languages makes the difference between symbolic and statistical/ML-based AI obvious. In symbolic AI we try to document the rules of both languages so that we can translate from one language to the other. In statistical AI, we might not know anything about the rules of the languages before we start. Instead, we would have millions of examples of texts in one language and their translation into the other. By feeding these examples into a machine learning algorithm, we let the algorithm figure out what rules are actually used in the example translations, instead of providing it with rules we tried to directly encode. It turns out that statistical AI works much better for many messy tasks such as teaching a car how to drive, teaching Amazon's Alexa to understand what we say, and teaching a camera to recognize a face. AI has taken off with our recent ability to have computing power provided by the cloud and massive amounts of data generated by the Internet and Internet of Things (IoT) sensors.

How does this relate to "analytics"? Analytics is the science and process of transforming data into knowledge. This means that analytics is at the core of what AI needs to work—namely, to create the knowledge in the first place. Analytics is much more than machine learning. While machine learning is an important part of analytics, there is also, for example, experimentation, causal inference, and other ways to create knowledge that don't rely on what is known as machine learning. At the same time, while analytics is at the core of AI, it does not imply anything about automation. An analytics project can be a one-off investigation into the success of a marketing campaign; it can be a single experiment to test a new production process at a plant. AI, in contrast, adds an automation layer to analytics. And this automation layer, powered by analytics, enables systems to perform actions that, if performed by humans, would be considered intelligent.

AI scales analytics. But if you don't understand analytics, you don't understand AI. And that is why we will show you a process for AIA, centered on how analytics gets you from data to knowledge in order to make informed managerial decisions and then scale them in your business.

THE AIA FRAMEWORK

After working with numerous companies on analytics, it became clear to us that most lacked a clear understanding of the fundamentals of analytics and the process for tackling an AIA project. As trained data scientists with PhDs from MIT, it seemed obvious to us how to approach an analytics project. But as we started working with leaders who were new to AIA, we learned that the C-suite mandate of "create value with data, AI, and analytics" was crippling. Most organizations struggled to connect business priorities with AI and analytics because they lacked a clear, valid process for doing so.

To solve this problem, we looked for existing frameworks that could shape our thinking and help business leaders. But we found the existing frameworks lacking. One popular approach, for example, describes analytics as a "journey of maturity" where firms gradually progress from descriptive to predictive to prescriptive analytics. Another describes the process of gradually building capability to handle increasingly complex analytics. These frameworks are limited and ultimately less useful because:

- They suggest that analytics maturity or complexity delivers business value
- They fail to connect analytics with business priorities and problems
- They blur and, worse, obfuscate important but subtle distinctions among analytics methods, which can lead to bad business decisions
- They fail to integrate AI and analytics in a cohesive manner

Our framework, the "AIA Framework," is a logical starting point to building a vocabulary and process for AI and analytics in your organization. Note that while our framework is a good starting point, leaders should customize it to meet their specific needs.

We ground our framework in the idea that the emergence of analytics and AI has *not* altered the general process of how leaders make decisions. Nearly every management decision starts with a business objective, after which one asks, "What is the impediment that is preventing me from achieving the business objective?" From there, managers ideate and generate a set of business ideas. These ideas are then vetted using a bit of data and models and *a lot* of intuition and judgment. After assessing various options, a decision is made. Visually, the process looks something like what's captured in Figure 2.1.

Figure 2.1   Traditional Business Decision-Making Process

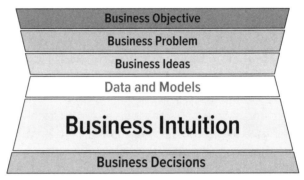

So what's different when you insert analytics, or a rigorous way of getting from data to knowledge? Before, the analytics layer was very thin, containing only limited data and some models, but now it's very thick. There are many opportunities to use data and models to analyze ideas, and even to generate ideas. This analytics layer is where we transform data, through learning, into knowledge.

Our framework is summarized visually in a diagram (Figure 2.2) that we informally call the "Lexus Grille." Why? One of us (Zettelmeyer) loves cars and noticed that the diagram looks a lot like the front of Lexus-brand cars!

Our grille presents a repeatable process that connects business outcomes with decisions informed by analytics. While the overarching process for how you make decisions hasn't changed from the past, the goal in using the AIA Framework is to replace intuition with evidence derived from analytics. The framework helps you do that in a systematic way.

We focus on three specific types of analytics, using the following terms:

Figure 2.2   The AIA Framework for Business Decisions

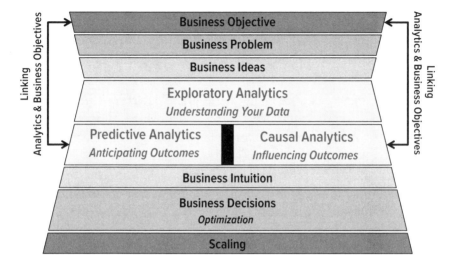

- *Exploratory analytics:* Describing your data, explaining how the data was generated, and understanding variability within the data
- *Predictive analytics:* Using AIA models to *anticipate* future outcomes
- *Causal analytics:* Using AIA models to *influence* future outcomes

The distinction between predictive and causal analytics is subtle. Say you're an online clothing retailer like Bonobos or Bombas who wants to forecast how many orders you'll receive next month. That requires a predictive model through which you can anticipate future outcomes under the normal course of business. But suppose the CMO asks whether the firm can drive 5 percent more orders with a new marketing campaign. Now, you've moved squarely into causal analytics, where you are trying to influence a future outcome. As we will emphasize repeatedly, this distinction is subtle but important. First, the business questions you can address with predictive analytics are quite different from the ones you can address with causal analytics. Second, the resources required to support a predictive versus causal analytics project can be very, very different. If you, as a leader, don't understand this distinction, you will struggle to align business priorities and investments with analytics (don't worry if this is not obvious yet; it will be as you progress through the book).

Our framework's final components are to determine the best decision (action) and then scale this across the business. Finding the best decision involves optimization or "what-if" scenario planning, which is simply choosing the best option among a set of them. Predictive analytics and causal analytics are merely inputs for the optimization. Remember: analytics is not the end goal. To determine the best action, you need to link analytics with your business objective.

Scaling the best decisions ties back to our discussion of the role of artificial intelligence. An AIA-driven business initiative may lead to a good decision today. But how do you refine and improve the decision over time? How do you integrate AIA-driven insights into day-to-day decision-making? This is where AI plays a central role. While AI has many definitions, the key part of AI from a business perspective is to scale and automate both learning and the creation and use of knowledge throughout an enterprise.

As decisions are made and scaled across a company, leaders need to recognize that virtually every analytics model can be optimized—in some cases the optimization can be challenging, but an answer is always generated. The fact that this somewhat mysterious black box of AI and analytics generated an answer is often viewed as a success in and of itself. But in many cases, a leader's job is to integrate model recommendations with their own business intuition. Blindly following the recommendations of a system can lead to poor outcomes, as we'll discuss in detail later in the book.

The AIA Framework, around which this book is organized, provides a systematic approach for using analytics and AI to achieve your business goals. After teaching thousands of participants, we realize that simply tossing out AIA-related definitions doesn't necessarily lead to mastery of concepts. So, let's turn to an industry case study we created to show the framework in action.

ZERO UNPLANNED DOWNTIME: BOOSTING WIND FARM VALUE

Wind farms, those large fields of modern-looking windmills in open areas, provide an increasing percentage of renewable energy worldwide. But the core energy-creating wind turbines behind the technology are subject to costly failure. So wind farm operators are eager to pursue the overarching goal of "zero unplanned downtime," given that as much as 60 percent of wind turbine downtime is unplanned.[3] This means that operators know turbines will fail at some point, and want to perfect their ability to predict failure and thus be able to address it immediately—such as by deploying engineers, technicians, and equipment to fix the problem—thus dramatically limiting the costs of failure. Consider the key steps to effective analytics in the context of this industry example.

Perform Exploratory Analytics (to Develop a Business Objective)

Exploratory analytics, as the name suggests, is where every analytics journey starts. Sadly, it's a step that is often overlooked. Great decisions follow from great analytics, but this only happens when you understand what is possible. Exploratory analytics enables you to understand the ways in which analytics may, and may not, deliver business value.

Exploratory analytics is about three issues:

- Describing past outcomes
- Understanding how your data was generated
- Understanding variability in your data

To illustrate these concepts, let's return to the case. Specifically, the wind farm operator may have a goal of increased profitability and may explore the data to assess various ways to improve the business. This includes reviewing reports that describe past outcomes related to inventory (variation in days of inventory of spare parts over time), labor costs (how these vary by season and other factors), and unplanned downtime (days that a turbine is not operating).

Based on this initial analysis, the wind farm operator may decide to focus on unplanned downtime as the most promising area for improvement. For example, the operator might have explored the metric "days that a turbine is not operating" and discovered that during the previous 12 months, 14 percent of turbines were unexpectedly offline for one or more days. The first question to ask, then, is whether 14 percent is high or low. Benchmarks with competitors suggested that for a typical wind farm, 10 percent of turbines were predicted to be unexpectedly offline for one or more days.

This illustrates a simple point: *comparisons* are pervasive in all types of analytics. Best practice in descriptive analytics, or describing past outcomes, is to make comparisons easy and obvious to those who aren't experts, as we'll discuss in the next chapter. Too often, reports are littered with tables and numbers with no clear explanation of which comparisons are critical. Best-in-class descriptive analytics homes in on the key comparisons that matter, makes these comparisons obvious to every decision-maker, and leaves "nice to know" facts out of reports.

Now suppose that a data scientist at the wind farm operator created a simple figure (a histogram) to illustrate that there was tremendous variability in the number of days that a turbine was offline (see Figure 2.3).

If a turbine was offline, most often the downtime was one day. But there was tremendous variability in this metric, with some turbines offline for more than three weeks, as the figure suggests. Perhaps a single day of downtime is not a problem, but clearly there are lost profits when a turbine is offline for several weeks. As such, the figure immediately identifies a potential business opportunity to reduce variability in downtime.

For leaders building their DSIQ, here is the first critical insight. Variability in this outcome metric is a must-have for analytics to be effective. The model will look at situations where turbines are working perfectly (no downtime) and compare these with situations where the turbines are unexpectedly offline. We must observe *both* situations for analytics to succeed.

Figure 2.3 Frequency of Unplanned Downtime

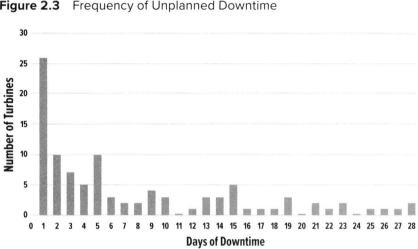

But how will the model learn which factors are leading to unplanned downtime? This brings us to a second concern that is easily uncovered by exploratory analytics. We need data on factors that may influence whether the turbines are unexpectedly offline, *and* there must be variation in this data as well. In the case of our wind turbines, evidence shows that explanatory factors can include turbine age, vibration, oil level and quality, weather, and operator and maintenance team skill and motivation.[4] We have data on hundreds of variables for each turbine, but is this data going to be helpful? Consider a variable such as "turbine manufacturer." It turns out that our wind farm has always bought turbines from the same manufacturer, and as a result there is no variability in this metric. So, while we may record this variable in our system, it doesn't help the wind farm operator predict unplanned downtime. In contrast, "age of a turbine" varies significantly, and might therefore help explain whether a turbine is likely to be offline.

This type of insight, though intuitive, is often overlooked by leaders. Leaders with low DSIQ simply assume that AIA will create valuable insights if they just throw lots of data at these systems. This could not be further from the truth. What matters is getting the *right* data.

To illustrate this point, let's switch examples for a moment: think about the type of data typically captured by a salesperson. First, does every salesperson take care to record a win or successful sale? Of course! This is because the salesperson is paid on sales. Second, does every salesperson track unsuccessful sales with the same diligence? In many organizations, the answer is a resounding *no!* While wins are tracked diligently, losses are tracked much less carefully. If you're in a situation where your data contains only wins, it is impossible (or at least very hard) to build a model to help your sales team improve their win rate. While we can create a model for win rates, our data doesn't have the comparisons (variability) needed to fuel the model.

Worse, *good* business processes are designed to squeeze out variability in all metrics. If Amazon, for example, wants to learn how number of delivery days impacts retention of Prime members, the company won't get very far because Prime delivery is optimized for two-day delivery for almost all orders. Similarly, a retailer like Lululemon may believe the best everyday price for a pair of women's yoga pants is $100, and as a result they likely have never tried different prices. With no variation in price, analytics cannot help the retailer assess whether $100 is indeed the best price. Remember, models learn just like humans. To find the best answers, we need to observe many different types of situations.

Back to our wind farm example. So far, we have identified a potential opportunity in the business (turbine downtime) where analytics may help us improve performance. Exploratory analytics helped narrow the focus to improving unplanned downtime, but reducing downtime is not our business objective. The point of reducing downtime is to increase profitability. Notice the subtle shift. A business leader should care only about the analytics metric (downtime) if it also improves the business metric (profitability).

To link the analytics metric with the business metric (as in Figure 2.4), we need to create a "scoreboard." Most organizations we work with don't systematically do this. What typically happens is that a data scientist builds a model that yields an analytics metric and then hands this off to a financial analyst or manager, who creates a profit analysis. This is problematic because nearly every decision-maker knows how to use the analytics metric to tell different stories.

What starts as a scientific, evidence-based analytics project may quickly become a biased political exercise. This is not the fault of data, models, or data scientists—it's evidence of bad business process.

Ideally, you should define the final final key performance indicator (KPI) or business metric before the analytics results are known. Also, the KPI should be specific. "Profitability," for example, is not specific enough. What is the time horizon over which we calculate profits? Similarly, you should define the costs and benefits included in the scoreboard in advance and make sure that everyone agrees on these. Once you agree on the final business KPIs and the scoreboard, a data scientist can perform the analytics *and* can evaluate alternatives using the agreed-upon scoreboard.

Figure 2.4   Linking Analytics and Business Outcomes Models

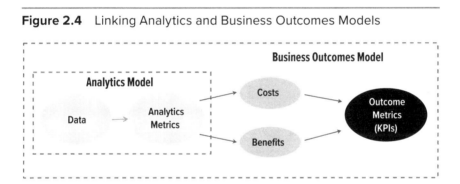

In our experience, many organizations don't define the business outcomes model before executing the analytics. What started as data science then becomes political because, knowing the analytics results, different stakeholders can pick KPIs and scoreboards to suit their political needs ("We think that a one-year profit horizon is more appropriate than a three-year profit horizon" or "We don't think we should consider fixed costs in the scoreboard"). Agreeing on KPIs and the scoreboard is much less political if no one knows yet how the analytics results come out and, therefore, who is likely to be a winner or a loser in the end.

Also, as you develop your business outcomes model, beware of "balloon effects"—the idea that pushing on a balloon's side relocates air within it. In business, improving one metric may unintentionally affect another, such as an example we witnessed where a large tech firm scaled a successful unit-level initiative firmwide, only to discover that it was detrimental to another division. You should be particularly concerned with balloon effects if you are part of a large organization where business units operate independently, with little coordination among them.

Anticipate Outcomes (to Make Better Decisions)

In our wind turbine example so far, we have identified a business problem, we have determined that the analytics may be feasible, and we have specified a business outcomes model. Now let's turn to using predictive analytics and building models. Recall that predictive analytics is about anticipating the future—in this example we are trying to anticipate unplanned downtime of a wind turbine.

To start, suppose that data scientists have created a table (below) that summarizes unplanned downtime by average vibration level, an important factor in wind turbine performance. For example, you see that when vibration levels are lower, downtime is lower.

Downtime	Average Vibration
1 day	0.050
2 days	0.265
3 days	0.408
4 days	0.360
5+ days	0.744

Now ask yourself, is this table exploratory analytics or predictive analytics? The answer is that it can be both! What matters is the business question you are asking. For example, suppose you are asking: "In the past, was there a relationship between vibration levels and unplanned downtime?" We are simply describing the past, which is part of exploratory analytics. But instead, suppose you ask:

"If a turbine has a high vibration rate, is it more likely to fail in the future?" Using just our simple table, the answer is *yes*. Here, we are using the same table, but this time for predictive analytics. Remember, the same data can be used for both exploratory and predictive analytics—it's the question you ask that matters.

But a single explanatory variable is rarely good enough for effective predictions. For example, suppose you use vibration levels only to predict days to next failure. Now plot *actual* "days to next failure" against *predicted* "days to next failure." If the prediction were perfect, the data would sit on a 45-degree line. Instead, we get a chart like the one in Figure 2.5, which shows poor-quality prediction.

Figure 2.5   Predicted vs. Actual Unplanned Downtime Using Only Vibration Level

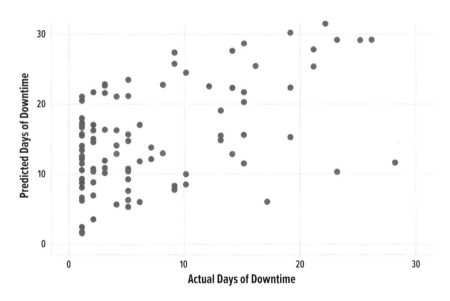

The model improves when you add more variables, for example, turbine age, oil levels, and operator/maintenance team experience and skill. Now the predicted and actual days to next failure line up much better, as shown in Figure 2.6.

Figure 2.6   Predicted vs. Actual Downtime Using All Variables

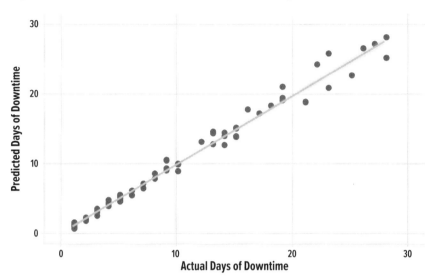

As a leader, it is not your role to build a model like this, nor is it your role to understand the details of the science behind the model. But, much like reading a balance sheet in finance, you do need to have an intuitive understanding of analytics. Being able to distinguish a poor-fitting model from a better-fitting model falls into that category. As we will argue in the coming chapters, a good intuition is critical to ensuring that your analytics efforts are aligned with and support your business goals.

We also think that leaders with a high DSIQ need to have a broad understanding of the type of predictive model their data science team has built. Later in the book we'll talk much more about predictive models. But for now, keep in mind that there are two broad classes of predictive models:

- *Data-driven models*, where the user specifies a set of variables and the model identifies potentially complex relationships among them. Examples include regression trees, neural networks, and most other forms of machine learning.

- *Analyst-driven models*, where the user specifies a relationship among variables and the results summarize those relationships. Examples include regression and count models, which have their origin in statistics.

From a leader's perspective, the advantage of analyst-driven models is that they make it easier to explain your predictions because there is often a clear mapping from data to prediction. Data-driven models, in contrast, may provide a more accurate prediction but can be very difficult to interpret. From a leader's perspective, you need to understand whether you need to unpack the "why" behind the prediction. In our wind turbine example, if you need to understand why wind turbines are failing, then you may nudge your team toward building an analyst-driven model. But if you simply want the best prediction and don't care about why, you may nudge your team toward a data-driven model. In many cases, you will ask for both types of models. Again, your job as a leader is not to build these models but to know what to request and why it matters.

Suppose you now have a well-performing predictive model. What decision do you make? As our AIA Framework suggests, you need to link the analytics model with the business model. In our ongoing example, suppose that the data science team decided to build two different predictive models. The first model predicts whether a turbine is likely to go offline unexpectedly, and the second predicts the number of days the turbine is likely to be offline.

The current practice was to dispatch repair technicians after a turbine had failed. How could the company use the models to, instead, dispatch repair technicians proactively—before a turbine failed?

Note that some dispatch decisions don't require a formal business outcomes model. For example, if a turbine has a near-zero probability of failure in the next 30 days, we should not dispatch a technician. Similarly, if the model predicts that failure is imminent and is likely to last for many days, we should dispatch a technician immediately. The business outcomes model becomes invaluable in the less extreme cases. For example, if the model predicts that the failure probability is 20 percent and the failure will last for one week, should we proactively dispatch a repair technician? For situations like this, the business outcomes model enables you to weigh business costs and benefits. If a repair technician is currently in the same geographic location as the turbine and has time available (i.e., low cost to dispatch), you should dispatch the technician immediately. If there is currently no technician in the area (i.e., high cost to dispatch), then it may be worth delaying, and scheduling a proactive repair in the near future, even if this increases the risk that the turbine fails in the meantime.

Remember, you can only translate the analytics to a decision by connecting the analytics models to the business outcomes model!

Influence Outcomes

Thus far, the wind farm has used analytics to proactively send out repair technicians, which presumably reduces downtime. Let's imagine that the models show that when turbines display early signs of failure, the probability of failure jumps quickly from zero to near one. Assume further that the firm intervenes quickly with proactive maintenance to avoid any catastrophic failures.

If this occurs, notice that we still have a business problem to address. Turbines are still beginning to fail, and we are dispatching technicians at the last minute to avoid actual failure. One might ask: Is there anything the wind farm can do to prevent turbines from starting to fail? If the turbines went into a state of near-failure less often, then there would be less need for proactive visits from repair technicians.

To address this issue, a team of engineers began looking at the regular maintenance schedule. The current strategy was to perform a thorough inspection of each wind turbine annually. These were extensive visits that required anywhere from half a day to a full day to complete. But it was believed that these annual visits were essential to preventing failures. One person on the engineering team asked, "Would it make sense to visit all or some of the turbines on a more frequent basis? Maybe we should be visiting older turbines twice a year?" Another engineer suggested an alternative approach: "Should we eliminate annual maintenance visits and just rely on proactive visits that are dictated by our model?" Notice that both options have merit. Can analytics help evaluate which of these options is best?

Let's first focus on the idea of increasing our maintenance schedule from once a year to twice a year on some turbines. Suppose we want to understand how failure rates are affected by a change in maintenance schedules. Is this predictive analytics or causal analytics? The first thing to recognize is that we want the analytics to generate a prediction. But are we trying to anticipate a failure or influence a failure? In this example, we are clearly trying to influence the failure rate by changing our maintenance schedule. As a result, this is clearly causal analytics.

Now ask yourself: Can we tackle this business problem with the data we have? Right now, we maintain every turbine once a year. Do we have any previous situations where preventative maintenance was sometimes done once a year and in other cases done twice a year? Clearly the answer is *no*. As a result of a very well-functioning maintenance program, every turbine has been visited exactly once for many, many years. Is there anything in our data that will tell us how turbine failures will change if turbines are visited twice a year? Definitely not. And the reason is simple: business practice has led to no variation in maintenance visits, a common issue discussed earlier.

This is one of the most important lessons for leaders. Notice that in the domain of wind turbines, we can use analytics to solve one problem (generating proactive technician visits) but cannot solve a related problem (whether to shift from annual to semiannual maintenance). Leaders who have a high DSIQ understand why they can easily solve one problem with existing data but related problems remain virtually unsolvable using the same data.

Moreover, such leaders understand what it takes to learn whether semiannual maintenance is a good idea. Here, data in hand won't suffice. Instead, the operations team will need to design a test (or experiment) where some turbines are maintained twice a year. The test results will then inform a model that can measure the impact of semiannual maintenance versus annual maintenance. High-DSIQ leaders who understand the need for an experiment also quickly realize that this process will take a minimum of one year.

With this understanding, we can also glean some insight into whether analytics can help us evaluate the alternative proposal of eliminating annual maintenance. Do we know anything about this from our data? Again, the answer is *no*. We have never tried not maintaining a turbine. Our gut instinct tells us failures may go up if we were to eliminate annual maintenance—but exactly how much may be an open question. Again, it may require some experimentation to learn how failure rates change when annual maintenance is eliminated.

Last, suppose we decide that it is worth running a small pilot test to learn how semiannual maintenance affects turbine failures. Suppose we discover that failures are reduced from 14 to 11 percent. Should we implement the semiannual maintenance program? Similar to our previous analysis, we need to integrate this analytics outcome with the business outcomes. What are the benefits of a reduced failure rate? We clearly save money by having fewer proactive maintenance visits. But what are the costs? If our maintenance costs doubled, is it still profitable? Again, good decisions follow from integrating analytics with a business outcomes model.

TWO CRITICAL TAKEAWAYS

For those new to analytics, there is a lot to digest from this use case. So we want to emphasize two key points as you absorb the information.

First, the importance of a *focus on business outcomes*. The idea is that analytics is often problem-driven, such as reducing wind turbine downtime or customer churn, but it's critical to understand the business objective and tie everything back to metrics that represent achievement of that objective. In the wind farm example, the broad objective is to improve profitability. So, while reducing unplanned downtime may be about changing maintenance schedules or the composition of maintenance teams, as we discussed earlier, all associated costs must be taken into account. That is, we may be able to reduce or even eliminate unplanned downtime, but at what price based on the initiatives proposed? The model simply tells you the turbines will have unplanned downtime, but you have to decide what business outcomes matter, as part of a "scoreboard" of the costs and benefits you'll use to determine priorities. Your role as a leader is to be clear on the business outcomes of consequence before you implement initiatives, or you won't be able to measure their value.

Second, the *distinction between predictive and causal analytics* is important but subtle, and something we'll come back to repeatedly. Pure prediction is simply about understanding the relationships between variables: how vibration relates to unplanned downtime in our wind farm example, or how time spent on a retail website is associated with likelihood of purchase, or whether call-center hold time predicts customer satisfaction levels. Causal analytics, in contrast, is about influencing the outcome in question: Will changing maintenance schedules reduce unplanned downtime? Will hiring more call-center employees improve customer satisfaction? So predictive analytics is about anticipation of an outcome during the normal course of business, whereas the causal variety is about intervention aimed at influencing that outcome.

If you've understood these two key takeaways, you're well on your way to boosting your DSIQ!

GETTING STARTED WITH ANALYTICS IN YOUR ORGANIZATION

Through the past five years, we have conducted many workshops with leaders all the way from CEOs to line managers. Our experience is that if you are new to analytics, it is often quite difficult to link this framework to a business problem. In other words, getting started can be challenging.

In response, we have developed a simple taxonomy for how analytics can create value; it goes by the acronym IEE, which stands for "ideate, enable, and evaluate." Analytics can be used to generate new business ideas, or ideate. Analytics can be used to enable new or existing business functions. And analytics can be used to evaluate whether a new or existing business initiative is working.

As an example of *ideation*, California-based El Camino Hospital reported using a predictive model of patient length of stay. In real time, the model scored patients on their predicted length of stay in a hospital ward. The predictions were then shared with nurses and unit supervisors who were asked, "Why are some patients predicted to stay longer than normal?" The nurses and unit supervisors knew the business very well—they had detailed information about the patients, their families, and their personal situation that the model was lacking. We call these people "domain experts." They brainstormed and came up with ideas for how to reduce length of stay. Two of the ideas were to do more outreach to patient families soon after admission and to explore increasing capacity in skilled nursing facilities, which proved to be a bottleneck in the system.

Notice the role of analytics in coming up with these ideas. We could have gone to the domain experts and said: "Please help us reduce length of stay!" This is a broad, open-ended question that could have gone in many directions. Instead, the analytics suggested that our domain experts focus their brainstorming on comparing patients with high length of stay versus those with low length of stay. Analytics narrowed the aperture from a broad lens (all possible issues on the ward) to a narrower one (specific patient comparisons). This presumably facilitated the ideation.

A second way that analytics can create value is via *enabling* a business function. Think of an existing business process like sending out emails to clients of a financial services firm. The firm regularly sends out emails and wants to use analytics to determine the best subject line for every email campaign. A subject line is critical because it encourages a client to open the email, read the information, and take action. At present, this is determined by judgment and the firm wants to use analytics instead. The firm ran an experiment that lasted for one week and included a small fraction of clients. At the end of the week, the optimal subject line was identified, and emails were sent to all remaining clients. Here, analytics was used to take an existing process and simply make it more effective. This is what we call enabling.

A third way analytics can be used is to *evaluate*. Suppose a retailer wants to launch a new marketing campaign that consists of digital ads, in-store merchandising, and local newspaper advertising. Everyone believes the program will be effective, but we want to use analytics to evaluate whether it actually is. A data science team works with the marketing team to create what is called a phased rollout of the marketing campaign. We will explain this technique later in the book, but the basic idea is to strategically stagger the launch of the campaign across geographies. Why? To evaluate whether the new campaign is effective.

As you think about getting started with analytics within your company, the IEE framework is very useful, and we will return to this in Chapter 13, "Organizing for Success." Too many managers think of analytics as some mysterious black box that involves radical new understanding and skills. That couldn't be further from the truth. We want managers to feel comfortable using data to generate new, creative ideas that may improve their business. Analytics can help narrow the aperture and provide inspiration for ideation. We want managers to use analytics to take an existing process and make it better. And last, think about how you can use analytics to evaluate whether the initiatives you launch actually meet your business goals. And even better, how you can use analytics to evaluate existing business processes and determine whether they are actually effective.

In summary, we want you to take away from this chapter that analytics projects should start with business issues, rather than data and models—you should clearly define your business initiative *and* the outcomes model before you begin an analytics project. Our AIA Framework will support your use of exploratory, predictive, and causal analytics to develop AIA-driven business initiatives to help you achieve your business goals.

Consuming AI and Analytics

Before you are ready to take an active role in AI and analytics (AIA), we want to provide some pointers on how to be a more educated consumer of AIA. This is a skill every decision-maker should have, in a world where decisions are increasingly backed up by data. In our workshops we hear comments like "I am getting inundated with data and analytics from my teams and other business leaders, and I have a really hard time knowing whether I should believe the results. The problem is even worse when I have to evaluate vendors." If you have the same problem, this section is for you.

In Chapter 3 we give you a systematic way to understand what is going on with your data. Can it answer the business questions you are interested in? Is it good data or bad data, and what does that mean for AIA? Chapter 4 then explains why managers often misinterpret analytics results, and provides you with a solution—a checklist that enables you to properly interpret reports, charts, and figures. We call this process distinguishing good from bad analytics.

CHAPTER 3

EXPLORATORY ANALYTICS
What Is Going on with My Data?

Exploratory analytics is about understanding what's actually *in* your data—a critical first step in any analytics project. Specifically, you need to determine quickly whether the data you have in hand can answer your business questions. As we discussed earlier in the book, many important business problems cannot be addressed even with the massive amounts of data today's companies store. Performing exploratory analysis is an imperative, so that projects can be quickly scoped and assessed for feasibility before committing resources to try to solve a problem for which the right data does not yet exist.

In short, exploratory analytics will help you understand the difference between having a large volume of data and having the *right* data. In turn, this knowledge can help you develop a plan for securing the most useful data for future projects.

WHAT IS EXPLORATORY ANALYTICS?

There are three key activities involved in exploratory analytics:

- Describing the past
- Understanding how your data came to be
- Understanding variability in your data

Let's take a closer look at each of these.

Describing the Past

Every company needs to understand what happened in the past. For example, were the business plans that were put into place actually fulfilled? Did the firm meet specific targets, financial or otherwise? Because of this need, most firms have armies of personnel dedicated to creating reports that summarize what happened during the past months, quarters, years, and other time frames.

At many firms, the job function associated with this kind of reporting is called "business intelligence," or BI. In our experience, when firms start the journey of building their AI and analytics capability, they often begin with an assessment of their personnel. What they typically discover is that many employees who self-classify as data scientists or data analysts perform the job function of business intelligence.

These employees are highly skilled at finding data, extracting it from systems, combining datasets, and then creating reports, figures, and charts that describe the past. Our very rough guess based on our experience and observation is that at many companies the vast majority of self-classified "analytics" people fall into this category—as much as 80 to 90 percent at some firms. This is not ideal. For example, the AIA leader of a B2B firm recently told us, "We need our CEO and the other leaders to understand that analytics is much more than just reporting."

Indeed, it is. To make this point, we looked at more than 5,000 postings for data science jobs posted on Indeed.com.[1] We found that only 31 percent of the jobs are for data analysts who tend to have skills in SQL (for data extraction) and Tableau (for reporting). The remaining 69 percent of jobs are for experts in data management and storage (data engineers), sophisticated data analysis and model building (AI, machine learning), or other technical skills well beyond reporting.

The task that most folks in BI groups and departments perform is referred to as *descriptive analytics*. The outputs of descriptive analytics are typically tables, charts, and figures that summarize what happened in the business at or over a given time point or period. Firms use these items to monitor the current health of the business and assess whether business goals are being achieved. For example, if a business or business unit was expected to grow top-line revenue by 3.5 percent year to year, this can easily be evaluated using yearly revenue figures.

Not surprisingly, most of what shows up in C-suite and board-level reports is based on descriptive statistics. For example, a CEO whom we work with told us he tracks his cash position daily to ensure he has sufficient liquidity to run the business comfortably. A retailer we know regularly monitors changes in margin, while a steel manufacturer keeps a close eye on capacity utilization. Every business has critical numbers to keep track of; descriptive statistics help leaders do this.

Descriptive statistics also form the foundation of online dashboards many companies use to monitor business health beyond the C-suite. A big advantage of such dashboards is that they allow managers to drill down more deeply into the data and view different cuts of the full set of numbers they have on hand. This enables them to grasp a more nuanced picture of what happened in a given time period by asking and answering specific questions. For instance, if total revenue falls short of a previously established 3.5 percent annual growth target, was one particular geography or business unit more responsible for the outcome than others? Or was this a common trend across the entire business? If the problem is related to one outlier geography, for example, this may suggest the need to dig into that market more carefully; but if every business market or unit is down, the underlying cause may be a macroeconomic trend or a broad strategic issue such as the arrival of a new global competitor.

No doubt there's value in using descriptive analytics in your business. But here is the sad, sobering reality. Many reports are time-consuming and rarely used for decisions. The explanation for this is simple: Descriptive analytics tells you about the journey you have taken and whether you are on course; but if you are off course, such analytics often provides little or no insight for how to get back on track!

Worse, once these reports are birthed, they tend to live forever. Some time ago, Duncan Fulton, former senior executive with leading Canadian sports retailer Sport Chek, became frustrated by this dilemma and took an extreme position. He mandated that reports would no longer be created automatically or routinely, but only on demand. "From now on, if you want a report," he told managers, "you have to ask for it." As such, reports weren't truly eliminated, but people had to have a good reason for asking for one.

What happened? Overnight, 80 to 90 percent of all reports went dormant. No one missed them! And people who truly needed a report were still able to get it. That means large savings of time, money, and effort formerly spent on routine report creation without any noticeable sacrifice of needed information. The success of Sport Chek's "no routine reports" policy suggests that good management requires not just the creation of reports, but the systematic "care and feeding" of these reports. So think carefully about what reports your organization or operation really needs, and consider a process for adapting reports or eliminating them altogether, like Sport Chek did.

As noted previously, despite the large effort many businesses spend generating reports, the reports often turn out uninformative. For example, a report may contain myriad semi-related numbers, charts, and other figures, leading to confusion and ultimately less value for the organization, or even waste. So, what makes a good report, chart, or figure in the first place? We have summarized three learnings that we have found helpful, along with some additional resources, in the following box.

Three Tips for Great Visualizations

- *Make comparisons easy.* Insights are usually derived from comparisons. Build your report around those comparisons that deliver actionable insights.
- *Keep it streamlined.* Pick only comparisons that are "key to act on," and ditch those that are merely "nice to know."
- *Visualize for simplicity.* Our visual system is incredibly good at deriving insight from comparisons that are similar to tasks we have performed, for example comparing the size of grapes on a vine, but has a very hard time with other comparisons.

Two great resources for visualization tips are the book *Making Data Visual* by Danyel Fisher and Miriah Meyer,[2] and a quick reference guide available at www.experception.net.

While this book is not primarily about data visualization and descriptive statistics, here are questions that leaders like you can ask in your organization to make reporting truly helpful:

- Do we need a report?
- If we need a report, what is the insight or set of insights we want to communicate?
- What is the best way to communicate those insights?
- Does my organization understand how to use this information appropriately?

Answering these questions thoughtfully will take you a long way toward driving business value with reports. In particular, starting in the next section, we will spend considerable time laying the foundation for you to ask the last question above. Many managers believe that descriptive analytics directly provide insight into how to improve their business. Sadly, this is usually not true. Your job as a leader with high DSIQ is to know when and how you can use descriptions of the past for decisions, and when you should instead rely on forward-looking predictive or causal analytics.

Understanding How Your Data Came to Be

The second component of exploratory analytics is to understand how your data came to be. This is perhaps the single most important task to determine whether descriptions of the past provide actionable insights.

Understanding how your data came to be starts with a simple question: Why are some types of data captured while other types are not? Imagine the example of a commercial salesforce. What type of data does every firm work hard to capture about its salesforce? Typically, wins or sales. Sales translate into commissions, so there is a clear incentive for every salesperson to record every win; moreover, finance and accounting need to report revenue, costs, and profit, meaning that every win and commission paid must be tracked with great care.

Now consider a harder question: What types of data may *not* be captured related to a given firm's salesforce? One likely set would be sales activities that don't lead to a win. While many companies require the recording of any client contact in an online system like Salesforce, there is usually far less incentive to track the full pipeline of activities that may lead to a win, including sales visits to prospective customers that ultimately don't pan out. Spending time recording such information is extremely useful for analytics and could uncover how salespeople should allocate their scarce time in the future. But recording lost opportunities does not help salespeople earn their commissions today. As a result, many salesforce databases have extensive data on wins, but incomplete or virtually no information on losses.

You may wonder: Why is it not enough to have just data on wins? The reason is that most analytics depend on comparisons. A data scientist can only tell you what salesperson behavior might lead to a win if she observes what behaviors are associated with wins *and with losses*. To prove that a behavior leads to a win, the data scientist also needs to prove that if a salesperson does *not* engage in that behavior, a loss follows. This shows that the win was not caused by something else.

Understanding how salesforce data is captured enables you to determine whether analytics can help you answer the question you are interested in. In our experience, it is important to convince those who control the data capture that the analytics can help them personally. For example, if the purpose of the analytics is to help your salespeople allocate their time more effectively, this may provide motivation for them to record *all* sales visits to customers and prospects, not just those that lead to wins.

This discussion brings up another important question: Who in the organization knows how the data came to be? Is this the responsibility of IT, data scientists, or business leaders? If the reason data is captured is driven by behavioral choices of managers, customers, and clients, then the understanding of how the data came to be typically resides with those who have domain expertise and understand the business. Instead, if data collection is driven by technical issues, such as storage cost, then IT people generally know best.

In the salesforce example above, business leaders are the ones who know most about the incentives offered to salespeople, which should enable them to understand why data is missing. As such, if data scientists request the missing data, business leaders are the ones who know what needs to be done to capture it.

In contrast, consider an example where data scientists, rather than business managers, hold the knowledge about how the data came to be. Meet Nellie, a data scientist who worked in IT for a large online retailer with whom we consulted. Nellie had years of experience with the company and knew the data inside and out, including how the business handled customers' household-level demographic data such as age, income, and gender.

In the course of our consulting, we noticed that any given household was always classified as either male or female, regardless of the genders of those who made up the household. So we asked Nellie how the company determined the "gender" of a household. She told us that they first captured customer-level data on all members in the household who were over the age of 18. Next, to create the demographic variables for a given household, they randomly selected one adult from that household and used that adult's characteristics to describe the entire household. So a household with, say, one male (father) and three females (mother and twin 19-year-old daughters) could be classified as male in that business's database if the lone male household member was chosen randomly. Similarly, a household where one adult earned $100,000 a year and the other (such as a stay-at-home parent) had an income of $0 would appear in the data as associated with zero income if the latter adult was chosen. To be clear, we are not advocating this approach—it's just how that business did it!

The immediate implication of this scenario is that it would be misguided to use such data to segment households by these gender, income, or age variables, since the information takes into account demographics only for a single household member chosen at random. In this case a data scientist like Nellie, rather than a business leader, is key in understanding how the data came to be.

As a leader, you need to not only understand the origins of your data at a single point in time, but also to put in place appropriate controls and processes that monitor continuously how your data comes to be. For example, we worked with a Fortune 500 firm that built a very cool analytics model that linked results from a customer survey with customer retention efforts. The basic idea was to gather customer feedback from a short survey and then, based on the customer responses, to deploy customer service proactively if a customer was deemed at high risk of churn. A survey and model were developed and tested, with tremendously positive results when the system was deployed to the field.

But about a year after the company deployed the system, a manager called the head of data science and said, "We've stopped using your system. You are telling us to call people that we believe have no intent of leaving, and worse, we think we are *not* calling clients who our people are pretty sure are at high risk of leaving." The data science team then spent a considerable amount of time trying to determine what was going on. They discovered that the manager was indeed correct that the system was broken because of one simple change in the survey: the order of questions changed. The most important question in the survey, from the model's perspective, was the last question. But someone decided to change the position of the question within the survey without updating how the data field was described. So, the same kind of customer data continued to be collected, but the wrong information was fed into the model.

While this is an extreme situation, it highlights nicely the importance of leaders understanding and managing the process of how data is captured and utilized in decision-making. These types of problems are not new. However, as we move to a world where data and models are scaled across the enterprise, these issues have much larger consequences, and are therefore critical for leaders to think about. The examples here highlight a need for better collaboration among data scientists and business leaders on data governance, a topic we will return to in Chapter 13, "Organizing for Success."

Understanding Variability in Your Data

The third activity in exploratory analytics is to understand the variability in your data. Variability refers to whether and how the values of a variable or set of variables change over time or across markets or customer groups. The term "variability" may sound a bit technical and perhaps unfamiliar. You might be asking yourself: Why is this a leadership issue? The reason is that variability is the rocket fuel of analytics, the metaphorical gas for the analytical engine. If you pour low-octane gas into your engine, your AIA will sputter. With rocket fuel you're more likely to speed to impressive financial results.

So what does variability look like?

Think about variability as relating to two key parts of your data: outcomes and inputs. Example outcomes are the sales of a product, the efficiency of a steel plant, or the length of stay (LOS) for hospital patients. If you are interested in using analytics to understand how to improve these outcomes, the outcomes *have to differ* over time or across groups.

Data scientists like to measure variability using a histogram, or bar chart. For example, going back to the El Camino Hospital example from earlier in the book, say that a histogram of length of stay shows that most hospital patients admitted for a particular procedure stay for fewer than 5 days, but there are also many patients who stay for 10 or more days. This is the prerequisite for asking "Why are some patients staying longer in the hospital?" which, in turn, is what you need to answer "How can I reduce length of stay?"

As a result, variability in outcomes is *the* prerequisite for using analytics to improve outcomes. To see why this true, consider what you could learn about changing length of stay from the data if every patient stayed for exactly four days in the hospital. (Answer: nothing!)

A general guideline in data science projects is that greater variability in outcomes means greater opportunity for analytics to create value. In the length-of-stay example, analytics may help us identify patients who are predicted to have high length of stay; then we can work to reduce the time they spend in the hospital.

For analytics models to work, we also need variability in *inputs*. For example, we may try to explain changes in annual sales over time by linking sales to marketing spend. Or we may explain an output like hospital length of stay using an input like doctors-to-nurses staffing ratios. In the case of steel plant efficiency, we may use an input such as the speed of the main conveyer belt used in production. Every analytics model needs variability in the inputs to generate meaningful insights. Again, to see why this true, consider what you can learn from your data about how changing the speed of the main conveyer belt affects efficiency if the belt speed is always the same. (Once again: nothing.)

Here is why these two issues are important for leaders. Business processes are designed and optimized to reduce and eliminate variability. In other words, everything you are doing to run your business more efficiently and profitably may be inherently reducing the ability of using AIA to create value.

Because your business seeks consistency in execution, you may find that all your inputs are set systematically, meaning with minimal planned variability. All prices for a given product may be the same across markets, for instance. Or the conveyer belt in our steel-production example is programmed to move at one consistent speed at all times. Amazon Prime packages are optimized for two-day delivery, or as close to that time frame as possible. What you should be realizing is that business execution is squarely at odds with analytics. Indeed, we find that firms with the most consistent execution often have the worst historical data for analytics, due to the lack of variability among inputs.

As a leader, it is your job to understand and manage this issue. If decisions are highly systematic in your business, then you need to assess what analytics projects can be tackled with the data you have in hand. To preview one of the key learnings we offer in this book, if consistent execution has eliminated data variability, leaders need to step up and purposely design variability into the data to make analytics useful.

TOWARD BETTER DATA AND ANALYTICS

In general, performing exploratory analytics enables you to start building the scaffold you need to use and benefit from data in the long run.

For example, when analytics projects start, they often rely on historical data captured for the purpose of regulation, finance, accounting, or inventory management. The data was not captured for the purpose of analytics. So understanding how your data came to be—the second exploratory analytics activity we discussed in this chapter—will help you identify gaps in the data. Later, you can prioritize whether and how you want to fill those gaps. Similarly, if you observe a lack of variability in your outcomes or inputs, you may begin to consider why this is the case and take steps to generate more variability, such as varying prices or delivery times.

Understanding your data in depth can also reveal two very common problems. First, managers don't all use the same agreed-upon data elements. One of the benefits of performing good exploratory analytics for a project is to learn whether or not data is used consistently throughout the company. For example, two divisions of a company may create divergent financial reports because they use slightly different metrics or time periods. This may reveal the more serious problem that data is not used the same way throughout the company, making it more challenging to compare performance measures across units and other groups.

A second common problem that good exploratory analytics can uncover is that managers mistake "data quality" for "truth in data." Not surprisingly, exploratory analytics often reveals missing data or errors in data. The reality is that no dataset is perfect. Therefore, every company should have a data governance strategy that seeks to improve the overall quality and consistency of data. But a narrow focus on data quality is problematic as well. Our experience is that it's critical to establish what we call "truth in data" and to distinguish this from data quality. Having higher-quality data is always desirable, and every organization should seek to improve on this dimension. But every organization that is moving toward evidence-driven decisions using analytics needs to establish a separate, parallel standard: what's considered "good enough" for making decisions. Don't let perfection in data become the enemy of the good when it comes to analytics. Your role as a leader is to help your organization determine when good enough is truly good enough.

The stakes are high. When leaders don't agree on truth in data, we have observed, companies spend several months working on an analytics project only to have managers declare that the results and recommendations are not trustworthy because the data is flawed. This is evidence of a broken analytics process. Managers cannot be allowed to throw the "data quality penalty flag" when they disagree with recommendations at the end of a project. Establishing a truth-in-data standard and ensuring the data you're using for a given project meets this standard *before* the project begins will go a long way to avoiding this problem.

We cover a full range of organizational challenges to using analytics, along with practical solutions, in the last chapters of this book.

CHAPTER 4

DISTINGUISHING GOOD FROM BAD ANALYTICS

The number-one reason for bad analytics is that data not generated as part of a true experiment is presented and interpreted as if it was.

That's our big takeaway from this chapter—one we wanted to present right away.

Today, the vast majority of business decisions are based on descriptive analytics, which involves interpreting reports, charts, and figures. As a leader, you are able to access more and more of this information through dashboards and other tools. But here's the challenge for every leader: you want to use this information not only to tell you what has happened but also to course-correct when a business is off-track. The problem is that leaders often misinterpret descriptive analytics when they try to make improvements or course-correct.

In our experience, many managers jump to the wrong conclusions for a simple reason: they mistakenly interpret a report as if it came from an experiment. In this chapter, we illustrate the challenge and then help you build your DSIQ by providing a checklist that will allow you to quickly make good decisions with reports.

Let's turn to a narrative example, inspired by a prominent sporting goods retailer, to help you understand these issues.

PENTATHLON

Colin Starke, the chief marketing officer of Pentathlon Sports, was wrestling with two competing opinions on his senior executive team. As part of a review of the European sporting goods retailer's digital marketing tactics, he'd met early in the week with Anna Quintero, the firm's recently hired director of digital marketing. "I'm frustrated," Quintero said to open the meeting. She explained that she'd been trying to convince the firm's seven department directors (who oversaw product lines such as Endurance Sports, Water Sports, and Winter Sports) to limit the number of promotional emails sent to customers. "Before I joined the company," Quintero continued, "the directors made independent decisions about promotional emails for their individual departments. When I looked at the departments collectively, I began to suspect we were sending customers too many emails."

She presented Starke data from a recent audit she'd led of all Pentathlon promo emails. The numbers seemed to back up her case: on average, customers received 3.8 emails per week, significantly higher than the industry average she'd observed. "But to be sure, I also sent a survey to over 85,000 of our recent online customers," Quintero said. "Look at what I found."

Starke examined Quintero's table of data (see below). Based on 3,642 survey responses, 72 percent of customers felt Pentathlon sent them too many promotional emails—very much in line with Quintero's assertion.

All consumers	Result
"I receive too many promotional emails from Pentathlon."	72%
"I receive just the right amount of promotional emails from Pentathlon."	21%
"I receive too few promotional emails from Pentathlon."	7%

Among Pentathlon's most profitable customers, the results were even more compelling. "I also looked at these metrics by sales volume," Quintero said, "and the finding held up." Pentathlon's highest-revenue customers felt they received too many promo emails (see the following table).

Consumers among top 25% total euro sales (last 12 months)	
"I receive too many promotional emails from Pentathlon."	87%
"I receive just the right amount of promotional emails from Pentathlon."	10%
"I receive too few promotional emails from Pentathlon."	3%

Quintero also found that among Pentathlon's less desirable customers, those in the bottom 25 percent in sales volume, fewer people felt dissatisfied about the email volume, as suggested below.

Consumers among bottom 25% total euro sales (last 12 months)	
"I receive too many promotional emails from Pentathlon."	52%
"I receive just the right amount of promotional emails from Pentathlon."	31%
"I receive too few promotional emails from Pentathlon."	17%

"Our most valuable customers are clearly frustrated with our volume of promotions," Quintero said to Starke to close the meeting. "So here's what I propose: We institute a strict, companywide limit of two promotional emails per week per customer. I hope you can approve it soon before we damage our brand any further."

Starke appreciated Quintero's passion about the issue. And her data did suggest that key customer segments were unhappy about the email volume. But over the past week Starke had also heard from several department directors who were highly skeptical of Quintero's suggestion. "A lower volume of emails means a lower volume of sales," the director of Water Sports had written Starke by email. Several others pointed out that the directors would have to coordinate promotional activities in the face of a limit—a likely time-consuming effort.

Starke understood their resistance but was tempted to institute Quintero's limit nonetheless, given the data she'd presented. He began to prepare a memo outlining the new policy but stopped short after a meeting with François Cabret, director of Endurance Sports. "You're going to want to see this," Cabret had said excitedly to Starke before even sitting down.

After conversations with his fellow department directors, Cabret conducted a new analysis, this time looking at the relationship between email frequency and purchase behavior—again from a random sample of the same 85,000-plus recent online customers Quintero had used.

Cabret's analysis split customer respondents into three categories based on the number of promo emails they received per week: 1 to 2.9, 3 to 4.9, and 5 or more. Roughly one-third of customers sampled fit into each group. Next Cabret had calculated the average number of orders and dollar sales in the past 12 months for each category.

"As you can see," Cabret said triumphantly, "consumers who received more promotional emails placed many more orders than those who received fewer promotions" (see table below).

Average weekly email frequency	Number of orders during last 12 months
1–2.9	3.5
3–4.9	9.9
5 or more	17.3

"That means Anna's email limit would definitely cost us sales," Cabret continued. To back up his argument further, he showed Starke results for total sales volume. Again, customers who received more promo emails ordered more.

Average weekly email frequency	Total euro sales during last 12 months
1–2.9	€41.64
3–4.9	€210.40
5 or more	€498.12

"It may be true that customers feel they're receiving too many emails," Cabret said near the meeting's end. "After all, how many consumers actually *like* ads? But my data show that we can't take the risk of sending fewer promotions, because we'll surely lose sales. We have to take the profit-maximizing approach, right?"

Starke felt stymied about the decision he had to make. Quintero and Cabret had presented compelling but highly conflicting analyses of Pentathlon's promotional emails. The numbers suggested that customers, especially the company's most valuable ones, weren't happy about the email volume, but also that such promotions were associated with greater sales.

This is a common situation in organizations of all types. A manager or department provides data in support of their favored approach, while another offers completely contradictory recommendations, with their own seemingly corroborative analytics results. To compound matters, *both* pieces of evidence may be correct. That's the case here for Pentathlon, as high-volume customers are legitimately dissatisfied with the volume of promotional emails, but they also represent the most valuable segment!

As a leader, whether making your own case or deciding between two conflicting ones, you have to be able to reconcile the evidence and make a good decision. We see leaders with low DSIQ falling into two traps. First, they pick their favorite story without thoroughly evaluating the evidence. Second, they suggest that there are flaws in the analytics and propose new but unfruitful types of new analyses. Neither path helps them make the right decision.

CMO Colin Starke faced exactly these challenges. He had to make a decision about whether to impose a limit on promotional emails and loved Quintero's compelling story: customers are upset and we need to react. But the business-focused evidence Cabret offered made Starke pause, understandably. When we discuss this case study in our AI and analytics workshops, executives often feel vaguely uneasy with the evidence provided by Anna Quintero and François Cabret. This leads them to request more data—for example, a breakdown of emails and sales by department. Or participants feel the data is flawed and ask for higher-quality data, such as an improved survey among respondents who they believe are more representative of the target audience. We push back. Asking for more data or higher-quality data may be a good idea, we tell the participants, but you first need to understand what exactly is wrong with the data you already have.

The analysis Quintero and Cabret presented, it turns out, didn't address head-on the question of what level of promotional emails is best for driving sales. Quintero's data was about whether customers were happy about email volume (they weren't). We can ask her survey questions different ways, and we are probably going to find the same result: many customers are unhappy with promotional email volume. Nonetheless, the fact that customers are unhappy does not mean that the firm is not behaving optimally. For example, major TV networks typically show 15 to 20 minutes of ads per hour. Would consumers be happier with only five minutes of ads? Of course, but fewer ads means less ad revenue, so reducing ad volume may not make sense from a business perspective.

Cabret's analysis relied on historical data, and one might take issue with how he analyzed the data. But no matter how you cut it, the evidence François Cabret relies on does *not* show that getting more emails drives higher revenues. Why?

Suppose a customer buys a pair of skis. Because each Pentathlon department handles email separately, this customer now starts getting promotional email from the Winter Sports department but not from others. Now, suppose this same customer buys cycling gear from the Endurance Sports department. The customer now gets promotional email from two departments, Winter Sports and Endurance Sports. Now suppose the individual buys from a third department; that department will start sending emails too. We hope the pattern is clear.

Looking across the business's customer base, some consumers buy from many departments and therefore get emails from many departments. Other consumers buy from only one department and therefore get emails from only one department. Who do you think spends more, on average? Probably those who buy from many departments. So the consequence is this: consumers receive many emails because they buy from many departments and therefore spend lots of money with Pentathlon. This means that revenues drive email frequency instead of email frequency driving revenues. The key insight is that we have *no evidence* in this case that more emails cause greater revenues.

The fact that some customers receive more promotional emails than others is a result of Pentathlon's historical decentralized mailing policy. The best customers today are more likely to be targeted with emails tomorrow.

Importantly, the data that Quintero and Cabret present does accurately describe the reality that Pentathlon faces: high-revenue customers today are more likely to receive a higher volume of promotional emails and are more likely to be unhappy about this. But what the data fails to explain is how changing the email policy will affect either profitability or customer satisfaction.

Like CMO Colin Starke in this example, you need to be able to "get under the hood" of seemingly simple data analytics to understand whether the implications and conclusions are valid. That is, you need to be able to distinguish good from bad analytics, or the kind that generate ideal data for decision-making versus figures and "findings" that may inadvertently lead you astray.

What is ideal data? Data generated by *experiments*—a special kind of comparison that helps you make valid conclusions about cause and effect. As suggested by the quote with which we opened this chapter, the problem with many analytics conclusions is that data that was not generated by an experiment is presented as if it was. This was the case with the Pentathlon results, and it happens countless times in businesses and other organizations.

This chapter helps you understand how to distinguish good from bad analytics, largely by using the concept of an experiment as your cornerstone for understanding when data is valid for answering a specific question or making a specific decision. And experiments, by definition, have their own cornerstone: randomization, which we'll discuss next.

THE MAGIC OF RANDOMIZATION

An ideal world for analytics would look very different from the real world: it would have at least two identical versions of the same consumer or product or factory, so we could test how each would react or change in circumstances that are exactly the same except with regard to what we want to study. For example, we could place two identical people into the exact same worlds but show one an ad for jewelry, a car, or deodorant and make sure not to show it to their "clone" in the other world. If the former is more likely to purchase the item than the latter, we could then attribute any increased likelihood to purchase to the ad itself. A clear cause-and-effect relationship.

Unfortunately, we live in the real world, and there's only one of each person! We can't place the same person or product or factory into two worlds simultaneously. Once someone sees an ad, they can't unsee it, as much as they might like to. Similarly, there is virtually no way to implement a new manufacturing process in a factory and compare it to the same factory at the same point in time without the new process. So there's no way to observe the differential effects of ad exposure and no ad exposure in the same person or to compare a new manufacturing process to an old manufacturing process within the same factory at the same point in time. This makes it more difficult to determine causal relationships in your business.

Luckily, there's a solution—not the perfect, clone-the-world solution, but a good-enough one. Rather than using truly equivalent people or other subjects of study, you can use a randomized experiment to create *probabilistically equivalent groups*. That is, you assign a given person randomly to one "world" (say, ad exposure or no ad exposure), then repeat that process again and again, until each group (ad vs. no ad) is large enough (we will talk about what that means later). The key objective is to create two or more groups that have no systematic difference in their characteristics or in how they would respond to the outcome of interest, which in our example is the likelihood to purchase after seeing an ad. Probabilistic equivalence is a foundation of good analytics because it enables causal conclusions and thus supports related arguments or recommendations.

Imagine you work with a company that sells jewelry and you run a randomized experiment to see if people exposed to an ad for a certain necklace or bracelet are more likely to buy it. Imagine further that you find that 24 percent of those in the group exposed to the ad end up purchasing the item, whereas only 11 percent of those in the group that's not exposed to the ad do so, as depicted in Figure 4.1. Through bad luck, is it possible there are more people likely to buy

Figure 4.1 Jewelry Purchases After Exposure to Ad or No Exposure

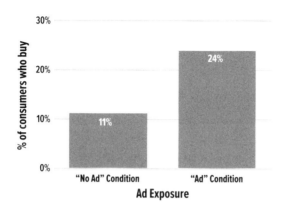

the jewelry in the ad-exposure group than the non-exposure group? For example, is it possible that there are substantially more women in the ad group, and that women are more likely to buy jewelry? Clearly this is possible if you are sloppy with analytics. If your test is well designed, randomization precludes this possibility. Moreover, if you are concerned about this possibility, you could examine the groups before launching the experiment to ensure they are equivalent on known influential factors like gender.

The great news about randomization is that you don't even need to know all the factors that might affect the outcome when you're creating randomized groups. A large enough sample will make it extremely unlikely that some unmeasurable variable you may not have thought of underlies any difference between groups. Indeed, randomization is about as close to *magic* as you're going to get in data science because you don't need to know anything about the people in your randomized groups—other than that they're actually people! Having large enough groups means you can run a test as if you had two versions of the same consumer in identical worlds that differ only on the feature of interest (ad vs. no ad). That's the power of randomization.

But before you assume randomization is the analytics cure-all, you should know that it is not easy to truly randomize—we'll discuss why later in the book.

MOST DATA IS NOT RANDOMLY GENERATED

Our core takeaway from this chapter is worth repeating: the number-one reason for bad analytics is that data not generated as part of a true experiment—with randomization as described above—is presented and interpreted as if it was. In the Pentathlon case, for example, the data presented was about as "nonrandom" as you can get. Consumers were not randomly assigned to receive different numbers of emails. Instead, how many emails consumers received depended on the number of departments they had previously purchased from (and therefore how good a customer they already were). This yielded flawed conclusions about causality and a major headache for the CMO.

We saw a similar example in the first chapter, where executives of a supplier of digital services to auto companies concluded that seeing an online car ad for a given manufacturer made people dramatically more likely to purchase that car. In reality, ads were more likely to be shown to people who had already expressed interest in purchasing a car (through online searches, for example), again making the groups (ad or no ad) nonrandom and invalidating any causal conclusions. None of this data was generated by true experiments, which requires randomization.

Unfortunately, much of the world we want to study is designed to be *nonrandom*. Google's whole advertising model, for example, is to avoid showing ads to people unlikely to be interested in them; the platform systematically targets those assumed to have some interest in an offering based on demographic or behavioral factors, to deliver to advertisers consumers who are more likely to click and buy, and ultimately to sell more ads. That results in highly nonrandom samples that make it difficult, and in some cases impossible, to draw causal conclusions. In the car ad example above, for example, interest in purchase drove ad exposure, as intended, which invalidates any causal conclusions about the effectiveness or ineffectiveness of advertising. We know that car ads are associated with more sales, but we just don't know why.

At the same time, randomized experiments are one of several tools in the data science toolkit for reaching causal conclusions. We'll discuss many other options in this book. But we emphasize here that people too often interpret nonexperimental data as experimental, and present it that way. Leaders with high DSIQ recognize this critical difference.

At its core, most causal analytics is about comparing outcomes such as purchase behavior, revenue, factory output, or units sold between groups (people, stores, factories, products) that differ on some key factor of interest. Continuing this line of thought, the factor of interest may be ad exposure versus no ad exposure among people; new versus old store formats; new versus old manufacturing plants; high versus low product prices. You want to be able say that the factor of interest is *causally* responsible for changes in the outcome. That requires that the groups are probabilistically equivalent, as we suggested earlier, and our examples in this chapter make clear that many analyses fail to meet that criterion.

A "GOOD FROM BAD ANALYTICS" OR CAUSALITY CHECKLIST

The good news is that once you have a high DSIQ you will be able to tell good from bad interpretations of charts, tables, and reports. But here's the trick. An experienced data scientist is much like an experienced CFO. Show the CFO a balance sheet, and she can quickly tell you about the financial health of the firm. Leaders with a high DSIQ can tell good from bad analytics in less than 5 minutes—not 60 minutes. So the issue is not that you can tell good from bad, it's that you need to do this quickly. Why? In 60 minutes, the meeting is over and the decision is made. You won't have the luxury of going back to your office, thinking things through, and then arriving at a solid conclusion. You need to first learn to discern good from bad analytics and then hone your skills so that you can do this quickly.

To assist you on this journey, we've created a systematic checklist to help you build your analytics muscle. By mastering this checklist, you will learn to quickly tell good from bad analytics.

The checklist (see Figure 4.2) takes you through a series of questions to ask about all types of analysis, using a clear process. Once you have mastered the checklist it will gradually become automatic—much like a CFO reading a balance sheet.

Figure 4.2 The Causality Checklist

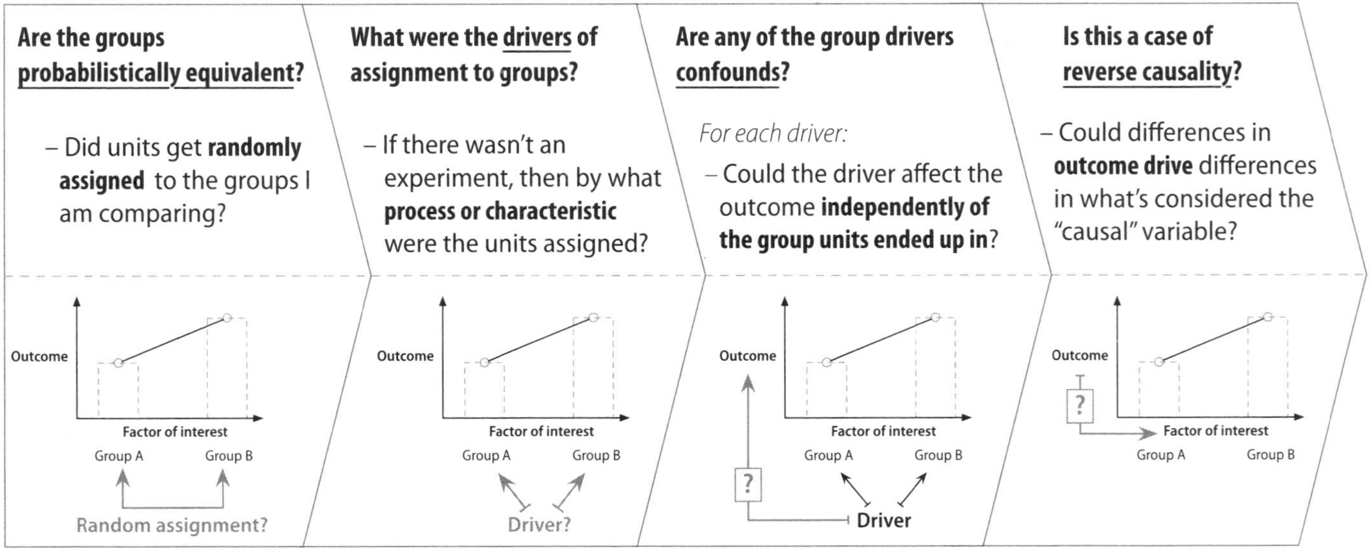

Are the groups probabilistically equivalent?

– Did units get **randomly assigned** to the groups I am comparing?

(diagram: Outcome vs. Factor of interest, Group A, Group B; Random assignment?)

What were the drivers of assignment to groups?

– If there wasn't an experiment, then by what **process or characteristic** were the units assigned?

(diagram: Outcome vs. Factor of interest, Group A, Group B; Driver?)

Are any of the group drivers confounds?

For each driver:

– Could the driver affect the outcome **independently of the group units ended up in?**

(diagram: Outcome vs. Factor of interest, Group A, Group B; Driver)

Is this a case of reverse causality?

– Could differences in **outcome drive** differences in what's considered the "causal" variable?

(diagram: Outcome vs. Factor of interest, Group A, Group B)

Checklist Item 1: Are the Groups Probabilistically Equivalent?

The first question on the checklist is, "Did units get randomly assigned to the groups I am comparing?" If you are new to analytics, like many participants in our programs, this question sounds a bit intimidating. After we break things down, you will realize it is quite intuitive.

First, the word "units" is short for "units of analysis," and this is a common term used among data scientists to refer to "what or who is being compared." For example, in the Pentathlon case described earlier, we are comparing the spending pattern among groups of consumers buying sport equipment, so "units" are individual consumers. In the ultrasound case in the first chapter, we are comparing the duration of ultrasound exams depending on what machine was used. So "units" are the individual ultrasound exams performed by technicians. Data scientists often think of "units" as being the rows of data in a data table or spreadsheet.

When using the checklist, we want to know whether units were randomly assigned to groups, which would make them probabilistically equivalent. If the answer is *yes*, that means causal conclusions may be drawn from the table, chart, or figure you are analyzing, and you can set the checklist aside. Unfortunately, in most cases the answer is likely to be *no*. That was the case in the digital car ad example from the first chapter, where people weren't assigned to ad or no-ad conditions randomly, but rather based on their previously expressed interest in purchasing an automobile. If the answer to checklist item 1 is a "no," which will happen most of the time you are reviewing results, you have to proceed to the next checklist question.

Checklist Item 2: What Were the Drivers of Assignment to Groups?

If the first question felt awkward, then this second question will seem very wonky. But again, with some practice it will feel more natural. Ask yourself, "If there wasn't an experiment, then by what process or characteristic were the units of analysis assigned?" Let's make this concrete by looking back at the car ad results presented in the first chapter (Figure 4.3).

Figure 4.3   Car Ad Example Results

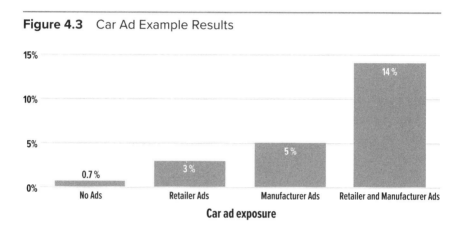

Car ad exposure

Recall that the groups were made up of consumers who saw "No Car-Related Ads," "Only Retailer Ads," "Only Manufacturer Ads," or " Retail and Manufacturer Ads." Remember, every row in a spreadsheet belongs to one of our four groups.

How did a customer end up in the No Ads group? Answer: they weren't searching for a car. How did a customer end up in the "Retailer and Manufacturer Ads" group? Answer: they were searching for a car (triggering a manufacturer ad) and a location (triggering a dealer ad). So, "Interest in Buying a Car" is a "driver" (the concept, not the person) that determined consumer search behavior—a consumer not interested in a car may search for "Yoga Mats," whereas a consumer very interested in a car may search for "Jeep Grand Cherokee, Boston." This search behavior affects the ads shown to consumers and, in turn, the groups they belong to, for purposes of our analysis. Again, in our framework, a driver is "interest in buying a car," as this is what ultimately makes the groups differ beyond their exposure to car-related ads.

If you had a different story in mind about why consumers end up seeing different ads, don't worry. As you will learn in a moment, there can be many drivers. For now, make sure you grasp the concept of a driver and our new language or terminology.

Checklist Item 3: Are Any of the Group Drivers Confounds?

Once you've identified what drives assignment to groups, you need to consider your outcome metric. A confound occurs when a driver, which influences group membership, also influences your outcome metric *directly*. Again, let's make this concrete using the car ad example.

Our outcome metric was the sales conversion rate of buying a car in a 90-day window. For the No Ad group it was less than 1 percent, and for the Both Ads group it was 14 percent. Our driver was "Interest in Buying a Car." Checklist item 3 forces you to ask the question, "Is interest in buying a car related to sales conversion, *independent* of whether consumers saw any car-related ads?" If the answer is "yes," then you have a confound.

In the car ad example, we have a clear confound and would thus be reluctant to draw causal conclusions. Here is why: when a confound is present, you can no longer confidently attribute changes in the outcome to the factor of interest. The reason is that we now have two plausible stories. Our first story is that the increase in car sales was due to advertising; our second story is that the higher car sales among consumers who saw ads was because these were the customers who were interested in buying a car in the first place. It's entirely possible that either story is correct, or that they are both going on at the same time. That is, consumers who see car ads are more interested in buying a car; in addition, ads are increasing their likelihood to buy even further. As a result, you might find yourself in a meeting where folks advocate for their favorite story, as happened in the Pentathlon example earlier. High-DSIQ leaders realize that we simply cannot tell, using our data and evidence, which story is correct. You may like the advertising story, but that is an opinion and not a fact. Good data science makes this distinction.

Answering the checklist questions presented so far is fairly straightforward in the car ad example—and the executives who were initially fooled by the data would have benefited from the checklist! But as we emphasized in the first chapter, assessing the validity of any kind of analytics often requires domain expertise gained through managerial experience. Data scientists may not know the business well enough to understand why a given person ends up in one group or another. Your role as a business leader is to fill in such gaps.

With that in mind, let's apply the checklist to another, more complex analytics example, again from the auto industry.

THE CAUSALITY CHECKLIST IN ACTION: HOW TO OPTIMIZE AUTO-INDUSTRY INCENTIVE SPENDING

Auto manufacturers spend *a lot* on purchase incentives. Consider that General Motors lays out about $3 billion annually on advertising, but three to five times that on incentive spending—lease incentives, interest rate incentives, cash incentives, and others.[1] The two most important incentive types go to customers (manufacturers give customers some amount of cash "back," toward their down payment or in some other form) and dealers (manufacturers retroactively rebate some portion of the invoice price back to the dealer).

So, if manufacturers have a fixed amount to budget toward incentives, how should they allocate it between customers and dealers to maximize profits?

A Problem of Pass-Through

The problem is that dealers tend to argue that more of the incentives should go to them, as they are closer to the customer and can thus know better when the money clinches the deal. But manufacturers who buy into this argument run the risk of enabling dealers to keep a significant portion of the cash for themselves, to boost their own bottom line. There's a lot of money at stake: dealers make an average profit of less than $1,000 on cars they sell; manufacturers in late 2019 offered on average $4,600 in incentives per car, so grabbing a sizable portion of that can increase dealer profits considerably.[2]

A key thing for manufacturers to understand, then, is the actual *pass-through* of cash incentives that dealers receive from manufacturers—or put differently, the amount of the incentive that is being passed to customers rather than kept by dealers. Getting an accurate sense of that critical figure is one factor manufacturers consider to allocate incentives in a way that maximize their own profits.

Determining the pass-through amount of course requires analysis of sales data.[3] For example, suppose that in a one-year period a sample of dealerships sold 38,456 Toyota Priuses with a promotional incentive paid to the dealer, while 94,560 were sold without such incentive. Say that the average incentive amount was approximately $2,000. For cars sold with no incentive, the average purchase price was about $25,000. In contrast, Priuses for which there was an incentive sold for about $23,000.

On the surface, that looks like 100 percent of the dealer incentive was passed through to the customer: the dealer incentive of $2,000 reduced the price paid by the consumer by more or less that exact amount. Dealers would argue that the incentive they received "caused" the lower purchase price because they passed the incentive fully to the customer, as the manufacturer would have hoped. But as you've learned from previous examples, when it comes to analytics, things often aren't as they seem, especially the validity of causal conclusions.

To understand this, let's put this example through our Causality Checklist.

First, are the two groups in question—customer purchases with and without the dealer incentive—probabilistically equivalent? That would require that the units, or in this case car buyers, be randomly assigned to the incentive or nonincentive group. We know that wasn't the case as customers made the buying decision themselves. As discussed earlier, a "no" answer to the first question means we have to ask the second: How did car buyers end up in different groups? What were the drivers of being in the incentive or nonincentive group?

To answer that we have to dig a little deeper into the practical realities of how and why incentives are offered to consumers.

Like nearly every action taken by a firm, incentives are offered for a specific business reason. Understanding this reason is critical for distinguishing good from bad analytics.

In the auto industry, manufacturers assess multiple factors to decide when to offer dealer incentives. As you can imagine, when demand for specific cars is high, there's no need for any incentives, as offering them would erode profits. So promotional incentives tend to be offered when demand is weak, to move cars that may have become less attractive to buyers, often because newer models have become available. This means promotional incentives are generally offered only in periods of weak demand. So now we have identified one driver: *demand* determines whether cars will be offered with or without an incentive.

Some drivers are easy to discern and understand; you may be able to come up with them off the top of your head. But in our experience, many are very subtle. So here are three systematic questions to ask about drivers, to help you identify them and assess their effect on an analysis (Figure 4.4). After the figure we present detailed descriptions of each question.

Figure 4.4   Three Questions About Drivers

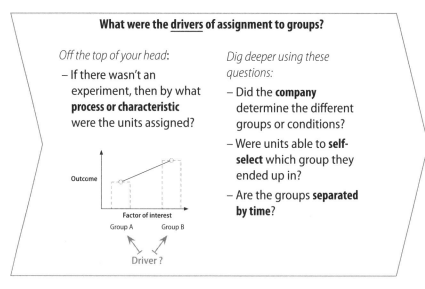

Did the company determine the different groups or conditions? In this case, yes, because the manufacturer decided whether to offer a dealer incentive in a given time period. In times of low demand, the manufacturer offered incentives, which we just discussed.

Were units (in this case people) able to select which group they ended up in? That is, did car buyers decide whether they would buy during a promotional period? Again the answer is "yes." For one, car buyers may have a sense for when a promotion will be more likely. For example, many people wait until the transition to the new model year (usually in the fall) to buy the previous model year at a discount. But even if buyers don't deliberately time their purchase to coincide with a promotion, their price sensitivity may make them more likely to buy when incentives are offered. In general, price sensitivity will drive people to *self-select* into the promotion or nonpromotion group, acting as a secondary driver.

Are the groups separated by time? This is a critical question because any separation of groups by time can leave room for other factors to affect the outcomes under study, with seasonality as a prime culprit. As we discussed above, dealer incentives tend to be offered only when demand is weak, so you can't have a time period when such incentives are simultaneously available and unavailable! So yes, the groups are separated by time, and promotions coincide with periods of weak demand. Demand is the driver that leads to the separation by time.

Having explored the drivers at play in depth, you can return to the third Causality Checklist question: Can any of the drivers be considered confounds? Recall that our outcome metric is the purchase price of a car. We now ask whether any of the two drivers we identified, namely *demand conditions* and *price sensitivity*, affect the purchase price of a car independent of whether it's in a promotional period. Absolutely. Weaker demand will result in lower negotiated prices because dealers want to get rid of cars that are not selling as expected, regardless of whether manufacturers offer promotions. Similarly, if a group of car buyers has higher price sensitivity, this is likely to result in lower negotiated prices because dealers lower prices when consumers are willing to walk away, irrespective of whether manufacturers offer promotions. So it's fair to argue that these drivers are likely confounds. We now have three stories that may explain the difference in price paid between the promotional and nonpromotional periods. We simply cannot separate the stories, so it's not necessarily valid for dealers to claim that they've passed through 100 percent of the incentive to customers. As we will discuss later in the book, further analytics may help us disentangle these stories. But, for now, the exploratory results fail our checklist.

CONFOUNDS, CONFOUNDS, EVERYWHERE

Because confounds are ubiquitous across settings, let's apply what we've learned to two more examples.

High-Speed Snow Blower Sales in New England

Imagine you work for the manufacturer of a popular high-speed snow blower that has experienced much poorer sales than expected in late 2014 in the New England region. To improve revenue, your company decides to offer a $200 sales incentive for blowers purchased in January and February of 2015. As hoped, sales go up 53 percent compared to November and December 2014 sales. Managers in charge of the promotion attribute the increase in sales to the design of the digital promotional campaign, which was integrated with in-store merchandising.

But can we declare success from just this data? By now you know that this would be a premature conclusion. Let's apply the Causality Checklist, including the expanded set of driver-related questions presented earlier.

Were purchasers randomly assigned to buy a snow blower during the late 2014 (no promotion) or early 2015 (promotion) period? No, people decided on their own when to purchase a snow blower.

Since the purchasers were not randomly assigned, the hunt for drivers begins. This example feels a bit similar to the pass-through example. The manufacturer offered the promotion after observing poor sales in November and December (demand is a driver). It's possible that the shoppers in late 2014 are different from those in 2015, due to the seasonal nature of snow blower sales. Deal-seekers, for example, may be more prevalent later in the season than earlier in the season.

But here is the added twist. Let's ask: *Were the groups separated by time?* Yes, the promotions happened in January and February 2015, rather than in the previous two months. Was there anything unique about the time period of the promotion that may have affected snow blower sales? If you lived in New England, you should immediately recall this historical winter period. Winter storms Juno and Marcus dumped nearly 50 inches of snow on the region! Can weather in general and snowfall in particular be considered confounds that affect whether and when people buy a product used to remove snow? Absolutely. A massive snowstorm will almost always drive higher sales of snow blowers and other snow-removal equipment in a region, promotion or not (especially for higher-speed blowers that can remove greater snow volume quickly).

So now we have four stories that each may claim some credit for the difference in snow blower sales. Story 1 is the new, integrated promotion. Story 2 is that demand slumped severely in late 2014 and naturally bounced back to normal levels in early 2015. Story 3 is around deal-seekers. Story 4 is "it snowed an unbelievable amount." While our promotions team may have done a great job, we cannot tell which of these four stories led to the massive increase in sales.

Weight, Weight, Don't Tell Me

Take a moment and look at the stylized graph in Figure 4.5, which depicts a positive association between weight and reading ability. One of the authors (Zettelmeyer) loves seeing this data because as a child he was often the heaviest kid in class and he was also a very good reader. It turns out kids at a higher weight tend to read better than those at lower weights. Why might that be?

When shown this data, participants in our programs offer all kinds of hypotheses: reading more makes children exercise less, leading to weight gain; kids who aren't physically active might gain weight but also read more; overweight children may have fewer social opportunities, which gives them more time to read.

Figure 4.5 Weight and Reading Ability

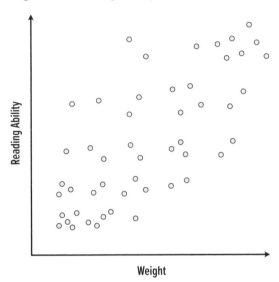

The real answer is much simpler: *age* affects both how much you weigh and how well you read. Seven-year-olds read better than six-year-olds and weigh more, on average; eight-year-olds read better than seven-year-olds and weigh more. All this data tells us is that older kids tend to read better than younger ones—an obvious fact. Age is the clear confound here because it varies systematically with the factor we think of as the cause (weight level) and the one we think of as the effect, or outcome (reading ability).

And here is why this story is so important. When first presented with an association like this one, especially if it's framed in a way that pulls for us to believe the causal implication ("Overweight kids should take heart—they read better than other kids"), it makes us more likely to accept a flawed conclusion. We assume age is held constant in the graph—that is, it includes only kids of the same age—and become more likely to accept a causal connection.

When presented with analytics of any kind, we tend to rationalize the data, even filling in missing pieces to make better sense of the world. We often surround data and analytics with a story, filled with assumptions, and once you buy the assumptions you are hooked! If you believe that "age is held constant" in the figure of weight vs. age, you immediately are led to the hypotheses we listed above.

This is why having a systematic process for interpreting data and analytics is so critical. Everyone has a story they want to tell with data and analytics. Part of your job is to determine whether there are plausible alternative stories that may explain the results. Following our systematic Causality Checklist enables you to do this quickly and efficiently.

In the final section, we look at the special case when the *outcome itself* is the driver, or what we think of as "reverse causality."

Checklist Item 4: Is this a Case of Reverse Causality?

Recall the Pentathlon example from earlier in this chapter: department managers were arguing that sending customers more promotional emails led to higher sales. In reality, it was the other way around, as people who bought sports equipment from more departments (higher sales) tended to receive more emails! This is a clear example of reverse causality, or when what you think of as the outcome (higher sales) is actually the driver of what's considered the "causal" variable (more emails). It's the last question on the Causality Checklist:

Could differences in outcome drive differences in what's considered the "causal" variable?

Here, a "yes" answer will invalidate causal conclusions drawn from the original analysis, as the hypothesized "cause" and "effect" are actually reversed. Let's consider reverse causality from an anonymized real-world case from one of the world's best-known companies.

Social Media and Customer Value at ComputerTech

In 2014, when Sunil Khosla started his position in digital marketing at ComputerTech, the name we use for a large tech company where we saw the events in this example unfold, he worked hard to apply insights about digital and social marketing to ComputerTech's customers across a massive array of products and services. For example, he considered the implications of a Bain & Company report about social media:

> Our recent survey of more than 3,000 consumers helped to identify what makes social media effective. We found that customers who engage with companies over social media spend 20 percent to 40 percent more money with those companies than other customers. They also demonstrate a deeper emotional commitment to the companies, granting them an average 33 points higher Net Promoter® score [common measure of customer loyalty].[4]

Would increased social engagement drive similar benefits for ComputerTech, Khosla wondered? How could he find related data? He'd heard the in-house ECOM Analytics group was good at tracking and reporting on consumer behavior. The group's charter was to create visibility into all products and services that resided on ComputerTech's sites. Moreover, the group now used tags that spanned all of ComputerTech's properties to track individual consumer behavior platform-wide, keeping up to four years' worth of data to inform the tactics of more than 150 internal teams.

Eager to learn from the data, Khosla reached out to the ECOM Analytics group. He asked for data on how much visitors to different ComputerTech properties shared, and how much revenue each visitor generated the previous quarter.

Two hours later, the ECOM Analytics group replied, sending the data in the following table.

	Visitors (millions)	Social Shares (millions)	Shares per Visitor	Revenue ($millions)	$ per Visitor
Total Site	324.1	n/a	n/a	$118.7	$0.37
Social Visitors	2.6	3.4M	1.3	$6.03	$2.41
% of Total	0.8%			5.1%	6.5x Avg.

Studying the table, Khosla was excited about the apparent association between social media activity and revenue: social visitors outspent the network average six-to-one, and generated more than 5 percent of revenue while representing less than 1 percent of the total population. Sharing, though not that frequent (1.3 shares per visitor, on average, in the last quarter), seemed powerful.

Moreover, Khosla had observed untapped potential for social engagement on the ComputerTech site: many pages contained no social options, such as links to share content through Facebook or Twitter. Armed with these facts, Khosla urged the digital marketing team to invest heavily in social engagement across all digital properties. He argued that social engagement reliably increases customer value, pointing to the data showing that customers who shared socially were much more valuable than others. "In fact," Khosla concluded, "doubling the number of visitors who share socially should drive a $6 million revenue increase next quarter, more than enough to cover the cost of adding Twitter and Facebook links on all pages of our site."

His presentation convinced the team to approve his suggestion, and within 30 days social links appeared sitewide. At the next quarter's end, Khosla and his digital marketing colleagues were eager to see the results of the strategy. The ECOM Analytics group first provided the data below for visitors and revenue.

Total Network	Visitors (millions)	Revenue (millions)	$ per Visitor
90 days prior to change	326.7	$124.7	$0.37
90 days after change	320.1	$120.6	$0.365
Q/Q Change	–2.0%	–3.3%	–1.4%

The decrease in overall visitors and revenue were not surprising, and in line with seasonal expectation. The bigger questions, then, were whether social visitors were up, whether sharing had increased, and whether revenues from social visitors were up. But the results were a big disappointment to Khosla. Creating more opportunities for sharing had increased shares per visitor from 1.3 to 1.7. But, there

was no effect on the number of visitors who shared or total revenues—that is, no evidence of the positive impact he'd promised the
organization. Where had he gone wrong?

Khosla had to understand the situation quickly, as he was
expected to explain it at the upcoming digital marketing meeting.
Before reading further, put yourself in Khosla's shoes and use what
you've learned from this chapter to identify any flaws in his approach.
Take some time to think.

As you may have realized after some deliberation, Khosla made a
critical assumption: that the act of sharing would increase affinity to
ComputerTech. Instead, once you use the Causality Checklist to get
into the drivers at play, you'd likely understand that *affinity to ComputerTech* is what determines whether someone is a social visitor or
not—those with more affinity tend to share more. So Khosla's argument that increasing social options on the site would lead to more
visitors who shared and, ultimately, greater revenues was not sound.

In fact, going deeper into the checklist should lead you to an
important conclusion akin to that in the Pentathlon example, based
on the checklist's last section: social activity wasn't driving greater
affinity (expressed as spend), it was the other way around—consumers with higher affinity share more. Thus, while adding more sharing
options increased levels of sharing, it didn't turn nonsharing visitors
into social visitors or increase the spending of already social visitors.

This is an excellent example of reverse causality, where the
perceived cause and effect are actually switched, resulting in often-
painful lessons like the one Khosla learned. As a standard practice,
you should literally flip the X and Y axes of a chart to stress-test the
proposed causal relationship. If you can tell a reasonable story in less
than 30 seconds that explains the relationship with the flipped axes,
you should be skeptical about the original causal claim. The ComputerTech example is an example of that (if you consider revenue a
measure of affinity, which is fair).

To avoid making mistakes like Khosla's—and so many other
executives who derive flawed causal relationships from invalid analyses—use the Causality Checklist for any analytics you encounter. If
the groups are truly probabilistically equivalent, you're all set. If not,
then you must be able to rule out any of the other issues—confounds

and reverse causality, specifically—before deriving causal conclusions. Sometimes you may not know the answer to a given checklist question and will need to gain more domain expertise to get to it. Most of us already know that the presence of more firefighters doesn't increase the likelihood of a fire breaking out (it's the reverse of that), for example, but we need more expertise to make judgments in domains we're less familiar with.

The more you use the checklist and other tools in this book, the more you'll be able to distinguish good from bad analytics, and to assess the validity of any conclusions about causality. In other words, when someone hands you a chart and makes an argument based on the data within it, you'll know exactly what to do next.

One final note. When we talk about the Causality Checklist in our executive workshops, we often hear things like, "With enough creativity, can't you always come up with drivers and confounds to throw the penalty flag on any proposed causal relationship?" Indeed, you often can. But the purpose of the checklist goes well beyond throwing penalty flags. It turns out that there are several great ways to prove a causal relationship, even if there is no probabilistic equivalence and the analysis initially failed the checklist. All of the solutions, however, require a reasonably complete list of possible confounds to find the right way to establish causality. You will learn how to do this in future chapters.

Actively Participating in AI and Analytics

N ow that you understand how to critically assess data and analytics quality, this section prepares you to *participate* actively in AI and analytics. We organized the chapters around three subsections, which follow the AIA Framework. The first subsection, "Predictive Analytics," shows you techniques for anticipating outcomes, and illuminates the inner workings of AIA predictive models like machine learning and neural networks. The second subsection, "Causal Analytics," introduces techniques that help you determine how to influence outcomes using experimental data as well as your existing, on-hand data. In this subsection, we also introduce a framework to help you connect predictive and causal models. The third subsection, "Making Decisions," helps you make the best analytics-driven decisions and scale them in your company.

CHAPTER 5

ANATOMY OF A CRYSTAL BALL

How can you anticipate outcomes?

That's the question predictive analytics seeks to answer. Like a crystal ball, predictive analytics presents a window into the future. Specifically, it's about using data that you have to predict an outcome that you don't yet know using statistical or machine learning approaches. To remind you, predictive analytics is one of the key components of the AIA Framework we presented in Chapter 2, in addition to exploratory analytics and causal analytics.

Consider some examples of predictive analytics in action. As you read, keep the key phrase "anticipate outcomes" in mind.

First, the aerospace division of Fortune 500 firm Honeywell manufactures auxiliary power units (APUs) that power aircraft like the Boeing 737 and many other commercial and military jets when they're on the tarmac.[1] In the past, technicians would have had to climb onto aircraft exteriors to inspect APUs and similar electronics on a regular schedule—say, monthly—to check for failure and replace parts or the whole unit as necessary. But today, as just one component of their "connected aircraft" strategy, Honeywell is able to instrument APUs with sensors that monitor key variables such as temperature to better predict performance. By anticipating future failures before they happen, predictive analytics models help reduce downtime for aircraft and allocate technicians strategically to provide the greatest business value.

Banks, too, can benefit greatly from predictive analytics, as you can imagine. One large area of application is loan defaults: What factors are most likely to predict someone will fail to repay a mortgage loan, for example? Citibank, Wells Fargo, and other consumer-focused lenders have many thousands of mortgage loans in their portfolios, and can benefit from understanding which are most at risk of default, to make related financial and other decisions. To do that, they can build a predictive model using factors such as household income, home price, loan-to-value ratio (size of loan compared to value of the property), home equity, type of mortgage (such as fixed-rate versus adjustable-rate, and length of term in years), and many others. Similar predictive models can help gauge the risk of approving a given mortgage loan in the first place.

Finally, consider a different kind of prediction: travel time. Most of us have used Google Maps or some other digital map technology to understand how long a given trip will take by car—whether you're traveling to a new restaurant just outside town or moving across the country for a new job. Along with providing the most direct (or scenic) route, the application will offer your ETA, or estimated time of arrival, if you were to leave now. How does it do that? Predictive analytics, of course! Google and other map-app providers use data including official speed limits, recommended speeds, historical average speeds, time of day (such as rush hour), weather conditions, and real-time traffic information (such as from Google's Waze app) to predict trip time, again as part of a model refined over time. When possible, they fine-tune their algorithms by comparing predicted travel time with actual time. Not surprisingly, the more data available, the better the predictions, and the more likely people are to use the app, which generates more data to improve the predictive model, as part of a virtuous cycle.[2]

This chapter will help you understand how to use predictive analytics by describing the "anatomy" of such real-life crystal balls—specifically, how predictive models work. We will consider predictions for continuous variables, such as revenues, earnings, and stock price, and binary variables, such as "yes" versus "no" and "buy" versus "not buy."

Many predictive models are grounded in a statistical approach called regression, which you've likely heard of. Soon, we'll get into that technique in detail. Here, we want to emphasize that while the data science behind good predictions can be complicated, the intuition needn't be. Predictive models are very understandable, so keep an open mind as we dive into the material here, which will surely increase your DSIQ!

Let's start with the case for continuous variables, using a fictional narrative example from a telecom carrier call-center operation.

IMPROVING CUSTOMER SATISFACTION AT BRIGHTSTAR MOBILE: LINEAR REGRESSION MODELS

Maria Cruz was excited.

Soon after she joined US mobile carrier BrightStar Mobile as director of customer service, her manager, VP of customer experience Tim Chan, tapped her for a high-profile assignment: improving customer satisfaction with BrightStar's call-center operation. Specifically, Net Promoter Scores (NPS; customers' willingness to recommend a product or service to others) had dipped from 45, well above the industry average of 32,[3] to 35 over the past year; that concerned the C-team, to whom Chan reported. The top leaders asked Chan to consider potential causes of the decline, and he had zeroed in on the call center, where hundreds of technical and customer service representatives answered thousands of incoming calls daily about technology issues, billing questions, and others. Chan was concerned that several call-center variables might be affecting the NPS, including hold time, representatives' knowledge, and other factors.

In an initial meeting, Cruz and Chan had decided to focus specifically on hold time, which had risen sharply over the past year as BrightStar's customer base had grown. They suspected that the call center no longer had adequate capacity to manage call volume effectively, leading to longer hold times and decreased satisfaction. Presumably, if hold time went down, NPS would go up. But was this indeed the case, and if so, how much business impact could

BrightStar expect—that is, how would an improvement in hold time translate into an improvement in NPS?

That was a critical question to answer, as it could help leadership better manage the "supply" of call-center representatives as related to the rising demand, or the growing volume of incoming calls. Maintaining too few representatives would mean longer hold times and reduced satisfaction. Overstaffing, in contrast, may improve hold times and NPS, but would potentially increase costs unnecessarily.[4]

To better understand the relationship between hold time and satisfaction, BrightStar needed a predictive model, one that could associate changes in hold time with changes in NPS. Cruz knew that NPS was calculated by surveying customers and asking the question, "On a scale of 0 to 10, how likely are you to recommend BrightStar to a friend?" NPS was calculated as the percent of customers whose "likelihood to recommend" rating was 9 or 10 (the "promoters") minus the percent of customers whose "likelihood to recommend" rating was 6 or lower (the "detractors"). Figure 5.1 shows the "likelihood to recommend" ratings in a sample of 500 BrightStar customers. If you calculate the NPS score based on this data you get 35.

Figure 5.1 Distribution of BrightStar "Likelihood to Recommend" Ratings

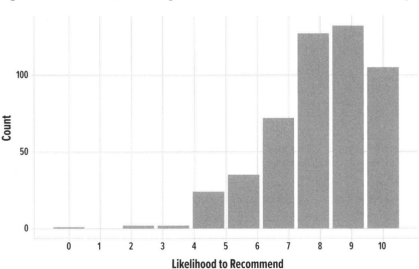

Luckily, Cruz had just completed a training course in predictive analysis and was eager to apply what she'd learned. That meant developing a simple model linking individual customers' hold times to their "likelihood to recommend" rating. To do that, she first asked BrightStar's data group to provide her with call-center data for hold times and likelihood to recommend ratings—customers heard an automated survey asking them to rate their likelihood to recommend BrightStar after the call, so Cruz was able to get a sample of 500 customers' hold times and likelihood-to-recommend ratings.

She used the data to create a simple graph (Figure 5.2) including both variables in question: hold time and likelihood to recommend.

Figure 5.2   Plot of BrightStar Hold Times and Likelihood to Recommend Ratings

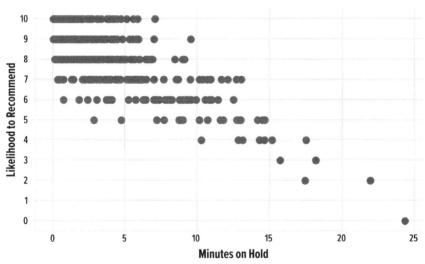

As shown in the figure, hold time is measured on the x-axis, and likelihood to recommend on the y-axis, so that each data point represents a given customer's hold time at the BrightStar call center, along with the likelihood-to-recommend rating they provided after the call. Take a look at Cruz's graph and think about how you'd predict the likelihood to recommend rating of a customer who had to wait, say, five minutes before connecting to a representative. This is where the statistical technique of *linear regression* comes in: Cruz used a regression to create a prediction for likelihood to recommend based on hold time. Once you run, or "estimate," a regression, you can figure the best-fitting line for the data and then write an equation for that line, as in Figure 5.3.

Figure 5.3   Regression Plot for BrightStar Data

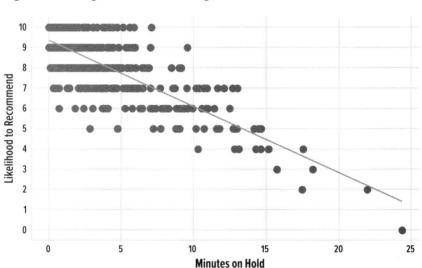

In BrightStar's case, the line that fits best (solid line in Figure 5.3) is characterized by the equation

Likelihood to Recommend = 9.4 – 0.33 × Minutes on Hold.

Let's take that apart. The 9.4 is what we call the intercept—or where the line crosses the y-axis. So for a hold time of zero minutes, customer satisfaction would be expected to be 9.4. The 0.33 number is the slope, which helps you understand how likelihood to recommend changes as hold time rises or fall. In this case, for every additional minute of hold time, you can expect satisfaction to drop by one-third of a point.

The equation, as you probably guessed, helps you make predictions. For example, if you want to know the likelihood to recommend associated with a hold time of 9 minutes, you'd just plug 9 into the equation to get 6.36. You can do the same for any specific hold time: 2 minutes, 4.5 minutes, 6.3 minutes, and so on. Most important for BrightStar's purposes, the team might want to predict the effect of staffing levels that lead to higher or lower hold times. That knowledge could prove critical to Chan and the C-team in deciding appropriate call-center staffing levels.

Cruz was excited to show Chan her regression model linking hold time to likelihood to recommend, and the predictions it yielded. "Nice work," Chan said after Cruz went over the model in detail. The VP, too, felt it was a valuable tool to help understand Bright-Star's call-center dynamics and to make related predictions. It was clear from the model that longer hold times were associated with decreased NPS, and the rising call-center hold times in recent years suggested satisfaction was only going to decline further. Convinced the company needed to hire more call-center staff to get control of hold times, Chan took Cruz's model to the next C-team meeting, ready to make his case.

But at Chan's next check-in with Cruz, he looked less confident. "The C-team agreed the regression model was reasonable," Chan told Cruz. "But the COO raised a great point. He asked how much likelihood to recommend even mattered. For example, customers who are likely to recommend may still cancel their contract with us if they get a better deal. And customers with a really low likelihood to recommend rating may stick with us for years despite that." Cruz understood the feedback, and together the two managers thought about its implications.

They quickly recognized that the link between hold time and likelihood to recommend was only part of the story of the call center's impact on BrightStar's business: hold time may relate to likelihood to recommend, as the linear regression suggested, but they needed to know whether either variable related to customer churn, which had the largest impact on profits. Specifically, they had to get a better handle on the relationship between likelihood to recommend and customer behavior—was there a measurable link between likelihood to recommend and churn, or the likelihood of a customer leaving the company, say, in the next six months? If so, Brightstar could perhaps identify customers who were at risk of leaving and do something about it proactively.

Cruz understood that likelihood to recommend, the predicted (or dependent) variable in the original regression, now became the predictor (or independent) variable, with churn as the predicted one. But that introduced another wrinkle: while likelihood to recommend is a continuous variable, churn (does the customer stay or go) is a binary one because it can only take two values. Luckily for Cruz, she once again knew how to create a predictive model—but this time it involved a different technique, as we discuss next.

LIKELIHOOD TO RECOMMEND AND CHURN AT BRIGHTSTAR MOBILE: LOGISTIC REGRESSION

In the previous section we described how linear regression could help predict telecom customer satisfaction based on call-center hold times. Specifically, the model created an equation showing that likelihood to recommend was estimated by 9.4 − 0.33 × minutes of hold time. This equation enabled us to predict likelihood to recommend for a customer who was placed on hold for any given amount of time.

Now BrightStar director of customer service Cruz faced a different challenge: predicting churn, a binary variable, using a customer's rating of likelihood to recommend BrightStar to other customers. Understanding this relationship would help determine how much likelihood to recommend mattered for retention. Using this model as a starting point, Cruz also planned to answer business questions like "How much money and effort should BrightStar invest to improve satisfaction?" and "Should BrightStar hire more call-center employees to reduce the average hold time?"

Remember that likelihood to recommend can take values between 0 and 10, and we want to use this variable to predict churn, which can be only a 0 (remains a customer) or 1 (churns). So let's take a look at a simple plot of churn versus likelihood to recommend for a sample of 500 BrightStar customers (Figure 5.4). As we will discuss next, this plot is *not* the best way to view this data.

Figure 5.4   Scatter Plot of Likelihood to Recommend and Churn

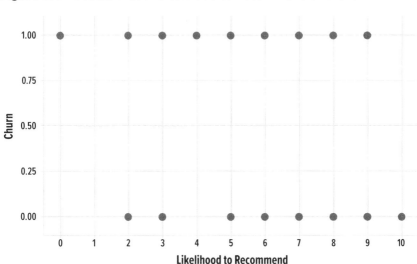

This time Cruz placed likelihood to recommend along the x-axis (predictor) and churn along the y-axis (predicted), because that was the relationship she wanted to understand. If you are new to data science, you may find this graph strange at first because you're probably used to seeing an upward or downward pattern emerging from data points scattered throughout the quadrant. So the pattern of dots in horizontal lines appears a bit odd. But if you think about it for a moment, this picture makes perfect sense. Numbers on the x-axis (likelihood to recommend) can take the values 0, 1, 2, 3, etc., and those on the y-axis (churn) can equal only 0 or 1.

Because many points on this graph lie on top of each other, it is hard to see how likelihood to recommend relates to churn. Each dot in Figure 5.4 could represent a single customer, or it could represent many customers. Our solution to the visualization challenge is to use a plotting technique called "jitter," which is great for understanding graphs like this. The idea is to plot each point with a small random change to separate the dots so that they don't lie on top of each other, as shown in Figure 5.5.

Figure 5.5   Jitter Plot of Likelihood to Recommend and Churn

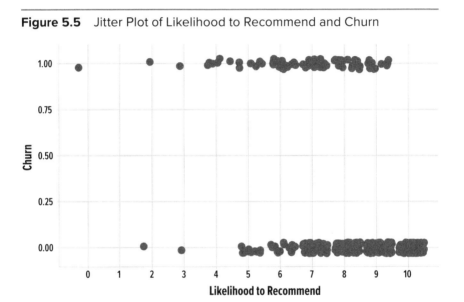

With the jitter technique, our dots become small clouds. Look, for example at the value of 9 for likelihood to recommend, and you see a dark cloud for the churn value of 0 (stays with BrightStar), which tells us there are many customers in this situation. But the small cloud associated with this likelihood-to-recommend rating for the churn value of 1 tells us there are far fewer customers who provide this rating and leave. Overall, we see that customers who stay tend to have high values of likelihood to recommend versus customers who churn. There are, of course, many exceptions, as the BrightStar COO pointed out; but there appears to be some meaningful association between likelihood to recommend and churn, based on this data.

Seeing the plot, Cruz was fairly confident there was a relationship between those two variables—meaning that likelihood to recommend did indeed matter—but she needed to measure that relationship more specifically to be able to make decisions related to hold time and other satisfaction-influencing factors. That is, *how much* did likelihood to recommend influence churn?

As a first step, she put a regression line through the data (Figure 5.6), similar to what she'd done in the previous graph. But it looked odd to her at first. Can you think about why?

Figure 5.6 Linear Regression Plot of Likelihood to Recommend and Churn

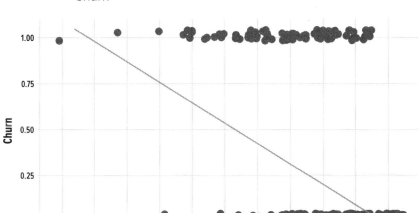

If you're like many people, you may not be as enthusiastic about the line we drew this time because it can take values all along the range between 0 and 1, but the outcome in question can be only 0 or 1. That turns out to be a good thing—a *feature* of the model, rather than a bug! Think of it this way: if you were to predict the likelihood of someone with the highest-possible likelihood-to-recommend score leaving BrightStar (churn), you'd probably go with 0 percent or close to that; similarly, for someone with the lowest-possible score, you'd say 100 percent chance of churn, or something really close to that. For those with ratings in the range of 5 to 7, you'd be less sure, maybe in the 40 to 60 percent range. Those numbers correspond to probabilities, so what we really have here is a prediction of the probability that a customer with a given likelihood to recommend will leave BrightStar in the next six months, which can take any value between 0 and 1, even though the *actual* outcome can only be a 0 or 1. That's a pretty useful predictive model to have.

But Cruz wasn't done yet. It turns out there are significant problems with using linear regression to predict binary outcomes like churn. First, notice that if a customer has a likelihood to recommend of 0 or 1 on the customer survey, then the model suggests that the probability of churn is around 1.05 or 1.10. Any high school math teacher would object to this, since probabilities are always between 0 and 1. A linear regression model like this can generate what we call "out-of-range" predictions, which are predicted values below 0 or above 1. This is not good.

Second, and more subtly, think about the effect of going from a likelihood to recommend rating of 1 to a rating of 3. Or from 7 to 9. How much does either of those change the likelihood of churn?

Take a look at the figure and think about it for a moment.

As you may have guessed, not a lot! But if you were to go from 5 to 7, it's a different story: the likelihood of churn may change significantly. The problem is that the linear model doesn't account for that difference: no matter where you are on the line, a given increase in satisfaction will always predict a proportionate decrease in the probability of churn. That's not a good thing if you want accurate predictions.

So what we want is something that looks much more like the graph in Figure 5.7.

As you can see, the reverse S-curve never goes below 0 or above 1, so it doesn't have the out-of-range problem. Moreover, it predicts a very small change in probability of churn when you move between two satisfaction ratings that fall at either the high or low ends of the scale (i.e., 0 to 1, or 9 to 10), but a much larger change when you move between points in the middle of the scale, which resolves the proportionality issue.

Figure 5.7   S-Curve Graph of Likelihood to Recommend and Churn

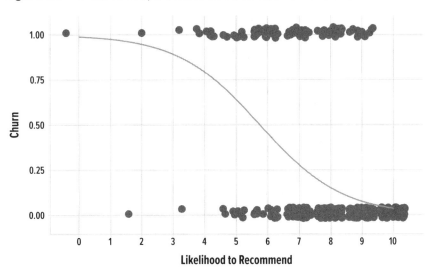

In the figure, the reverse S-shaped line is created by a "logistic function," which was invented in the 1830s. Over time, the function became the basis for what is now called "logistic regression," popularized by economist Dan McFadden in 1973. He showed how valuable the analysis was for understanding the theory of discrete choices by consumers, receiving the 2000 Nobel Prize in Economic Sciences for his contributions in this research area. Logistic regression continues to be a workhorse model among data scientists for predicting binary valuables: customer churn (stay/go), purchase (buy/don't buy), electronic parts failure (fail/doesn't fail—relevant to the Honeywell auxiliary power unit example described in this chapter's opening), and many others. From a data scientist's point of view, it works very similarly to regular regression, can be estimated on large datasets, and is very fast. As a result, it is one of the most popular analytics models when faced with understanding discrete choices.

The equation for logistic regression is a bit more complicated than the one we saw earlier for linear regression. In this case, it's:

$$\text{Probability of Churn} = \frac{e^{(A \,+\, B \,*\, \text{Likelihood to Recommend})}}{1 + e^{(A \,+\, B \,*\, \text{Likelihood to Recommend})}}$$

Solving this equation for a given value of likelihood to recommend gives you the probability of churn. So what's *e* in the equation? Consider it the second most famous constant—with pi as the most famous. It takes on the value 2.718. Your stats program can calculate *A* and *B* for you (in our example *A* = 4.4 and *B* = − 0.77), then you can plug in different predictor-variable values (for likelihood to recommend, in this case) to calculate the predicted variable (churn). Generating a prediction is actually very easy to do in a spreadsheet, despite the equation's more complicated appearance. The table shows the predictions.

Likelihood to Recommend	Probability of Churn
0	98.8%
1	97.5%
2	94.7%
3	89.3%
4	79.4%
5	64.1%
6	45.3%
7	27.7%
8	15.1%
9	7.6%
10	3.7%

Maria Cruz showed her manager Tim Chan the logistic regression model she'd generated to explain the link between likelihood to recommend and churn. She highlighted that likelihood to recommend was related closely to customer departures, with "detractors" more likely to leave BrightStar for another carrier. Chan, in turn, used Cruz's analytics model to calculate customer profitability, which helped prioritize different incentives that may have improved call-center metrics like customer hold times.

Cruz's final model incorporated a rich set of predictor variables beyond likelihood to recommend: customers' tenure, prior revenue, call/data usage, and many more demographic and behavioral metrics. Logistic regression models can help assign weights to each of these for predicting churn, shedding critical light on which variables to focus on in attempts to improve customer retention through call-center-related tactics. In addition to finding key variables, the predicted churn values are useful in and of themselves. For example, most of BrightStar's marketing segmentation had focused on demographics like age, income, and household size. The predictive model showed that customer behaviors were much more predictive of churn compared to these demographic factors. Ultimately, Cruz and Chan used the model proactively: they assigned customers with a high predicted probability of churn to a high-priority queue at the call center.

There you have it: a quick deep dive into the intuition of predictive analytics. It's meant not only to provide a useful tool, but to illustrate the key point we made at the chapter's beginning: while the data science behind good predictions can be complicated, the intuition isn't. Regression and logistic regression are the workhorse models for prediction of continuous and binary variables, and such models are ubiquitous, in business and beyond. If you grasped the intuitions in this chapter, you've just understood one of the most commonly used predictive models in data science, and boosted your DSIQ! Admittedly, we skipped many of the gory scientific details, and that is on purpose. Our goal in this chapter—and the entire book, really—is to ensure that if you get into a situation where data scientists tell you something you don't understand, it's probably on them, not you. That's because every leader can master the intuition behind most complex predictions.

THE PROCESS OF PREDICTIONS

Now that you are more familiar with predictive models, it's important to understand how to assess the quality of a given predictive model. Just because you can draw a line or S-curve through a given set of points on a graph doesn't mean the predictive model does a great job of characterizing the relationship between the variables in question. This matters a great deal when you apply your model in the real world. If Maria Cruz's models for understanding the relationships among hold time, likelihood to recommend, and churn aren't sufficiently accurate, for example, BrightStar could end up misidentifying what they think are "at-risk" customers, a potentially costly mistake.

To make this example concrete, suppose that at the end of 12 months, every customer has to decide whether to renew their contract. Among customers who have completed their first 12-month contract, we know whether they renew their contract or churn. Our business problem is to proactively manage churn: rather than waiting for customers to tell us they are going to leave, we want to predict it. In this context, let's say we have a sample of customers who have been with BrightStar for three months of service and will make their renewal decision at the end of 12 months. If we can predict which customers are going to renew or churn, we can design programs to intervene.

The general idea is that we want to build a model (also referred to as "training" or "estimating" a model) on one dataset. In BrightStar, this is done on customers for whom we know the outcome of renew versus churn. Then, we want to apply the model to *another* dataset that contains customers for whom churn is not known. Visually, the task looks like the diagram in Figure 5.8.

Figure 5.8   Prediction Problem for BrightStar Customer Churn

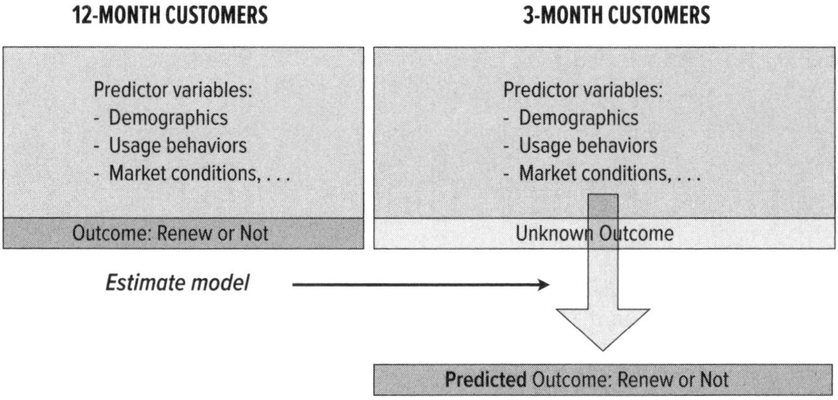

The subtle point in the diagram is that among our 12-month customers, we know the outcome: churn or renew. But among our new

customers with only three months of experience with the carrier, the decision to churn has not yet happened.

Remember that BrightStar's business challenge is to predict churn among customers for whom we don't know the outcome, and we have only three months of data. To mimic this situation, we use three months of buying behavior among our 12-month customers to build a logistic regression. With this model, we can now generate predictions for every customer who has been with us for three months.

At this point, you might think we are finished. We have a model. We have a prediction. Isn't that enough? The answer is *no*. What you should also care about is whether the model will generate accurate predictions. That's because you don't want to roll out your analytics model, generate predictions on all three-month customers, and then get a nasty surprise nine months later when customers who were predicted to renew end up churning.

Because obtaining accurate predictions is a very common challenge, data scientists have developed an intuitive, practical solution to resolve it. The solution is to split the original data used to build the predictive model into two separate samples. In BrightStar, we randomly divide the 12-month buyers into two groups: a training sample and a test sample (Figure 5.9).

Figure 5.9   Training and Test Sample Split for BrightStar Data

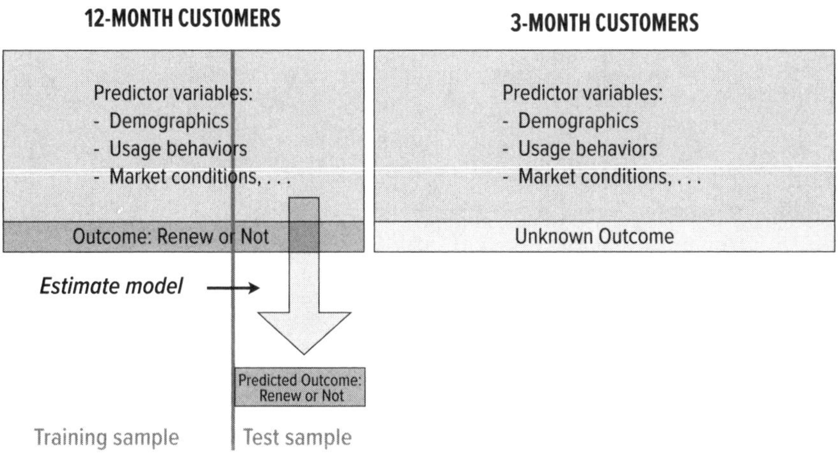

The training sample is used to estimate the model. The model uses this sample to connect demographic, behavioral, and market condition variables with churn. After this step, we have a trained model that can be used for predicting outcomes. This is where the clever twist comes in. Rather than roll out this predicted model, we first evaluate its efficacy. Notice that we actually know what happened in the test sample—that is, whether a 12-month customer churned. Moreover, we did not use any of the test data for building (or training) the model. Notice that characteristic is shared by our three-month customer dataset: it was never used to train the model. In contrast to the test dataset, however, the three-month customer dataset does not allow us to evaluate the quality of the model before the 12 months are up because we are only three months into the customer relationship.

Since we know what happened in the test data, we can compare our prediction of churn with whether a customer actually churned. To give you greater confidence that the model will work, your data science team will build a model that predicts well in the test sample (Figure 5.10).

Figure 5.10   Rollout Process for BrightStar Churn Prediction Model

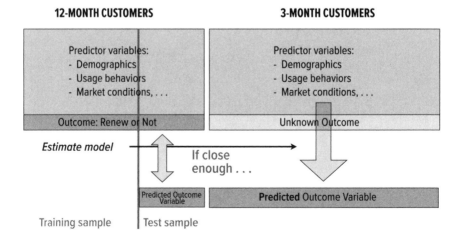

ARE YOUR PREDICTIONS ANY GOOD?

At this point, you have a good understanding of the general process for generating a prediction. Again, the key intuition is that we end up using three datasets. We train a model on the first dataset, we test the model on the second dataset, and we roll out predictions on the third. If this is already enough data science for your taste, we would recommend you skip to the next chapter now!

But for those of you willing to forge on, we believe it is very helpful to peek under the "data science hood" and extract one more piece of intuition: the metrics a data scientist uses to evaluate whether a model is predicting well or poorly. The reason we want to explain this in practical terms is to debunk the idea that data science is too complicated for managers. As you will read, the intuition for these metrics is rather straightforward—but at first it can be a bit intimidating. The final sections below introduce you to two very common metrics for assessing the quality of predictions.

Root Mean Square Error (RMSE)

RMSE, or root mean square error, is used to assess the quality of a model predicting outcomes measured on a *continuous* scale. In the vast, vast majority of linear regressions, the line you draw through the data points won't hit every single point. That is, while some points fall on the regression line itself, many will be at some distance from the line. That was certainly the case in the regression Maria Cruz used to create a prediction for likelihood to recommend based on hold time, as shown in Figure 5.11.

RMSE assesses the quality of the regression's predictions by capturing how far each given actual data point is from the predicted value. To understand RMSE, try reading the acronym from right to left instead of the traditional left to right. Start with E, which is Error. We calculate the error in a given model as the difference between the predicted and actual value. The next letter is S, which tells us to Square all the error terms. After that, we have M, which is the Mean or average, so we take the average of the squared errors.

Figure 5.11   Regression Plot for BrightStar Data

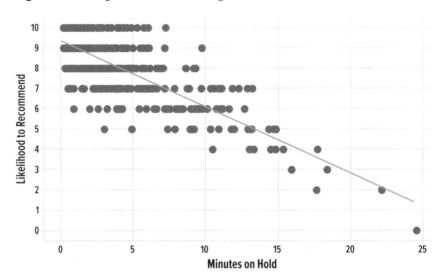

Finally, R stands for Root, which is short for square root. So we simply compute the square root, which generates the final RMSE value! More intuitively, RMSE tells you how concentrated the actual data is around the prediction. A smaller RMSE means there is less error, and the data is more concentrated around the prediction. When we look at RMSE, lower values mean better predictions.

An advantage of RMSE is that it uses the same scale as the predicted, or dependent, variable, which in our example is likelihood to recommend. Since the RMSE in our example is 0.99, this means that the likelihood-to-recommend prediction is, on average, about 1 rating point away from the actual likelihood to recommend value. If you had a predicted rating of 9 in the BrightStar example, the RMSE of 0.99 would tell you that the typical error is roughly plus or minus 1 rating point.

Area Under the Curve (AUC)

When you're predicting a *binary* outcome, data scientists typically use metrics like AUC, which stands for "area under the curve." Now let's look under the hood of the AUC metric, by using a sample of, let's say, 30,000 BrightStar customers. To create the training and test samples (as discussed above), we put 20,000 customers in a training sample and 10,000 customers in a test sample. We trained the model on our 20,000 customers, and now we want to ask whether the model is a good fit on the test sample of 10,000 customers.

When we look at the test sample, it turns out that 18 percent of customers, or 1,800, churned in the past six months. To illustrate AUC, we need to first imagine that we split the 10,000 customers from the test sample randomly into 10 equal-size groups or "bins" of 1,000 customers each (it will become clear in just a second why we do this!). Since we had 1,800 customers who churned in the test sample, how many should we expect in each bin? Well, because we placed customers randomly into the 10 bins, or about 10 percent into each, we should find roughly 10 percent of the customers who churned in each bin, or about 180 in each bin.

Now suppose we sorted the customers most likely to churn, based on the model prediction, into Bin 1, and those least likely to churn into Bin 10. So it's no longer a random assortment but one dictated by the prediction from the logistic regression model. If the model has good predictive power, we should see more customers who actually churned in Bin 1 than in the bins lower down.

The table in Figure 5.12 shows that the model helps you increase significantly the accuracy of churn prediction: if you look at the first bin, for example, where the random (no model) grouping of customers yields 10 percent of those who churned, the predictive model gets you to 30 percent, a dramatic improvement. For instance, if Bright-Star wants to target a promotion—such as a discount on monthly fees—at customers more likely to churn, the model would help them do that much more accurately.

Let's look at it visually, using what is called a "cumulative gains chart" (Figure 5.13). This chart depicts what we described above graphically by showing the percent of customers targeted (corresponding to the bins in Figure 5.12) along the x-axis and the related percent of responses (churn) in the case where no model is used and when the logistic regression model is used. For example, if BrightStar targeted the first 10 percent, or 1,000, customers in the test sample

Figure 5.12 Logistic Model Churn Prediction for BrightStar Customers

Decile	Number of Customers	Percent of Customers	Number of Conversions	Percent of Conversions	Number of Conversions	Percent of Conversions
1	1,000	10%	180	10%	536	30%
2	1,000	10%	180	10%	338	19%
3	1,000	10%	180	10%	296	16%
4	1,000	10%	180	10%	191	11%
5	1,000	10%	180	10%	176	10%
6	1,000	10%	180	10%	97	5%
7	1,000	10%	180	10%	73	4%
8	1,000	10%	180	10%	94	5%
9	1,000	10%	180	10%	0	0%
10	1,000	10%	180	10%	0	0%
Total	**10,000**		**1,800**		**1,800**	

using no model, they would identify only about 10 percent, or about 180, of those who churn. But using the predictive model to sort customers from most to least likely to churn gets them 30 percent, or 536, of customers who actually churned, a vast improvement.

Figure 5.13 Cumulative Gains Chart for BrightStar Churn Prediction Model

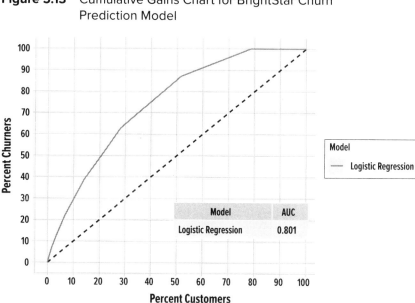

You may already have guessed that the better a model's predictive ability, the more churners it will sort into the top bins. This means that a better model will have a cumulative gains chart that is steeper at the beginning, or more rounded overall. This gives rise to a simple, clean way to summarize with one number how well any binary prediction model performs: the "area under the curve" (AUC) metric. This is a measure of the area under the curve created for the test sample (the curved line in Figure 5.13).[5] As evident from the chart, a no-model benchmark would be an AUC of ½, or about 0.5. If your AUC is below that, you're actually destroying value with a model that performs worse than chance!

An AUC of 0.5 is a model that selects customers purely randomly, and an AUC of 1.0 is a perfect model, which almost never happens. How do you judge intermediate values? Obviously a higher AUC is better, and in absolute terms one might say, very roughly speaking, that an AUC below 0.6 is poor, 0.7 is okay, 0.8 is good, and 0.9 is very good. More typically, AUC is used to compare among models. If one model generates an AUC of 0.68 and another generates an AUC of 0.82, the second model is a better fit. The next chapter presents an example of such a comparison.

Note that there are many different metrics of statistical fit, and these can seem complicated or even overwhelming at first. But our main point of walking you through RMSE and AUC is that the underlying intuition is fairly straightforward to grasp—don't be intimidated by these metrics! Remember, it is not your job to perform the calculation; you simply need to grasp the intuition so that you can make better decisions.

CHAPTER 6

A SMARTER CRYSTAL BALL

In the previous chapter, we helped you understand how to make predictions using linear and logistic regression—two workhorses of modern data analytics—and how to measure the quality of a prediction using metrics like root mean square error (RMSE) and area under the curve (AUC). Companies across sectors have used these types of predictive models for decades.

So what's new today? Why is there so much buzz around predictive analytics? The answer is machine learning (ML), a new class of models that often yield better predictions because of the highly flexible way in which they use input variables to predict an outcome. With better predictions comes enhanced business performance, which is the ultimate goal of most business leaders.

Today's advanced models include neural networks, deep learning, gradient-boosted decision trees, random forests, and others. These machine learning models form the core learning approaches that power AI. Many managers we work with are familiar with these terms and have a rough idea that these are better models, but that's about it. To many who aren't trained as data scientists, the models seem impenetrable, even mysterious.

Our goal with this chapter is to demystify these models. Yes, the science is sophisticated. But as we have said repeatedly in this book, the intuition for these models is something every leader can master. And, most important, with a mastery of the intuition, as reflected in a higher DSIQ, you will better understand whether and when these approaches are best for your business.

As we embark on this journey, keep in mind the terms "data-driven model" and "analyst-driven model." In the previous chapter, an analyst selected a set of variables (such as "likelihood to recommend" and "churn" in the BrightStar example) and selected a model (such as logistic regression) with a particular underlying mathematical formula. We call this approach an analyst-driven model because a human is not only making choices about which variables to include, but also specifying the exact mathematical relationship between the predictor and the outcome variables. In contrast, ML models are *data-driven* models. A human is involved in creating a fairly high-level, flexible algorithm, and also makes choices about variables to include in the model. But the algorithm itself determines how variables relate to outcomes, and in many cases the algorithm even decides which variables to use. The key is that the algorithm does this in a very clever, flexible manner that relentlessly maximizes predicted performance. And this is what leads to a better crystal ball!

THE 411 ON MACHINE LEARNING

So, let's dig into a specific example: suppose we want to train a machine to identify cats in pictures. To do this, we first have to obtain lots of pictures, some with cats and some with other animals, like dogs, rabbits, and squirrels. Second, we need to add "labels" for what is in each picture: is it a cat or some other animal? Such a dataset is referred to as "labeled data." Using this data we can train a model using a "machine"—or computer—to distinguish cats from other animals. Once our model is trained, we can show it a new picture, which the model has never seen, and allow it to predict whether the picture is a cat or some other animal.

Now let's nudge this example a bit. Suppose that you don't have the time or resources to label all the pictures. After all, manually labeling thousands of pictures is tedious work. In this case, all we have is a large collection of pictures of animals with no descriptions—data scientists refer to this as "unlabeled data." Could a machine still learn something from these unidentified pictures?

You should realize immediately that our machine has no idea about the types of objects in these photos—they could be cats, dogs, horses, unicorns, tigers, or lions, among others. To the machine, these are simply pictures of different objects that have no labels. As a result, the machine can no longer predict whether an object is a cat, but it may be able to tell you how many different kinds of objects are in the pictures, and what features "go" with certain objects. For example, it might understand that Group 1 objects tend to be pink and have a single horn (which we know as unicorns), and that Group 2 objects have fur, whiskers, and two pointy ears, which we know to be cats.

The distinction between having labels ("I know and tell the machine it's a cat") or not ("I don't know and therefore can't tell the machine what is in the picture") is critical in ML, and is the basis for two basic types of machine learning: supervised and unsupervised learning. In supervised learning, we have an outcome variable—called a "target" in machine learning speak—or something we want to predict. In the BrightStar example from the previous chapter, this was the customer's churn-versus-renew decision. In a manufacturing setting, this could be whether and how long a factory is unexpectedly shut down. We also have explanatory or predictor variables—"features" in ML-speak—that we use to predict the target, for example, time spent on hold in the BrightStar example, or sensor readings in a factory. The goal of the supervised learning model is to map, or link, features to the target. For example, what in-factory sensor readings predict whether a factory is likely to unexpectedly shut down? With our model, we can then use current sensor readings to predict future shutdowns.

In unsupervised learning, we don't have an outcome variable. We don't know if a customer has churned or renewed; we don't have data on whether and how long a factory is shut down. But we do have explanatory variables or features. As in the cat example, the goal of an unsupervised learning model is to discover groupings of data and the characteristics that describe them. For example, using unlabeled data, a model may identify groups or segments of customers. If you dive into the data, you may find that one segment has consumers with higher income and higher education. As a human, you interpret this as "It makes sense to me that we might group together customers with high income and education." But keep in mind that the machine simply puts these observations in a group because two variables have similar values. The machine has no idea about the meaning (or lack of meaning) of the variables—or even that the rows of data are customers. To the machine, it's just a bunch of data.

The name "supervised learning" comes from the idea that it is as if a teacher supervised the learning process: a machine learning algorithm makes predictions using training data and is then graded by a "teacher" who knows the right answers in the test data. If a prediction is correct, a teacher gives praise (a positive score); when a prediction is wrong a teacher imposes a penalty (a negative score). The model then seeks out predictions that will please the teacher.

Unsupervised learning, in contrast, has no teachers—and no correct answers, as such. Instead, the ML algorithm discovers whether there are patterns in a dataset. As in the previous example, the fact that several customers have high income and high education is just a pattern in the data.

Before we move on, there's one more important type of ML: reinforcement learning. To understand it, imagine you want a computer to learn to play a board game like Go or a video game like Mario Kart, where players drive through a racecourse. Driving a car through a course with competitors is a complicated, dynamic problem, and your success depends on your decisions and other players' decisions. Playing a board game like Go is similarly complex and depends on your actions and your opponents' actions. In these examples, it's virtually impossible to describe all possible scenarios to a machine, as we did in the cat picture example. There are simply too many possibilities.

So how have machines learned to solve these complex problems? And what data do they use? Broadly, here is how a machine may learn to drive a car in a video game with no competitors. The machine makes an initial decision like "drive very fast and don't turn." After one second, the car crashes and the game ends. Surviving for one second earns the machine one point. On the next try, the computer decides "drive slowly and gradually turn to the car right." This time the car crashes after three seconds and the game ends, but making it a bit further earns five points. With two attempts, the machine has learned a tiny bit about the racecourse. Penalties (crashing) tell the machine what to avoid; rewards (positive scores) tell the machine what works better. With lots and lots of trials, the machine is able to learn how to drive the course based on this feedback or reinforcement: avoid decisions that lead to penalties and favor decisions that lead to rewards.

One advantage machines have over humans is that they can learn to play against themselves, thus refining and enhancing their skills quickly. That's exactly what happened with the famous Google AlphaGo example, in 2017. An ML-enabled computer bested the top Go players in the world after studying human models of play, then a new version of the algorithm learned Go from scratch (with no human models) and beat the old version in 100 consecutive games.[1]

So why does all this matter? Well, it turns out that machine learning contributes to all three types of analytics in the AIA Framework: exploration, prediction, and causal inference. Within unsupervised learning models, we have statistical techniques like cluster analysis, which is used for customer segmentation and anomaly detection models. Segmentation analysis is often used to understand your data, which is part of exploratory analytics. Supervised learning models include well-known statistical techniques like linear and logistic regression, but also encompass tree-based algorithms, like decision trees and random forests, as well as neural networks and deep learning models. These models are typically used for predictive analytics but can be used for causal analytics in some cases, as well.

In practice, most ML models used for predictive and causal analytics fall into supervised learning. In the remainder of this chapter we would like to explain the "magic" of some of the most popular and widely used machine learning models for prediction: neural networks and tree-based methods such as random forests and XGBoost.

Neural Networks

Neural networks are called that for a reason: they're somewhat analogous to how our brains, which are made of neural tissue, work. The idea is that you have many connected nodes—like neurons—that can pass information to each other—like electrical signals—and that transmission can potentially lead to the activation of another node. But that's where the analogy ends. At its core, a neural network is just a set of equations and an algorithm to find the parameters of those equations.

The cool thing about neural networks is that the algorithm can learn rules that govern how to drive a car or play a game just from analyzing data, without a data scientist crafting any of those rules. This idea sounds a bit odd, so let's consider a very simple example. Nearly every society plays a version of the game called tic-tac-toe. In the United Kingdom, Australia, and New Zealand it's called "noughts and crosses," and in several other countries it's called "X's and O's." For a human, the rules of winning this game are straightforward: you win by placing three X's or three O's in a straight line in a nine-square grid.

In this example, we consider a simplified version of the game—"tic-tac"—where Player 1 puts a 1 on the board, and Player 2 a zero. Player 1 wins by placing two 1's *vertically* in either column. Yes, it's a pretty pointless game, but bear with us—this little game helps illustrate a big point!

As data, we collected several examples of played games, shown in Figure 6.1. In the leftmost board, Player 1 has scored zero because the 1's placed on the board are not vertically aligned. In the second board from the left, Player 1 scores a 1 because the 1's are vertically aligned. Notice that a few of the game boards, the third and last boards, actually represent player mistakes or illegal games.

Figure 6.1 Tic-Tac Board Examples

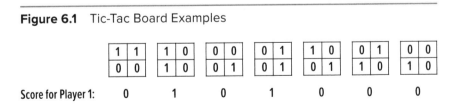

Our objective is to teach a machine to predict for any possible board what the score for Player 1 is. The rule for scoring a point is so simple in this example that we could simply write a rule that a machine could use to score each game. In the lingo of AI, this is referred to as "symbolic AI" or "rule-based AI." But the idea behind modern AI, machine learning, and neural networks is to learn the rules purely from examples or data! And this is partly why AI is so popular today—it shifts much of the burden to the machine.

To build our model, we turn our game-board examples into a dataset that our machine can understand. Machines are used to seeing data in the form of columns and rows, so we turn each 2x2 game board into one row in the following table, as shown in Figure 6.2.

Figure 6.2 Tic-Tac Game Dataset

	Features				Target
Board #	R1C1	R1C2	R2C1	R2C2	Score
1	1	1	0	0	0
2	1	0	1	0	1
3	0	0	0	1	0
4	0	1	0	1	1
5	1	0	0	1	0
6	0	1	1	0	0
7	0	0	1	0	0
Weights	a	b	c	d	

Notice that this looks like a regular spreadsheet or data table. The upper left corner of each game board is captured by the variable that we label R1C1 for row 1, column 1. Because there are four cells in each game board, we have a dataset with four variables. In addition, we have a variable that labels each game board, 1 thru 7, and a variable for Player 1's score in each game. Before proceeding, make sure you understand how the game boards are transformed into this data table. As an aside, if we were analyzing grayscale pictures of cats, the pictures would be like game boards and each pixel would be represented by a variable that contains the gray level of the pixel (with 8-bit encoding, the values would go from 0 for white to 255 for black). As a starting point, suppose we tried to use linear regression to predict whether Player 1 wins or loses tic-tac based on the four variables. You may recall from the previous chapter—and, potentially, your real-life experience—that a regression is a simple equation like this:

$$\text{Player 1 Score} = \text{Intercept} + a \times R1C1 + b \times R1C2 + c \times R2C1 + d \times R2C2$$

A linear regression will try to calculate coefficients (a, b, c, d) and an intercept to predict Player 1's score. Using just paper and pencil, try to see if you can find weights that perfectly predict Player 1's score.

What you will realize after a few minutes is that this is not possible. You might be thinking "Okay, the problem here is that Player 1's score is binary and we need a logistic regression." While this will help, it still won't work perfectly. We need something more sophisticated: for example, a neural network. As a friendly caution, things are going to get a bit wonky for a few pages as we dive into the terminology of a neural network. But bear with us, as it will pay off by building your DSIQ.

It turns out that a neural network is capable of running a linear regression, logistic regression, and much, much more. To illustrate, let's see how a neural network handles a linear regression model. We can write our regression as:

$$Z = a + b \times X + c \times Y \text{ (Linear Regression)}$$

Here, Z is our target, or dependent variable, and X and Y are features, or independent variables. To understand how a neural network handles this model, we need to introduce several terms: "input layer," "input node," "weight," "output layer," "combination function," and "transfer function." Each of these is shown in Figure 6.3.

An *input layer* is simply the collection of features (variables) that you plan to use to predict your target (outcome). The *input layer* consists of *input nodes*, each of which represents one feature. In tic-tac, each node contains a variable like R1C1; in our regression example,

Figure 6.3 Diagram of a Regression as a Neural Network

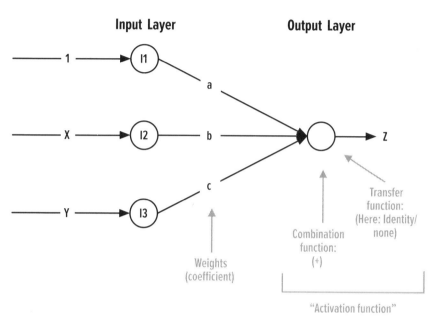

the input nodes take X, Y, and 1. Where does the 1 come from? Notice that we can write "Z = a + b × X + c × Y" as "Z = a × 1 + b × X + c × Y," hence, the features of our model are 1, X, and Y.

Weights are ML-speak for coefficients (a, b, c, d in the tic-tac example). Their purpose is to change the importance of the input by multiplying the weight by the input. A *combination function* tells us how to combine what comes into what we call the *output layer*, which in our example contains one output node. In the linear regression, we're going to use "addition" as the combination function, which simply means we add "a times 1" plus "b times X" plus "c times Y." Notice that the output node generates our prediction of Z, which we are trying to get as close as possible to the actual Z we observe in the dataset. The term *activation function* refers to two things: a combination function, which we just described, and a transfer function, which we will get to next.

Remember our logistic regression? It had an S-shaped, or nonlinear, relationship between inputs and outputs. In a neural network, this is handled with the transfer function. In our linear regression, we generated a prediction of Z. But what we can do next is pump Z through an S-shaped (or sigmoidal) transfer function—and voila! We can mimic our logistic regression!

To give you a sense of how the S-shaped function may work, suppose we made the S-shape extreme, meaning that the S becomes a "step function," as pictured in Figure 6.4.

Figure 6.4 S-Shape and Step Function

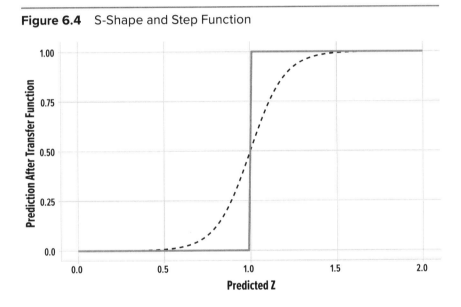

You can see that this transfer function implements the rule that if Z is any value less than 1, make it a zero; if Z is greater than or equal to 1, then make it 1. We implement this rule by setting a threshold of T = 1. This transfer function takes a continuous value, Z, and generates only a 1 or 0 by comparing Z with T. For fun, you may want to pull out your previous attempt to predict scores in tic-tac and see if your prediction got any better by adding a transfer function.

Here is our best attempt at predicting Player 1's score. Suppose we use an intercept of zero and weights a = 1, b = –1, c = 0.5, d = –1, and for our transfer function, we use a threshold of T = 1. As you can see in Figure 6.5, we predict six game boards perfectly but still have one mistake! So, even if we use a transfer function and estimate a logistic regression, we still cannot perfectly predict Player 1's score.

Figure 6.5   Simple Step-Function Model for Tic-Tac Score Prediction

	Features					Predicted Score	Target Score
Board #	R1C1	R1C2	R2C1	R2C2	+		
1	1	1	0	0	0	0	0
2	1	0	1	0	1.5	1	1
3	0	0	0	1	–1	0	0
4	0	1	0	1	–2	0	1
5	1	0	0	1	0	0	0
6	0	1	1	0	–0.5	0	0
7	0	0	1	0	0.5	0	0

a = 1   b = –1   c = .5   d = –1   T = 1
Weights   **Threshold**

And here is where things get really fun. The power of neural networks comes from applying nonlinear functions to linear combinations of inputs, to create what are called "derived features." Recall in the regression example above that we had three features: 1, X, and Y. Those became the input nodes, which were connected directly to an output node. We can make our neural network more powerful by creating what's called a "hidden layer." In this case, you take the three inputs and give them weights, like before; but now, instead of putting them directly into the output, we put them into a new node—what you can think of as an "artificial" node. In other words, our model starts with a set of features (the input layer) and then derives new features (in the hidden layers) from the original features (Figure 6.6).

Figure 6.6   Neural Network with Hidden Layer

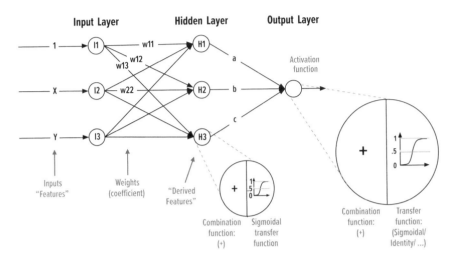

Remember that in our linear regression and logistic regression we had weights and an activation function. When we add hidden layers, we add more weights and more activation functions to the model. The addition of these hidden layers gives our neural network tremendous flexibility.

Suppose in tic-tac we create ("derive") a new feature, a "hidden node" that is equal to 1 whenever R1C1 and R2C1 are both equal to 1. We create this derived feature by choosing weights (a = c = 1, b = d = 0) and a threshold of T = 1.5. For those of you who are programmers, this hidden layer mimics a simple "AND" condition, which is also called an interaction effect. We need both variables R1C1 and R2C1 to be equal to 1 for the variable to "turn on." This new feature becomes our first hidden node and represents when Player 1 wins by having 1's in the first column. This is shown in the "Hidden Node 1" columns in Figure 6.7.

Next, let's build a second hidden node. When R1C2 and R2C2 both take on the value 1, then this new variable equals 1—otherwise it is zero. This derived feature captures winning scores for Player 1 when the second column is all 1's. This is shown in the "Hidden Node 2" columns.

Figure 6.7   Neural Network Model for Tic-Tac Score Prediction

Board #	R1C1	R1C2	R2C1	R2C2	Hidden Node 1 +	Hidden Node 1 >T?	Hidden Node 2 +	Hidden Node 2 >T?	Output Node +	Output Node Predicted Score	Target Score
1	1	1	0	0	1	0	1	0	0	0	0
2	1	0	1	0	2	1	0	0	1	1	1
3	0	0	0	1	0	0	1	0	0	0	0
4	0	1	0	1	0	0	2	1	1	1	1
5	1	0	0	1	1	0	1	0	0	0	0
6	0	1	1	0	1	0	1	0	0	0	0
7	0	0	1	0	1	0	0	0	0	0	0

Hidden Node 1	a1 = 1	b1 = 0	c1 = 1	d1 = 0	T = 1.5	T = 1.5	T = 0.5	
Hidden Node 2	a2 = 0	b2 = 1	c2 = 0	d2 = 1				
	Weights				**Thresholds**			

With these two hidden layers, can we now perfectly predict the score of Player 1? Clearly yes! To predict Player 1's score with these two hidden layers, we simply add their values, as shown in the "+" column to the left of the "Predicted Score" column. We then apply a threshold of .5 in the transfer function of the output node, and we are done!

We intentionally made our tic-tac example simple, but it still illustrates a key point. As a human, you understood the rules of tic-tac and immediately could score game boards. For a simple game, we could share those rules with the computer and let the machine score every game board. But the trick with a neural network is that the algorithm will find these rules using only the data. You don't need to describe the rules; the machine figures them out. In the case of our two hidden layers in tic-tac, the algorithm would iterate until it found these hidden layers—with no human telling the machine the rules of the game.

The hidden layers enable the neural network to create what we call "higher-order derived features"—or descriptions of a *pattern* of features, whether a column on a game board, ears and whiskers of cats, sentences in language, or even a human face.

Many of the models that power AI, from face recognition to language translation, rely on neural networks. Because they have not just one but thousands of hidden layers, these neural networks are referred to as "deep learning" networks.

We want you to understand the intuition of neural networks so that you can better assess their pros and cons and decide when they are right for your business. The good news about such networks is that they can describe arbitrarily complex data relationships. As "multilayer perceptron with sigmoidal transfer functions" (a mouthful, we know!) they are universal approximators, meaning that with sufficient time and computing power they can approximate any continuous function to any degree of accuracy. That's because nonlinear functions of linear combinations of inputs make good use of hidden relationships for predictions, relationships that we would never have thought of on our own or been able to describe with a basic set of rules, as we saw in the tic-tac example. This makes neural networks very, very good at prediction.

But here's the bad news: neural networks can't *explain* results. That is, these nonlinear functions of linear combinations of inputs make interpreting results nearly impossible. For example, look back at Figure 6.6 and think about how you'd explain the effect of input X on the final output. The problem is that X flows into hidden nodes 1, 2, and 3 with some weight, and at each node is combined with other features and put through some nonlinear transformation. This weighting and transforming happens repeatedly, such that the impact of X on the final output depends on the effects of all the other features as well. So, a neural network's amazing flexibility is also its largest disadvantage, as it renders interpretation extremely difficult—in many cases, virtually impossible.

An inability to interpret what drives predictions—or to answer "why" questions—is a major issue you must consider as a business leader. If you need to anticipate *only* a future outcome, then neural networks are extremely valuable and appropriate—think of authorizing or denying a credit card swipe. But when it is critical to understand and explain why a machine makes a particular prediction, then you need to think carefully about whether to rely exclusively on neural networks. For example, when you're denying a loan application, you must be able to show that you're in regulatory compliance. But that's really hard to do when you can't describe the specific effect of any individual feature, such as a credit score, on the outcome.

We hope that we have demystified one class of models that power today's advances in AI: neural networks. Now let's take a look at the other set of important ML models that are used for predictions.

Decision Trees

Decision trees and their extensions, "random forests" and "XGBoost," are another set of workhorse prediction models. As you will learn, random forests and XGBoost are simply a collection of many decision trees. These algorithms, or models, have been applied to numerous business problems, such as those in marketing, operations, and finance. Once you understand the intuition behind them, you will be able to assess whether these models are appropriate for your business.

The intuition for a decision tree is easy to understand if you first visualize a spreadsheet with many rows. The idea in a decision tree is to place every row of your data into a unique group. When you are done, each row has been assigned to a unique group and will share characteristics similar to those of the other rows of data that are in the same group. Observations are grouped by whether they have similar values for the outcome variable. So, if you are predicting churn using demographic variables like age and income, consumers in Group 1 may have very high churn, and those in Group 2 may have very low churn. Input variables, like age and income, will determine how to segment your data into groups.

How does a decision tree get its name? Because once the algorithm is complete, we can represent our data visually as an upside-down tree, as in Figure 6.8.

The "root node" at the top contains all the data, meaning every row in a given dataset. At Split 1, we create three groups of data, labeled a, b, and c in Figure 6.8. An algorithm determines that further splitting of the data is a good idea, and this continues until we have five groups. Note that every observation falls into one of these groups, and only one of these groups.

Figure 6.8   Decision Tree Diagram

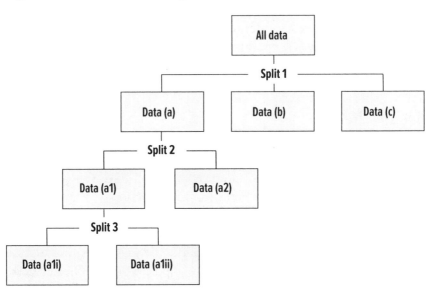

The last piece of intuition we need is a rough idea of how the algorithm creates groups. To illustrate, imagine you want to predict the response to a product offer based on customer demographics (age, income, and gender—for simplicity, binary in this example), as shown in Figure 6.9. Further, let's say we have data from 1,000 customers, where 20 percent, or 200, responded to the offer.

To start building the inverted tree, notice that we have three options. We can create three groups based on age (old, middle-aged, young) *or* two groups based on gender (female, male) *or* three groups based on income (low, medium, high). So which grouping is best? Also, can we refine these groupings? To answer these questions, we look at the response rates for each group (Figure 6.10).

For age, the response rates for young, middle-aged, and old people are 11 percent, 23 percent, and 26 percent, respectively. The algorithm uses a statistical test (chi-square) that shows middle-aged and old are statistically indistinguishable, so we can combine them into a new, compound category. That means that from the algorithm's

Figure 6.9 Variables in Decision Tree Example

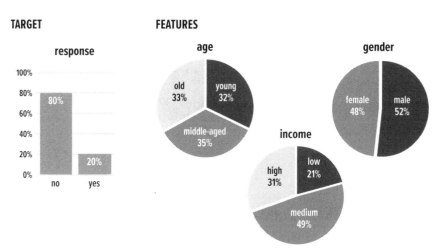

Figure 6.10 Response Rates for Each Variable

perspective, age has only two meaningful groups that differ by response rate: young and "not young."

Gender, the next variable, shows a statistical difference between categories, so it becomes another candidate for splitting the data at the root node. For income, we can again combine categories: this time, low- and medium-income groups are indistinguishable, so we combine them and have another candidate variable for the split. Figure 6.11 contains breakdowns for all three variables.

Figure 6.11   Splits for Each Variable

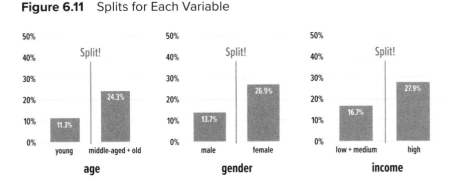

So which of these represents the best way to split our data? Intuitively, we want to create the largest difference in response rates among groups. If you subtract the response rate of 24.3 vs. 11.3 percent for the age variable, we have a gap of 13 percent. If we do this for gender and income, we see that the gap of 13.2 percent for gender is largest. It turns out our algorithm picks gender, based on a statistical criterion. What this means is that we take our 1,000 customers and put 517 men into one group and 483 women into a second group. Among men, we have a 13.7 percent response rate, and among women the response rate is 26.9 percent, as shown in Figure 6.12.

Figure 6.12   Split 1 for Decision Tree

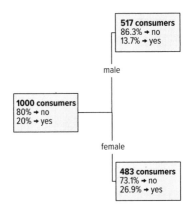

That's our first split. From here, things are rather boring, as we simply continue the basic process of looking at the best way to split our data. Next, the algorithm will try ways of splitting the "men group" into subgroups based on the variables that remain, namely age and income. If the prediction of response differs in these subgroups (men + age or men + income), then the algorithm creates a split. If you follow this process for each subgroup, and then for each of the "sub-subgroups" that are newly created, the tree keeps growing taller and taller (or longer and longer). When we no longer find meaningful ways to split our data into groups, the growth stops.

Figure 6.13 shows what the final decision tree looks like in our example.

Figure 6.13   Final Decision Tree

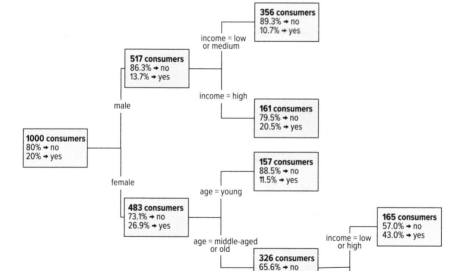

But how does this tree help us make predictions? Actually, very simply! To create a prediction for a new customer, you need to know that consumer's age, income, and gender. Then you just find the group in the tree the consumer belongs to. For example, men with low/middle income have a 10.7 percent response rate, but women who are older and low- or high-income have a 43 percent response rate. Remember, we generated our tree based on consumers who have responded to the offer. But the real purpose of creating the tree is to predict the responses of new consumers.

The approach you've just learned is a decision-tree algorithm called CHAID, short for "chi-square automatic interaction detector." But there are many others. If you go back to our final tree, you will also notice that the way age, income, and gender are used to predict response rate is quite flexible. For example, age is not a factor in predicting response among men, but it does matter for women. Also notice that for older women the algorithm grouped low and high income; however, for men it decided to group low and medium income. The algorithm—which is data-driven—uncovered these relationships without our having to intervene, because grouping the data this way yielded the most accurate predictions. While it is possible that you could find this relationship as a human, it would be very difficult. So, from a business perspective, these algorithms are best when you believe that there may be complex relationships between input variables and outcomes that a human may have trouble identifying.

Random Forests

Now that you understand decision trees, let's talk about a large set of such trees. While one can generate predictions from a single tree, it turns out that predictions from a collection of trees, or a "forest," perform even better. Because the way we generate these trees has some randomness, the next algorithm we describe is called a "random forest."

To understand the core intuition of random forests, let's first understand what we plan to do. First, instead of one, we will use lots of datasets—say, 500 (we will soon describe how we obtain these). Second, for each dataset we will build a tree. Since the datasets will all differ a bit from one another, the trees will be somewhat different. Third, we will generate a prediction for each customer in each tree, then average over all the trees to get a single prediction. These three steps are the first core idea behind a random forest.

You may be asking why we do this. Let's first look at the idea of using many datasets. The rationale for doing this is that small differences among samples of data can change the way a tree is built. In our example above, recall the very close call between gender and age for the first split: a 13.2 percentage-point difference versus a 13 percentage-point difference, giving gender a tiny edge. So perhaps age would have "won" had we used a slightly different sample of data. Because the order of splits can change the predictive model, this is a problem: your predictions will vary based on what sample you use to train your decision tree.

This insight motivated a truly breakthrough idea by Leo Breiman, a famous statistician at UC Berkeley: Why not create multiple decision trees, each based on a different sample of data, and then take the average of their predictions instead of relying on just one tree? That raises a related question: How are we supposed to come up with all these samples? We're lucky to have one sample, let alone 500 samples of data! Collecting additional datasets may quickly exhaust your IT resources. Luckily, you don't have to collect new data.

Instead, you use the original sample of data you have to create new samples of data, say 500 customers, with a statistical technique called "bootstrapping." So, using our sample of 1,000 customers, we would randomly generate a new dataset of exactly the same size by randomly selecting customers. But the trick that makes the new dataset slightly different is that we sample "with replacement." What this means is that we first take a random observation (customer) from the 1,000 customers and make this the first observation in the new dataset. Suppose Customer 412 is added to our new dataset. When we add our second observation, all customers are eligible to be picked—even Customer 412. Thus, by chance, we may select that exact customer again for the new dataset.

Following this logic, at each step, every customer is eligible for selection; this causes some customers to appear two, three, or even more times in the new dataset. Each time a customer is selected, we simply repeat that customer's data in the new dataset. That means that if Customer 412 appears once in the original data, that customer may appear three times in a new dataset. But notice that if a new dataset has some customers who appear multiple times, then other customers must be missing. As such, the algorithm uses a process of randomly repeating some customers and randomly omitting others. When we are done, we have 500 new datasets that are similar to our original dataset.

The random forest uses a second core idea, which is really clever and practical. It turns out that good predictions often follow from averaging over less-than-perfect models. In the AI literature, this concept goes by the terms "strong learner" and "weak learner." Just think of a weak learner as a simple predictive model. In our response rate example from earlier, we might just use gender to predict response, rather than all the variables. Clearly, this would not be the best decision tree. But the route to a strong learner, or the best pre- dictive model, is often to aggregate a group of so-so models, or weak learners. We think of this as akin to "the Borg" cybernetic organ- isms from the *Star Trek Enterprise* TV series (yes we know, this dates us!). Individually, the Borg were not very effective, but when linked together in a hive mind called "the Collective," they represented a formidable foe. The idea of building less-than-perfect models has another practical advantage: speed. If you don't try to build the per- fect model, you can generate individual models more quickly.

Leo Breiman operationalized these ideas in his random forest algorithm by allowing only a subset of variables to be considered at each split in a tree. So, if you had 100 features to build your tree, you might consider only 10 as candidates for a split of the tree. By chance, this means that some very good predictor variables are left out of the tree, which creates our weak learner. But, since we need to evaluate only 10 features for splitting the tree, the algorithm runs much more quickly.

Once we are done building our 500 trees, we generate predic- tions by taking an average over the predictions from all the individual trees. Say you want to make a prediction for a specific customer who's an older, middle-income woman. You will find the probability of purchase associated with that demographic in each tree (say, 23.9

percent and 28.6 percent), and then take the average (26.25 percent) over all the trees.

Random forests are among the best-performing machine learning models in practice today. More broadly, random forests are an example of what's known as "ensemble methods," because they work by using not one but a whole ensemble of trees. There's also XGBoost (extreme gradient boosting), which became a favorite of the data science community because it performed really well in hackathons and competitions. Compared to other ML-based models, XGBoost offers great scalability, speed, accuracy, and ability to handle both large and sparse datasets.

PREDICTING CONVERSION AT LEVEL UP GAMING

Now that we have built up your intuition on sophisticated models, let's apply what you've learned to a practical problem, which is patterned after a real example we encountered in the tech industry. Let's call the company Level Up, a video gaming company focused on mobile games. Suppose that you are a manager with Level Up, and you want to predict whether a customer will respond to an in-app offer. In many video games, it is typical to offer customers an opportunity to buy additional features, such as spaceships, weapons, or adventures. In this case, Level Up wants customers to purchase a unique adventure, Omega3, for $14.99.

To understand the impact of the in-app advertisement for Omega3, the data science team has run a small-scale test with 30,000 customers who were randomly selected from all users. Each consumer was exposed to ads for Omega3, and the data science team tracked whether a consumer responded. Using this data, the firm wants to predict which users should be targeted with an advertisement for Omega3.

Using the data, Level Up's analytics team developed four predictive models: logistic regression, neural network, random forest, and boosted decision tree (XGBoost). The team now needs to choose a model that satisfies two goals. First, they want a model that is scientifically sound and is good at prediction. Second, they want to understand whether using the predictive model will achieve business goals.

The Science of Prediction

How can you compare competing models on the scientific quality of predictions?

The good thing is that you already know the answer! Recall from Chapter 5, "Anatomy of a Crystal Ball," that we presented the RMSE (for continuous outcome variables) and AUC (for binary outcomes) approaches to assessing the quality of predictions generated by a given model. So now we can just calculate the AUCs of the different models to see which one performs best; we use AUC for the Level Up example because post-ad conversion (yes or no) is a binary outcome.

But there's a slight snag. Recall from the last chapter that we assess the performance of a prediction by splitting the available data randomly into training and test samples; we train the model using the training sample, then evaluate it based on its performance in predictions for the test sample. This means that we end up using the randomly chosen test sample to come up with an AUC measure for each model. So, it's entirely possible that the absolute and relative performance of models will change from random sample to random sample: for one test sample, a random forest might have the best AUC; but for another, neural network may come out on top; and so on.

The good news is that there's a simple solution to dealing with this randomness: we train and evaluate the models on many different subsets of our data. A popular approach for creating different training and test splits is called *cross-validation*. The idea is to split the original dataset into a specific number of "chunks" or "folds," and then to use all but one of these to build the models and the remaining one to test the model.

When we iterate through a process where each chunk is left out once (used for testing), we are using what is called "K-fold cross-validation." Here, K simply refers to the number of chunks. In Figure 6.14, we illustrate 5-fold cross-validation.

Figure 6.14 5-fold Cross Validation

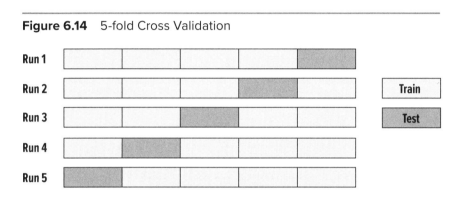

In each iteration, or run, we use four chunks of data to build our predictive model and one chunk to test the model. By the end of this process we have estimated and evaluated the model five times, each with slightly different datasets. For each iteration, we can compute the AUC of all our models and find a winner. For even greater accuracy, you can "turbocharge" cross-validation by repeating it multiple times. For instance, you could run the previous cross-validation five times, ultimately generating 25 different test datasets on which to compare 25 AUCs for competing models.

The Level Up team used multiple cross-validations to compare AUCs for the four predictive models. The graph in Figure 6.15 shows a head-to-head of the logistic regression (also called a "logit") and neural network models: the x-axis is the AUC of the logistic regression; the y-axis presents the neural network's AUC. Each dot represents the two AUCs for a given test sample on a single iteration.

For example, in one test sample the logistic regression achieved an AUC of 0.72, but the neural network came in at about 0.78 (see the arrow in Figure 6.15)—which is a big difference! A dot above the 45-degree line on the graph means the neural network outperformed the logistic regression for that sample. Since all 25 dots are above the 45-degree line, we know the neural network consistently outperforms logistic regression.

Figure 6.15   Logit vs. Neural Network for Conversion Prediction

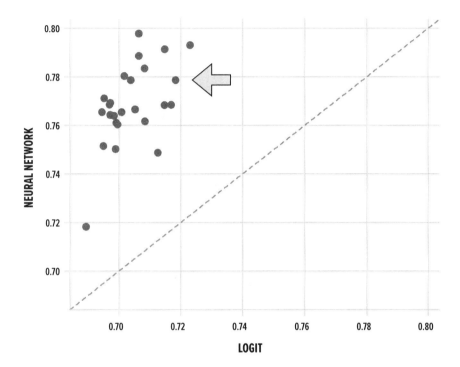

Similar graphs (not shown here) reveal that the random for-est and XGBoost also beat the logistic regression handily. That is, all three ML models outperform the regression. So which of the machine learning models is best? Level Up's subsequent comparisons show that the neural network underperforms the random forest and XGBoost, so they pitted the latter two against one another to deter-mine the winner. And it was (drumroll, please) . . . random forest! That model performed best for predicting whether users would pur-chase the Omega3 adventure after seeing an in-app ad—as shown in the graph in Figure 6.16 comparing the random forest and XGBoost AUCs. Note, however, that the random forest didn't beat XGBoost on every test sample, highlighting the importance of using multiple such samples, as the cross-validation does.

Figure 6.16 XGBoost vs. Random Forest for Conversion Prediction

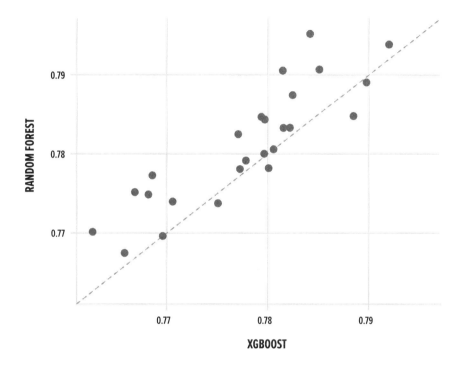

AUC

Keep in mind that it is very hard to tell in advance which model will perform best. So it's important to try a variety of models until you find the one that best suits your specific task.

The Profit of Prediction

Continuing with the Level Up example, now that we have a model that is best at the science of prediction, we need to understand whether the model will yield the desired business outcomes. At Level Up, conversion of users to Omega3 purchasers is not the KPI business leaders care most about. The marketing team wants to know the *financial benefit* of using a predictive model—that is, what model-based tactic will be best for the business. That requires linking analytics to business outcomes, or moving from prediction to profit.

In general, to link analytics to outcomes, you have to choose which KPIs matter most. Campaign profit? Cost objective? Market share objective? Picking one will provide the lens through which to evaluate the analytics model's success. In the Level Up example, campaign profit is the key indicator.

To calculate predicted campaign profits we need to understand the financial benefits and costs associated with conversions. In this case, that's straightforward: we know that each sale of Omega3 yields $14.99 in revenue; on the cost side, we know that annoyance related to seeing ads results in lower in-app purchases—specifically, about $1.50 less for a standard two-week ad campaign. So the Level Up team realized that each conversion yielded about $13.50 in profit, while each ad served without conversion meant about $1.50 lost. They used those figures to calculate the changes in profits associated with following each of the predictive models to target users with Omega3 ads.

The following table shows the conversion rates and profits when the business projected the profitability of sending the Omega3 ad to 750,000 customers, or 15 percent of the company's total 5,000,000 customers, based on the pilot.

Model	% Converted	Total Profit
No Model	13%	$336,525
Logistic Regression	33.2%	$2,607,510
Neural Network	36.6%	$2,989,755
Random Forest	36.9%	$3,023,483
XG Boost	36.5%	$2,978,513

As a benchmark, the marketing team showed first what would happen if they did not use a model at all and just randomly picked 750,000 customers for the ad. The profit was projected to be $336,525. Next, they showed what happened when the team used models to pick customers. The benefit was staggering! The logistic regression raised profits to $2,607,510. But machine learning models did even better. Using a random forest yielded projected profits of $3,023,483, an almost $416,000 difference just by using a better model!

The other machine learning models aren't far off. The bottom line: you should always encourage your AIA teams to give machine learning models a try. Often, they improve predictions. Sometimes they improve them dramatically, especially if you have complicated, nonlinear effects in your data. But you have to have a clear understanding of how to move from prediction to profit, as demonstrated by the Level Up example.

CHAPTER 7

DESIGNING YOUR DATA FOR ANALYTICS

Experiments and Quasi-Experiments

Our overarching goal is to help you move from a consumer of analytics to an *active participant* in analytics. In this context, recall that causal analytics is about influencing outcomes. That is, we want to use data and analytics to provide evidence about whether a business initiative worked. This could be running a marketing campaign to boost customer acquisition, or replacing a cooling fan to prevent an engine from overheating and failing. Too often, managers think that an initiative was successful without knowing for sure—we want you to know whether it worked, using data and analytics.

As you will learn in this chapter, *business experiments* are a critical tool for understanding whether an initiative works. This chapter will illuminate best practices in business experiments, which are a foundation of causal analytics. At some companies, large-scale experiments with random assignment to test and control groups are the norm. But in many business situations, these types of experiments are difficult, costly, or even impossible. In such cases, data scientists deploy another technique, *quasi-experiments*, which approximate a true experiment.

We'll cover both experiments and quasi-experiments in this chapter, with the following goals:

- To understand why creating planned variation in your data is essential for learning about cause and effect, for evaluating business initiatives, and for building and improving predictive and causal models
- To learn the methods to create planned variation in your data
- To recognize that planning ahead is critical for successful business experiments

WHY YOU NEED DESIGNED DATA

For senior leaders new to data science, the idea that you need to create new data can be a surprise—and not necessarily a pleasant one! After all, your company has invested in systems to store and retrieve massive amounts of historical data, which we call "opportunistic data." Isn't this sufficient? Unfortunately, the answer is typically *no!* To address many of your most important business problems, you will need to create new data, which we refer to as "designed data." The reason we need designed data is that we learn from comparisons, and the necessary comparisons are often missing in historical data.

Let's look at a few examples and then see what is missing:

- You may be interested in how customer satisfaction changes when delivery of a retail package takes two days versus five days.
- You may want to know how a 10-second decrease in manufacturing time, from 70 to 60 seconds, affects product quality.
- You may want to compare sales of an item when it's priced at $14.00 versus $9.99.
- You may want to measure the ROI of a new product launch by comparing sales from the same market with and without the product.

So, why aren't these comparisons in your historical data? First, business processes often eliminate the comparisons you need, as we mentioned earlier in the book. The very popular Amazon Prime service, for example, has optimized delivery for one or two days, not three or four. Second, some initiatives you might be interested in knowing about have never been tried before. A new manufacturing process may improve the speed of an assembly line from 70 to 60 seconds, but you have no idea if this will impact product quality. A new product has, by definition, never been launched. Securing designed data relies on a plan that creates the necessary comparisons in your data.

But what if the comparisons are *already* in your data? Isn't that enough? Again, often it's not! Simply observing differences isn't enough. As we saw in Chapter 4, "Distinguish Good from Bad Analytics," comparisons of groups that arise incidentally in the course of normal business may be insufficient to tell you much about cause and effect. The problem are confounds, where something else varies systematically in your data. For example, in Chapter 4 we saw how running a snow blower sales campaign in the winter is confounded by weather: you can't tell whether sales increase because of the advertising campaign or because of increased snowfall.

That means you need to *create* situations so that you have the right comparisons in your data. This chapter is about *designing* data to do just that: by implementing planned experiments or quasi-experiments.

PLANNED EXPERIMENTS: THE GOLD STANDARD

Planned, large-scale experiments are the gold standard when it comes to creating the ideal comparisons in your data. Such experiments go by multiple names: *A/B test*, *randomized controlled trial (RCT)*, and *field experiment*. But as we discussed earlier in the book, all planned experiments have several things in common. Critically, they rely on random assignment—for example, customers are randomly assigned to see one price or another—which leads to "probabilistic equivalence," a concept introduced, again, in Chapter 4. When we have probabilistic equivalence, we don't need to worry about confounds.

Moreover, an experiment enables us to establish two facts. First, when we take an action, like offering a 30 percent discount, we learn an outcome, such as the level of sales. It is tempting to believe that observing this first relationship establishes a causal connection—such as "the discount caused the sales." But it turns out that we need one more fact: when we *don't* take an action (i.e., there is no discount), we learn the alternative outcome (sales when there is no discount). A comparison of these two situations—test versus control—enables us to establish that an action *causes* the outcome.

Now that we've established that basic understanding, a note of caution: If you are new to data science, it can be tempting to simply dive in and start running experiments at your company. In our experience, this often leads to disappointment. And not because experiments are a bad idea—it's that executing experiments, while conceptually easy enough, can be very difficult in practice. We've used our experience to develop a list of key elements required for any business experiment, and "watch-outs" to highlight what can go wrong in your business, as described next.

THE EXPERIMENTATION CHECKLIST: WHAT YOU NEED—AND WHAT CAN GO WRONG—IN BUSINESS EXPERIMENTS

Setting up a business experiment requires careful planning. While there are many factors to consider, we believe there are five critical elements to every effective business experiment. Think of this as your experimentation checklist. For each item on our list, we'll discuss what you need, along with where you might be led astray.

Impactful Business Initiative

First, you need to bring a business focus to your experiment. On the surface, an experiment sounds like a pure data science activity. But your first challenge is to understand how the experiment relates to your business objective and/or business problem. Since resources for experimentation are typically scarce, you need a process for vetting experiments and choosing those that are likely to have the greatest impact on your business. This may sound obvious, but it is both important and difficult.

At some companies, like Canadian Tire, this alignment happens through a committee that prioritizes, selects, and strategically invests in experiments that align with business objectives. In this book's last chapter, we provide a Canadian Tire case study that explains this process. At other companies, this process is delegated and becomes the responsibility of line managers. And this is where you, as a leader, need to be very careful. Will your best line managers allocate their time to the most impactful business problems? We've found that the answer to this question varies tremendously.

What can go wrong? For one, managers tend to focus on experiments that generate "nice to know" insights, rather than more critical ones. Or they focus on insights that are highly relevant to them personally but may not align with the broader enterprise's top priorities. This is what colleagues told us happened at a large amusement park when they helped a manager launch an experiment to determine the best price to charge for photos on a thrill ride. If you've ever been to such parks, you've seen these photos as you exit the ride; they feature frightened, often comical expressions of riders. The manager who sponsored the price experiment ultimately discovered the best price to charge and then shared his findings with senior leaders. But the problem was that the pricing of these photos was not a top management priority in the first place, and there was no organizational buy-in on the new pricing strategy.

We see this example playing out at other companies as well. Business experiments that yield insight on low-impact ideas are likely to have only limited internal support, which means less likelihood of follow-through on implementation, even if an experiment reveals an initiative's effect. If your organization is resource-constrained, this step may be the most important: spend time identifying and prioritizing the most important and impactful business initiatives that you want to test.

Business Outcome Metrics

Next, it's important to consider the outcome metrics that will determine an initiative's success or failure. Here, you need to ensure that *experimental* outcomes, or the outputs of the data science, are linked clearly to the *business* outcomes, or KPIs, of interest. For example, if you wish to run an experiment to reduce customer churn, what are your associated business outcomes? Is the goal to increase revenue, profit, or market share? Over what time horizon—six months, one year, three years? Those are the kinds of questions you need to be able to answer up front.

There are several ways that things can go wrong in this domain. One is the presence of too many business-outcome measures, or KPIs, such as sales, profits, and growth. Rather than simply listing multiple KPIs, you need to decide which matters most. Moreover, problems arise if there's no up-front discussion of potentially competing or conflicting KPIs. For example, say you want to boost Net Promoter Score (NPS), which is a measure of customer willingness to recommend your products or services to others. But, since improvements in customer experience are costly, any changes would mean higher costs. Which outcome do you prioritize: NPS improvement or cost minimization? Similarly, you may take steps to enhance capacity utilization and throughput of a manufacturing facility, but this would likely reduce your average margin per unit sold. Again, this is a trade-off: greater capacity and throughput, but lower unit margin. In general, you need to decide, up front, which trade-offs you're willing to make, and use that to choose specific business-outcome measures.

Experimental Units

Third, to design your experiment you need to think about the experimental units you want to use—that is, are you looking at customers, stores, regions, or some other specific context for measurement?

Here, you need a clear understanding of what can be randomized and how many units exist in the testing domain. For example, suppose you want to test a new math curriculum in a school. Would you randomize the curriculum among students, classrooms, or entire schools? In many education-focused experiments, it's common to randomly assign schools to treatment and control groups, rather than assigning individual students to these groups. This makes sense logistically, as the children at a given school will all receive the same new curriculum or be part of the control group, which keeps consistency at the school level. The reality is that there are many, many children, but far fewer schools, and you will need to factor this into your experimental design. In business situations, it often makes sense to take the same approach by treating regions, states, or zip codes similarly. For example, a retailer may run an experiment on a new marketing campaign and use test and control regions rather than stores.

The reason you should identify your experimental units is that when planning your experiment you need to watch out for *spillovers*, or the movement of meaningful information or effects across boundaries among your experimental units. For example, imagine that two children go to different schools—one in the math-curriculum treatment group, the other in the control—but live near each other and do homework together. The treatment-group student may then share math study techniques from the new curriculum with the control-group friend, "contaminating" this member of the control group.

The spillovers come in two broad flavors. The first flavor is the one we just discussed, namely that experimental units in the treatment may communicate with those in the control. For example, a customer who receives a 30-percent-off coupon may share it with a customer in the control group, who received no offer; this will invalidate your experimental findings. But you also need to think carefully about spillovers within the test group. For example, do you care if customers in the test group talk to each other about a promotion? In some cases, this is exactly the kind of behavior you want—particularly if the discussion is positive! In other cases, it may interfere with measurement or invalidate an experiment. For example, if conversations take place about a discount, you are now measuring the combined effect of a discount and positive word of mouth.

Not surprisingly, social media has become a major problem in consumer studies, as people may share experiment-relevant information in highly public forums, again leading to spillovers. In a business context, similar information may be shared at trade shows, discussions in the field, or through other channels. Remember, a good experiment eliminates spillovers between test and control and assesses whether spillovers among test units is an issue.

Number and Division of Experimental Units

You also need to consider how many experimental units you need and how the total number will be divided among the target (or A) and control (or B) groups.

Luckily, there's an "app" for that: a power calculation, or statistical technique that helps you determine how large a sample size you need for a given experimental test. Broadly, three factors go into a power calculation: signal (or the strength of the effect), noise (factors attenuating the signal, or preventing the effect from being observed), and statistical significance level (the stringency of the test you use to determine whether you've found a valid effect). Holding the statistical significance level constant, you'll need a larger sample size for smaller signal-to-noise ratios, as you'd expect.

If you talk to a data scientist, a power calculation is a fairly standard tool used routinely. But it almost always ignores the costs and benefits of running an experiment—and this is where you, as a business leader, need to step in.

Suppose you want to run an experiment focused on launching a new product in a retail category, and learn that you'll need a sample size of 500 stores, based on the power calculation: 250 in the test group and 250 in the control. But what if everyone on your team believes that the new product will be hugely successful and grow category sales by 20 percent? Do you really want to offer the new product in only 50 percent of your stores? After all, you'd be losing out on the opportunity to grow category sales if you withhold the new product from the market. Our 50/50 split of stores is silent on this business consideration. Instead, the sample size calculation simply tells us the amount of data we need to measure an effect, which is a purely scientific view of the world. To put this another way, suppose your new initiative was very risky and could potentially damage a business. Would you want to split your sample evenly between test and control? Probably not.

So, the big "watch-out" here is a lack of business assessment: you need to understand the cost and risks to the business of running an experiment—and this is particularly important when you experiment on an infrequent basis. Fortunately, there is a well-established method for looking at experiments from a business perspective: real options. It turns out that every experiment can be thought of as a real option, where you pay a price to learn whether an initiative worked.

The details of experiments and real options are beyond the scope of this book, but the intuition is straightforward. If you think your ideas are more likely to work, you may want to nudge more experimental units into the test group versus the control. Why? To avoid the opportunity cost of not having a successful business initiative in the market. At the same time, if an idea is risky, nudge more units into the control group and out of the test group. Ultimately, your data science team can help you adjust your allocation of units to test and control groups to factor in both scientific and business concerns.

In our experience, shifting the discussion of experiments to a real option elevates the conversation to the CFO level. When you stop portraying experiments as yielding "nice to know" information and start thinking about them as "investments in real options," the CFO's ears are more likely to prick up. Think of every experiment as an investment today that provides valuable information to correct course in the future.

Random Assignment of Units

Finally, we come to random assignment of experimental units—customers, stores, regions, whatever—to the target and control groups; this is the key to ensuring probabilistic equivalence among groups, without which an experiment is most likely invalid, as detailed in Chapter 4. The goal here seems simple enough, but achieving it is one of the biggest challenges a business can face when ramping up analytics capabilities.

For example, assignment of a new approach or initiative might be determined by politics rather than science. As an illustration, imagine a biotech firm that rolled out a new sales initiative but limited it to their top salespeople, the proven performers. A comparison after the fact showed that those using the new approach drove larger sales, but the company was not able to conclude the initiative was successful because its implementation was confounded with the ability of the salesperson—only the best salespeople used it. Randomly assigning top, middle, and low performers to the initiative and no-initiative conditions would have enabled a true test of the sales initiative's effectiveness.

A further watch-out is that, as a business leader, you should feel empowered to ask: "How are we randomizing units to test and control?" What you should listen for are two things. First, you would like this to be done in an IT system (or process) and not in an unmanaged spreadsheet, as the latter introduces human error. Second, you'd like to know that the process of randomization is monitored consistently. A common problem is that an experiment fails and then in the post-evaluation someone determines that the up-front randomization process went awry. If you have a system for randomization and it is regularly monitored, you are more likely to achieve success with experiments.

PLANNED QUASI-EXPERIMENTS

As we mentioned at this chapter's outset, experiments are sometimes too costly, or logistically unfeasible. For example, the number of experimental units available may be too small for a valid test: a retailer may have only a small number of stores; a manufacturer may have only one plant; a wind farm may have just a handful of wind turbines in operation. In other cases, a firm may lack the infrastructure for an adequate experimentation platform, or there may be other operational constraints.

In such situations, you can resort to using a *planned quasi-experiment*. The core idea of planned quasi-experiments is to create limited variation in the data in order to *approximate* an experiment.

In the world of data science, planned quasi-experiments represent an enormous topic, worthy of an entire book. Our more modest goal here, then, is to build your DSIQ by focusing on three important techniques that will help you deliver business value with planned quasi-experiments:

- Matching
- Difference-in-differences
- Phased rollouts

Let's consider each of these in detail.

Matching

Matching is a powerful quasi-experimental technique that is useful when you have small samples. To illustrate, suppose that instead of having thousands or even millions of customers, you have only 20 B2B partners, which is a very, very small sample. In a randomized controlled trial, you'd simply generate a random number that would assign each partner to the test or control group—the A or B group. For example, you might assign odd numbers to the control group and even numbers to the test group. With large samples, this results in probabilistic equivalence, based on a statistics theorem called the *law of large numbers.*

The challenge is that if you use random assignment with a small number of partners, you can get very unlucky, such as having groups that are highly dissimilar in terms of key variables like partner size, location, or previous purchase behavior. For example, your control group may be 80 percent large partners and your test group 40 percent large partners, making the control and test groups unequal for partner size. Or you may end up with 15 partners in the test group and only 5 in the control group, due to your randomization procedure. This creates a problem for your analysis.

Matching addresses this problem by creating test and control groups that have "observational equivalence" but are not probabilistically equivalent. In other words, we try to create groups of data that are similar on various metrics in our dataset. To illustrate, suppose you have a small number of partners and want to create groups that are similar on partner size, location, and past purchase behavior. Rather than randomly assigning customers to groups, you create as many matched pairs as possible: two partners that are similar in terms of size, location, and past behavior. Once you have identified a pair, you randomly assign one member from the pair to the control group and the other to the test group. Notice that we still use randomization, but it occurs *after* we identify pairs of partners.

As you go through this process, you may eventually find partners for whom it is difficult to find a good match. They just differ too much on key variables and hence don't look similar to any other partner. This is fairly common—particularly when you have small samples, like the 20 partners in our example. How to handle "unmatchable" customers? In many cases, we simply drop such customers from the analysis.

We recognize that dropping data seems counterintuitive. We started with only 20 partners, and dropping any of these leaves us with an even smaller sample. Indeed, in many situations, excluding data is a bad idea. Having fewer observations lowers the statistical power of your analytics and makes it more difficult to find meaningful differences between groups. However, with matching, the logic for keeping only pairs that match on our key variables is that we hope to increase—not decrease—the quality of our experimental design. We end up with a smaller dataset that is very high quality because the test group looks very similar to the control group.

In general, matching creates two (or more) groups of customers that look similar on the variables used to create matches, approximating a true experiment. But note that the groups may not necessarily be similar on variables you don't prioritize in the matching; in our example the partners in test versus control may differ on age of the company or length of time since they first purchased. Why? We didn't prioritize this in matching—instead we focused on variables like size, geographic location, and annual order volume.

Notice that the partners may also differ on factors that we don't have in our data because they are difficult or impossible to measure. Remember that randomization handles these unobservables just fine—they are probabilistically equivalent in large A/B tests and other experiments. When we move to matching to create test and control groups, we lose this benefit. Now we need to assume (i.e., hope, as opposed to know) that unobserved factors are similar in test versus control—which is why a quasi-experiment is not as good as a true randomized A/B test.

Let's consider a brief example of matching in action, which will both illustrate the concept and point out a common pitfall. Say a lab equipment manufacturer sells specialty equipment to pathology labs. The equipment previously came with paper-based training material but, to save paper and related costs, the manufacturer recently shifted the training material online. However, the manufacturer soon noticed that buyers weren't using the online material as much as expected. This was potentially problematic, as less training could mean lower accuracy with the lab work, with negative implications for patients undergoing important health tests. Longer term, it could also mean erosion of the manufacturer's customer relationships if its equipment were seen as less effective or hard to operate.

So the company took two big steps: it developed new immersive digital training video content and established call-center support so labs could call in with technical questions. The business then designed a quasi-experiment based on clinics that had recently bought equipment; it consisted of one control group and two test groups. In the design, the control group of clinics continued to use only the existing online training; a second group of clinics (Test A) were offered the online training and digital video content; and a third group of clinics (Test B) were provided the online training, digital video, and call-center support.

Given the small number of customers, the company used matching instead of a true randomized experiment to assign clinics to groups. All clinics were located in midsized US cities, and the company asked the data science team to match clinics on five factors:

- Clinic size
- Revenue
- Number of employees
- Dollars spent on equipment in the prior year
- Previous usage of online training

Since there were control, Test A, and Test B groups, the matching algorithm searched for sets of three clinics that were as similar as possible on these metrics. Once a matched group of three clinics was found, one clinic was randomly assigned to the control group, one to Group A, and one to Group B.

After three months, the results revealed that the control group averaged 90 minutes of monthly training per site, Test A averaged 100 minutes, and Test B averaged 110 minutes. Based on these results, the company rolled out the practices in Test B, which was the combination of online, video, and call-center support. But they needed to ensure this was the right call. With a randomized experiment, all you need to believe is that the randomization was done correctly. With matching, what do you need to believe for this to be the correct decision?

Remember that we made our decision based on the KPI "monthly minutes of training." Imagine for a moment that the control and test groups are similar on factors like size, revenue, and number of employees but they differ somewhat on *historical* monthly minutes of training—the control group are light users and Test B are heavy users. Is it possible that this difference persists into the future? Absolutely. If the difference is only five minutes, maybe this isn't a big deal. But if the previous difference is 20 minutes, it invalidates our conclusion because the current observed difference could have been based on historical patterns alone.

Another possibility, although more remote, is that there is some underlying trend in Test B that differs from the control. That is, the control group may have a flat historical trend and the Test B group may be increasing at about five minutes per month, historically. If that trend continues for three months, this may explain a large part of the 20-minute difference between the control and Test B. Again, this may invalidate our interpretation of the results.

This example highlights how important your role in analytics is. You will be presented with results (90 minutes in the control vs. 110 minutes in Test B) to help you make important decisions. To do this effectively, you don't need to know the details of the data science algorithm, but you do need to ask: "What are the business assumptions that need to be true to believe this result?" In our example, two things need to be true. First, the clinics in the test group need to have similar historical levels of training usage. Second, if there is any historical trend in usage among clinics, this trend must be similar in the test and control groups. Your job is to ask the question, and your analytics team needs to provide the answers.

In observing examples of matching in the real world, we often see that the process of creating matches is not connected back to the actual business decision leaders need to make. Here, we saw that the business decision was made on the KPI "monthly minutes of training." Knowing this, the data science team should then prioritize the historic values of this variable in matching—"historical minutes of training" need to be identical in test and control groups. This is often counterintuitive, because it implies paying less attention to other variables like clinic size or revenue. And this is where you, as a leader, need to be involved. Managers who have less experience with analytics may believe that the clinics need to be similar on all metrics. Ideally, this is the case. But remember, we are in a world of small samples, which is by definition a less-than-ideal world. In these types of situations, you need to prioritize what you match on, so that the results are interpretable. And you need to convince others in the organization to trust the results when they find it odd that clinics studied vary widely in size but match on historical training. Again, we typically want all variables to match, but this may not be realistic in small samples.

In sum, your role is to understand enough about the science of matching to ask the right business questions, have confidence that you are making the right call, and be able to explain to others why they should trust your decision.

Difference-in-Differences

Difference-in-differences is a bread-and-butter quasi-experiment technique that combines two well-known methods: A/B comparison and Before/After comparison. To illustrate the difference-in-differences approach, or DiD, say you own a chain of 30 gas stations and want to understand the impact of placing advertising on the gas-pump video displays to drive customers to purchase coffee and other items in the store. You have sufficient budget to place video displays at 10 of your 30 stations. How could you test the prediction that the video displays increase in-store revenue?

This a perfect situation for DiD. We'll show you the analysis first, then explain the design. Let's imagine that you use matching to identify 10 stations for the test group and 10 for the control group; to keep things simple, we will not use the remaining 10 stations in our analytics. To measure the impact of the advertising, you may decide to use the KPI "in-store revenue" and compare the test and control stations. But remember, that approach comes with two business assumptions that you need to trust: that the test and control stations have similar levels of historical revenue, along with similar recent revenue trends. The advantage of using DiD, rather than just a simple comparison of test and control stores, is that we can remove one of these assumptions.

To see how this might work, let's create a 2x2 matrix to illustrate the data we need and how we could launch the program. The two columns represent our test versus control stores, and the two rows represent the time period before and after the launch of our new ad campaign. Our table looks like this:

	Control Stations	Test Stations
One Month Before	No Advertising $4,000	No Advertising $6,000
Month of Advertising in Test Stations	No Advertising $3,600	Advertising $6,300

Before we explain how to do the analytics, give it a try yourself. Grab a pen and paper and try to determine the impact of the new advertising campaign using just the numbers in our 2x2 matrix.

Now that you have given it a shot, let's explain how to analyze the data. Suppose we did not have a control group of stations and just compared the change over time of in-store sales for the test group. This mimics what you would measure without a quasi-experiment. What we see is that in-store sales grew by $300, or $300/$6,000, which is 5 percent. But notice also that our control stores don't have stable in-store sales during this same time period: revenue drops by $400, or 10 percent. You may also notice that our test stores are larger—and this was not an accident. We chose to test in larger stores because we felt the impact of the advertising would be larger. It turns out the test stores are 50 percent larger in terms of in-store sales. In sum, we have three different effects: a size difference (larger stores are in the test condition), a trend in the control stores, and the impact of advertising. Can we disentangle these?

Let's first look at our test stations. We know with certainty what happened when we launched our ad campaign—data scientists call this the *factual* outcome. What don't we know? We aren't sure what would have happened had we *not* launched the advertising—data scientists call this the *counterfactual* outcome. For example, would sales have stayed at $6,000 per month? We don't know. In a true, large-scale experiment the counterfactual is provided by the control condition (because it is probabilistically equivalent to the test condition). Could we use the control stores' in-store sales of $3,600 that occurred during the time that the test stores were advertising? Would this be a good counterfactual—that is, a good measure for what would have happened in the test stores had they not launched the advertising? The problem is that we chose smaller stores as our control stations. Hence, our test stores would most likely have generated higher in-store-sales than $3,600, even without advertising.

The trick with DiD is that we use a model to calculate, or approximate, what would have happened in the test stations had we left them to operate under business as usual. With a true randomized experiment we use data—our control condition—to create the counterfactual; in DiD, the model serves that role. To be clear, we would much rather use data than a model, so DiD is not as good as a true experiment, but often the best you can do.

Let's return to our control stations and note the downward trend of –$400, or –10 percent, in sales. Our thought experiment is this: "If we hadn't intervened in the test stores, do we think that they would have decrease in a similar way?" If you answer this with a "yes," then we can use the trend of the control stations to forecast what would have happened in the test stations. To keep our math simple, let's start by assuming that the loss of $400 would have happened in the test stores. This implies that test sales would have been $6,000 minus $400, or $5,600, if we had not launched the advertising. Knowing this, what is the impact of the advertising? I can take my fact—sales were $6,300—and compare it with $5,600, which is a difference of $700. So, my advertising had an impact of +$700 on in-store sales.

Notice that to create the counterfactual, we subtracted $400. What happens if we believe that the *percentage* change is a better way to assess how sales would have evolved? Notice that the control stores' in-store revenues decline by 10 percent. Hence, we take the pretest sales of $6,000 and subtract 10 percent, or $600, which gives us a counterfactual of $5,400. I take my factual outcome—sales were $6,300—and compare it with $5,400, which is a difference of $900. Thus, my advertising had an impact of +$900 on in-store sales. Since the stores are of different size, the percentage forecast seems like a better way to generate the counterfactual.

Earlier we identified three different effects that we needed to disentangle: a size difference (larger stores are in the test condition), a trend in the control stores, and the impact of advertising. Notice that so far we have considered only the trend and the effect of advertising. How do we account for store-size differences? Let's find the difference between the historical in-store sales of test versus control stations: $6,000 minus $4,000, or $2,000. Now let's take the control stations' in-store sales of $3,600, which is during the same time frame that advertising occurs. If we add the geographic effect of $2,000 to $3,600 we get $5,600, which is a guess of "what would have happened in the test stores." And, if you look back at our math, this is *exactly* the same answer we generated for the counterfactual when we assumed a trend of –$400. And, to blow your mind just a bit more, notice that the ratio of previous sales in test and control stores is 1.5 ($6,000/$4,000). If I multiply the control station sales of $3,600 by 1.5, we get $5,400, which is exactly the same answer when we used a –10 percent trend in sales! In other words, you can generate the counterfactual using either differences in size or differences in the trend. What matters is whether you think the best guess is an absolute difference or a percentage difference. Most data scientists like to think of this in terms of "trends."

Now that you understand the mechanics of calculating the impact of advertising, let's turn to your role as a business leader. First, please recognize a theme that we emphasize repeatedly: analytics *always* generates an answer. But you should never be impressed or satisfied with the fact that analytics generated an answer. Instead, in the example above, you should ask: "What needs to be true about the business to trust that the impact of ads is +$900 in my test stations?" What needs to be true in this example is that the trend we observe in the control stations is a good proxy for what would also have occurred in the test stations. This is a business assumption, because managers are usually in the best situation to assess whether the assumption is likely to be true.

For example, say that a large number of the control-group gas stations were located in a region where a competitor entered during the test period, depressing in-store sales, and that most stations in the test group faced no such competition. That would violate the assumption that the trend observed in the control group would transfer to the test group, making the result of the DiD model invalid. There may be nothing in a dataset that informs your data science team of this possibility—but managers are very attuned to this type of situation, particularly if they are involved in day-to-day operations. Again, your role is to ask the right questions and then assess the analytics results.

If you are new to DiD analysis, the assumption we just discussed is a bit tricky. To be honest, even among those who use DiD regularly the assumption can be difficult to understand. To help you get a better grasp of the assumption, we like to use the analogy of the summer experiences one of us (Anderson) had on Cape Cod in Massachusetts. For several years, we rented a cottage on a saltwater pond, with a dock. If you live on saltwater, you know that most docks float up and down all day long—at high tide they are up about three feet, and at low tide they are down about the same. As we looked out on our saltwater pond, there was a neighboring cottage a few hundred feet away that also had a dock. All day long our two docks would float up and down with the tide. We call this the "floating docks" assumption because this is what is behind DiD. Just like the two docks on the salt pond float up and down, the assumption in our gas station example is that the in-store sales float up and down the same way in test and control stations: if control stations go up by 5 percent, then we assume that test stations also go up by 5 percent. Notice that the level of sales does not need to be the same ($6,000 versus $4,000)—they just need to move up and down together.

Now that you have mastered the math of DiD and understand the business assumptions behind DiD, what else is required for success? Planning. For the math to be correct, we need to *assume* that in-store sales among test and control stations are "floating" up and down the same way. We could just get lucky, or we could plan so that this assumption holds. In particular, we can use matching to ensure that the floating docks assumption is likely to be true. How? We look at our historical data and choose test and control stores to match on the floating docks assumption—that is, to match on historical trends in our outcome variable. This becomes our priority in matching. If this assumption holds, you can be more confident that the results of your quasi-experiment will lead you to the correct answer. Later, we devote an entire chapter (Chapter 11) to the importance and details of analytics planning.

Phased Rollouts

Finally, we come to phased rollouts, a quasi-experimental method you can think of as difference-in-differences on steroids! To us, this is one of the most powerful tools in your data science arsenal. The reason is that with a phased rollout you can promise that an initiative will eventually be implemented or rolled out everywhere. But the trick is that by staggering how the initiative is launched—in phases—you are able to measure the business impact and ROI. In contrast, when you simply roll out an initiative in a single blast, measurement is usually very poor. Staggering the launch is what makes phased rollouts so powerful, by enabling you to both execute a business initiative and measure its impact. In fact, we believe phased rollouts should be the norm for executing nearly *every* business initiative.

Another cool feature of phased rollouts is that you already know all the tools you need to put them into action. That is, this technique simply extends what you have already mastered with the matching and DiD approaches described earlier!

To see how this works, let's go back to our gas station example. Suppose we decide to group our 30 stations into three groups of 10 stations each. Each month, we launch the video-screen advertising campaign at a group of stores so that after three months all the stations have the advertising. Our data now looks something like this:

	Group 1	Group 2	Group 3
One Month Before	No Advertising $3,000	No Advertising $5,000	No Advertising $6,000
Month 1 of Rollout	No Advertising $2,700	No Advertising $4,500	Advertising $6,300
Month 2 of Rollout	No Advertising $2,900	Advertising $5,300	Advertising $6,750
Month 3 of Rollout	Advertising $3,200	Advertising $5,300	Advertising $6,750

Earlier, we analyzed the impact of using DiD with 10 test stations and 10 control stations. With a phased rollout, after three months all of the stations will have the new video displays. In Month 1 of the rollout, our analysis mirrors the DiD from the previous section. Previously, we compared Group 3 (test) with Group 2 (control); now we add Group 1 to our analysis. Notice that our trend of minus 10 percent is true in both Group 1 and Group 2, which is another indication that the downward trend in sales is more likely to affect all the stations—not just a subset.

But to see one of the compelling aspects of a phased rollout, look at Month 2 of the rollout. We can see an upward trend of +$200 in Group 1, which is around 7.4 percent. We can use this trend to calculate the counterfactual for Group 2—or what would have happened in Month 2 had we not rolled out the advertising. This analysis would follow along the same lines of our previous discussion of DiD. On top of this, we can also use Group 3 to generate a similar forecast. Here, advertising is present in both Months 1 and 2, so ads are stable. A comparison of Group 3 sales tells us about the trend, which is +$450, or +7.1 percent. Again, we can use the percentage trend to forecast what would have happened in Group 2 without an intervention. Notice that we get similar, but not identical, answers and this gives us greater confidence in the data science.

As we move to Month 3, we can now use both Groups 2 and 3 to create a forecast. Here, the math is simple: there is no trend over time, as sales didn't change. As such, our forecast of the counterfactual for Group 1 is simply the previous in-store sales, so the advertising lift is +$300, or 10.3 percent. Again, having two ways to generate the forecast adds greater reliability to our analysis.

If you followed all of this, you will notice that in each month we can perform two DiD analyses; over three months, we can perform six DiD analyses. Your data science team will typically build a single model that averages over all of these comparisons to generate an average effect of the advertising. If they were to show you the model that generates this result, it is likely to be impenetrable—the data science is a bit messy. But you now have the DSIQ to understand the intuition behind the analytics. And, most important, you should understand how phasing in the rollout over three months moved us from a single piece of evidence to six pieces of evidence. Better business planning will power up your data science!

TWO BIG WATCH-OUTS

We hope this chapter has helped you understand the value and power of experiments and quasi-experiments as part of your analytics arsenal. But it's also important to keep in mind two significant hazards in running these kinds of analytics. After all, you want to avoid wasting your investment of time, money, and other resources.

Execution Can Ruin an Experiment

Coming up with the idea for an experiment or quasi-experiment is just the start. Proper execution makes all the difference between analytics that return useful information on business initiatives and those that simply do not.

To illustrate, consider a narrative example inspired by something very similar we saw in a different industry. Red is a European mobile phone carrier. Some time ago, Marco Vega, a manager at the company, developed a promising social media marketing campaign. The idea was to use Twitter as a source of new Red customers. Marco proposed that his team would analyze Twitter data and identify customers whose behavior suggested they had a broken phone, such as a statement of "I broke my phone," or a picture of a cracked phone screen. The team would then offer them a promotion for a 100-euro phone discount in return for signing up for a new Red contract for one year.

Before rolling this out to everyone, Marco wanted to run an A/B test to see if the promotion worked. In designing the test, he ran into a challenge. When customers signed up for a Red account, he would know their name and contact information. But he realized that for the analytics to work, he needed to link Red accounts with Twitter accounts. Soon, a member of his team came up with a very clever work-around.

First, all potential Twitter customers would be randomly assigned to a test group (100-Euro Promotion) or a control group. Among the test group, an offer would go out mentioning the 100-euro promotion; then, if consumers clicked on the link, it would take them to a page where they could enter their name and contact information. On this page, they would learn about the 100-euro credit and be told to go to a Red store or to the website to redeem their promotion. By entering their name and address, they were now eligible!

For the control group, Marco's team realized that they needed an incentive to encourage customers to give their name and contact information. So, in exchange for their contact information they gave a 5-euro prepaid Visa debit card that could be used anywhere. To prevent spillovers, there was no mention of Red for the control group.

Once the name and address were collected, Marco's team would monitor sign-ups for Red accounts for both test and control customers. With their name and address captured, it was straightforward to link account information from Red with the name and contact information database from the first stage of the experiment.

Marco was excited to share this new experiment with his leadership team. Finding new customers was a huge challenge, and this was a very clever way of tapping into a new group of prospects. As Marco presented the experiment, another manager asked, "So if 10 percent of the users who sign up for the 100-euro phone credit sign a contract with us versus only 2 percent of the other group, does that mean the phone credit caused an 8-percentage-point increase in customer acquisition?"

Now we would like you to pause and think for a moment. Use what you know about experiments and the Causality Checklist presented in Chapter 4. This experiment sounds cool, but is actually flawed—can you explain how?

It's tricky. This certainly looks like an experiment because consumers are randomly assigned to the test or control group once they are identified as potential customers. Indeed, those offered the phone credit are probabilistically equivalent to those offered the prepaid credit card. So far so good—we pass the Causality Checklist. But once we ask consumers for their name and contact information, the experiment breaks down.

Why? Think about who would give their name and contact information in response to a 100-euro phone credit—probably consumers who like Red and may be interested in buying a phone and signing a contract with the company. In contrast, people giving their name and address for the prepaid Visa debit card are likely to be those interested in money and less concerned about privacy. The key question, then, is whether interest in Red is likely to be correlated with buying a Red phone. Absolutely! That means interest in Red is a confound because it is highly correlated with signing up for a new Red contract. If we launched this experiment, what would likely happen? We would learn that people who already like Red are more likely to sign up for a new account! But we won't be able to tell whether sign-up is driven by interest in Red or by the promotion.

Fortunately, once the problem was surfaced in the planning stage, Marco and his team came up with a simple solution. First, they identified potential customers on Twitter. Second, all customers were sent an offer for a 5-euro prepaid Visa debit card in return for their contact information. Third, among the customers that provided their contact information, the team randomly created test and control groups. The test group was offered a 100-euro promotion, and the control group was offered nothing. This simple adjustment turned a fundamentally flawed experiment into a valid one: now the difference in response rates between the test and control groups became a valid indication of the initiative's impact on acquisition.

We see variants of this example in many companies. The reality is that many businesses face practical constraints that need to be addressed as you move from the idea of an experiment to the execution of an experiment. As a leader, you need to be vigilant that the experiment does not "break" as you move to implementation.

Don't Forget the Broader Business Context

In approaching any kind of experiment or quasi-experiment, you also need to think carefully about how the business initiative in question rests on both the *customer journey* (how are customers expected to act differently?) and *firm actions* (how is the firm going to behave differently?). In this sense, running an analysis is like setting up a large sequence of dominos to fall; if any single domino misses its mark, the experimental results may be invalid. You need to think through every step to make sure you haven't missed something.

The retail floral giant FTD learned this lesson during the Great Recession. New CEO Rob Apatoff faced the formidable challenge of growing the business amidst the economic turbulence of that period and the influx of new floral industry competitors like 1-800-FLOWERS, grocery stores, and warehouse clubs like Costco, which had commoditized floral products and driven down prices.

In this market context, Apatoff and fellow leaders developed a strategy to establish FTD as a quality leader, by both including new packaging conveying a higher-end feel and offering new, quality-based tiers of products: "good," "better," and "best" arrangements for Valentine's Day, Mother's Day, and other occasions. The better and best arrangements generally offered more flower stems than the basic ones.

FTD set up an A/B test in which customers randomly assigned to a control group saw only the "good" arrangements on the site, whereas those in the test condition saw "good," "better," and "best" arrangements. After four weeks of testing, everyone was eager to see the results—but they were quickly disappointed when they found minimal return on investment. Very few customers in the test group had opted for the better and best product levels.

Leadership had to understand whether their strategy was ineffective or if they'd run a flawed test. In this case, fortunately for FTD, it was the latter. The problem was that the company had launched the good-better-best strategy using its website's existing structure. But notice that the premise of such a strategy is that customers are able to quickly and efficiently compare the three options and make a choice. The problem was that the existing website did not have this capability—and as a result, the new strategy was not framing the value proposition effectively for customers.

As a remedy, FTD redesigned the website to enable customers to search in a new manner: customers first decided on a specific arrangement, and then saw an offer to add more stems as part of the better and best arrangements. Figure 7.1 illustrates the change.

A simple change to the website was all that was needed to make the value proposition clear to customers. The results of this modification were impressive. While the overall number of orders didn't change with the new strategy, FTD's total revenue grew significantly, as more than two-thirds of all customers upgraded from the basic product of interest to one of the higher-quality, more expensive ones.

The takeaway here is that while the core idea of the test was simple, the execution was more complex because the test was conducted in a broader business context. Success required not only offering new product types, with new photographs and descriptions—it also required redesigning the website to help customers understand the value proposition. We have often seen this blind spot in many companies. Businesses tend to focus quite closely on the customer journey and take for granted that business execution will simply follow. But when an experiment fails, how do you know whether you made the wrong assumption about customer behavior or the execution simply fell short? As a leader, you need to develop processes for tracking

Figure 7.1   FTD's Redesigned Website

both the customer journey and the firm journey so that you can tell these two apart.

* * *

In closing, we want to emphasize the importance of *planning* for experiments and quasi-experiments. With good planning, you can create variation that overcomes the limitations of using historical data and results in forward-looking analytics. But with any such analysis, make sure to attend to both execution details and the broader business context to ensure that the results you emerge with are indeed valid and applicable. We will provide a detailed road map for planning in Chapter 11.

CHAPTER 8

WORKING WITH DATA YOU HAVE PART 1

Using Opportunistic Data

This chapter is about using "opportunistic" data, or data that is collected in the normal course of business or under standard operating procedures rather than secured specifically for a given analytics initiative or series of these. As we noted in Chapter 3, "Exploratory Analytics," some firms have no shortage of historical data, but not all of it may be useful for analytics.

As context, recall that a goal of analytics is to progress from data to learning to knowledge and insight. A fundamental premise is that we learn from *comparisons* of groups or situations: time spent by different groups of consumers on a retail website, employee understanding and performance after going through two different training programs, and other comparisons. But not all comparisons yield the same type of learning. Specifically, some comparisons are useful for *predicting or anticipating outcomes* that have yet to happen. Other comparisons form the foundation for *causal predictions* that tell us how an action will influence an outcome of interest. Keeping this distinction in mind will help you understand and maximize the value in your opportunistic data.

LIMITATIONS OF OPPORTUNISTIC DATA

To start, it's important to understand the limitations of opportunistic data you may have on hand. Indeed, as noted above, there's a good chance that a large proportion of such data at any given firm is not useful for analytics. The reason, which we've highlighted repeatedly in this book, is that most leaders and managers emphasize the creation of business situations that yield desirable business outcomes, while working hard to avoid and minimize situations that result in undesirable outcomes. Sounds pretty logical, doesn't it?

Indeed, good managers are those who are able to craft the best strategy and implement business plans with near perfection, ultimately eliminating many business situations from historical data—those that are assumed to result in poor business outcomes. As a result of good execution, then, our data tends to contain mostly what we believe are good business situations. But the only way to know for sure that these are good business situations is to compare them to bad situations, or those expected to yield negative outcomes. The problem is that we often don't have any such situations with which to make the comparison. They're missing from our data because leaders do their best to avoid them! The irony here, as you've probably guessed, is that practices that appear good for business overall can be bad for analytics, given that analytics often thrives on using mistakes or missteps to make those all-important comparisons.

We joke with our executive participants that the best manager from an analytics perspective would be the Batman nemesis Two-Face, a former district attorney named Harvey Dent whose face was severely disfigured after a mob boss threw acid on him in court. Now the unfortunate character makes all important decisions by flipping a coin, his former lucky charm that was also damaged by the acid. In the business world, the Two-Face approach to decision-making would yield great data for analytics comparisons, as it would be "agnostic" about which option would be expected to yield a better business outcome, and would thus result in truly random decisions. That would yield a healthy mix of good and bad decisions in our dataset—perfect for analytics. Of course, no real-life manager would keep the job for long using that decision-making model!

NAVIGATING OPPORTUNISTIC DATA

Given these limitations, not all historical data is useful for analytics. This is often a surprise to business leaders who have the naive view that massive amounts of data will surely generate learning, knowledge, and business value. Here, your job as a leader is to understand whether and how your business questions might be informed by historical data. And to do this, we suggest asking yourself two important questions:

- Do I want to use my data to *anticipate* a future business outcome?
- Or, do I want to use my data to understand how I can *influence* a future business outcome?

As suggested by the emphasis above, what distinguishes these two questions are the words *anticipate* versus *influence*. Let's take a look at each of those options in detail.

Anticipating a Future Business Outcome

If you want to anticipate a future outcome, you are clearly in the space of *predictive* analytics, which we've discussed in detail in previous chapters. Let's look at a narrative example, patterned after similar circumstances at a travel company, to bring things to life.

Once-in-a-Lifetime Adventures (OLA) offers adventure trips ranging from African safaris to Pacific Islands diving to European hot-air balloon trips. Founded in the mid-1990s, the family-owned company has grown steadily, gaining customers through traditional (such as in outdoors-focused magazines) and digital advertising and positive word of mouth, including on sites like TripAdvisor and others.

Juan Rios, CFO of OLA, faced an ongoing dilemma: the accuracy of his annual financial forecasts. Over the past few years, his annual revenue estimates had been "all over the place"; some years OLA would exceed forecast, but in others the business would be well below forecast. A major factor that influenced revenue was cancellations. Customers could make reservations for OLA trips at any time, and secure their booking by paying a 5 percent deposit, ranging from $200 to $1,000 per person. Bookings were often made 6 to 24 months in advance, which provided Juan with great insight into expected revenue. The problem had to do with the fact that full payment—the trip cost minus deposit paid—was due four months before the travel date. This lead time allowed OLA sufficient time to finalize itineraries, air travel, tour guides, restaurant reservations, and other trip features with knowledge of exactly how many adventurers to plan for.

So, when Juan's team created revenue forecasts for the next *three* months, they were quite accurate, since bookings were very secure at that point—the payment had been received, and penalties for canceling after that point were high, yielding very few last-minute cancellations In contrast, there was tremendous variability in cancellations *four to six* months before departure, and this affected Juan's longer-term forecasts. Juan said, "The variability in cancellations is very high. Some trips we lose almost no customers, and on others we have lost so many that we had to cancel or postpone the trip. Trips with new destinations and many new customers are particularly challenging for us." Indeed, when Juan's team would learn—three to four months out—that their longer-term revenue forecast was off, there was a mad scramble to put the enterprisewide financial puzzle back together.

Given this ongoing challenge, Juan posed a question to his newly appointed head of data science, Julia Simpson: "My team needs to find a way to forecast revenue more accurately. Can you help us?" After listening to Juan's challenges, Julia directed her team to work on the problem. They quickly concluded that most of the variability in revenue was due to cancellations as Juan suspected. The data science team then assembled a dataset that could be used to build a predictive model. The variables included:

- Total cost of trip
- How long before the travel date the customer booked the trip
- Customer age

- Size of travel party (such as a solo individual versus a five-person family, which also changed deposit size)
- Items "bundled" into booking, including airfare, pre- and/or post-travel hotel, travel gear, and others
- How much time the customer spent on the OLA site before booking

The initial models showed that many of these variables were correlated with cancellation. For example, one predictor of cancellation was whether a customer booked air travel through OLA. Specifically, customers who reserved a plane trip through the company were about half as likely to cancel their trip as those who booked air travel on their own: the model predicted that while 17 percent of customers who purchased their own plane trip canceled, only 9 percent of those who booked their air travel through OLA did. This was the case even though customers paid the airfare only when the full payment for the trip was due, or four months before the actual travel date, rather than at the time of booking.

Juan's team was delighted with the efforts of Julia's data science team. With the old financial model, total bookings were aggregated for each trip and then an attrition rate was applied to account for the possibility of lost revenue. Small adjustments were made based on the nature of the trip. The predictive cancellation model was a game-changer. Knowing how cancellation rates varied with trip characteristics, customer characteristics, and past booking behavior, the OLA team was able to forecast expected revenue for every customer at the time of booking. To calculate the overall revenue associated with a specific trip and the overall revenue for a given quarter, the team simply added up the revenue expected for each customer. The results showed that this was far more accurate than the old approach.

Having demonstrated the value of predicting cancellations, Julia said to Juan, "You didn't ask me for this, but my team is using similar data to predict future bookings. We did a lot of the heavy lifting getting the data assembled for the cancellation model. Now that we have all the data organized, it should be relatively fast for the team to start forecasting bookings. I'll let you know how this works out!"

In the OLA example, notice that we used historical data, which is in abundance at most firms, to create an effective predictive model. But not all data will lead to successful models. What is needed? There are three critical ingredients in a predictive model. First, the outcome needs to vary for our predictive model to work. In the OLA example, customers either keep a booking or cancel a booking. Second, we need variables that may explain the outcome. The OLA team used size of transaction, customer age, and others. Again, these explanatory variables or features need to have variability (e.g., customers with different ages) for our model to work.

With these two ingredients—variability in outcomes and variability in explanatory variables—you can build a predictive model. Let's assume for the moment that the model predicts fairly well from a data science perspective. Does this imply that the predictive model will be useful from a *business* perspective? Not yet.

So far we have established that a predictive model can link *known* business outcomes with input variables. But remember, that's not our goal—instead, we want to predict something that hasn't yet happened—a future outcome. At OLA, we want to use booking to predict expected future revenue.

Specifically, for a past relationship to predict a future outcome, we require what is called "situational invariance": the business situation we observed in our data needs to reappear in the future. That is, while business outcomes and inputs must vary to create valid predictive models, the specific situation of interest must recur over time. Thinking through this last point can help you decide whether a predictive model is going to help you meet your business goals. Without a recurrent business situation, it will be hard to drive business value with a predictive model.

Continuing the OLA example, suppose our cancellation model is built on bookings and cancellations from 2018 and 2019. This model worked very well at predicting cancellations in January 2020. But, would a model built on data from 2010 and 2011 predict accurately in January 2020? Well, if the business was totally stable then possibly, but nearly every business evolves meaningfully over a decade. In this case, it's not that a model created a decade ago is wrong; it's that today's business situation is likely to be very different from the one in which that model was created. In most businesses, there is a lack of situational invariance over 10 years. So this is another thing to keep in mind: the "freshness" of the data and model in question. The closer the data and model are to the time frame to which the prediction applies, the better.

The importance of recurrence and recency highlights the criticality of having business managers involved in planning for predictive analytics. While data scientists can create a predictive model, they are less likely to know whether a given business situation will recur in the near future, because they're simply not as close to the day-to-day business. That's the domain of experienced business managers, not data science experts.

Influencing a Future Business Outcome

In the previous section, we built a predictive model to forecast future revenue. Now, we want to focus on a different problem: determining how to *influence* (not just anticipate) a future business outcome by using analytics for "what-if" analysis or scenario analysis. Here, we are in the domain of *causal* analytics. In a previous chapter, we illustrated how one could use an A/B test or a planned quasi-experiment to uncover a causal relationship. Now, we'd like to use our existing data—not planned data—to achieve this goal.

When applying data science to your business, many of you are going to be in precisely this situation. You want to improve the business by influencing a future outcome; but you may not have the luxury of a planned experiment or quasi-experiment. Here, we give you a framework for how to get causal insights from historical data.

To illustrate these points, let's return to the OLA example.

When CFO Juan Rios shared the success of his predictive cancellation model with the CEO and senior leadership team, there was a buzz in the room. The senior leaders had talked about using analytics before, and there had been anecdotes of success stories within OLA, but Juan's was the first real success story to make it into the C-suite. Inspired by Juan's success, CMO Ashwin Arora decided to tackle a related problem. If OLA now understood factors that predicted customer cancellations, was it possible to influence their behavior? In other words, what interventions might prevent or reduce cancellations?

Ashwin pulled his marketing team together for a brainstorming session with head of data analytics Julia Simpson and her team. The data scientists explained how the predictive model was able to anticipate cancellations, and then presented the top five variables associated with cancellation. These included how airfare was booked, whether the overall booking was direct or via a travel agent, price paid, size of travel party, and customer loyalty status. Ashwin then turned to his team and said, "I want you to come up with the best ideas to reduce cancellations."

Ashwin's team, working with the data scientists, spent the next hour brainstorming ideas to reduce cancellations. There was no shortage of ideas. One idea was to offer a $100 bonus to travel advisors if they persuaded consumers to book their airfare through OLA when consumers booked their trip. Another idea was to identify high-risk bookings and offer discounts on trip-related activities, such as excursions and special events. A final idea was to offer customers higher loyalty status on trips with high cancellation rates, which would lead to incremental benefits like private dinners and premium drinks.

This process at OLA illustrates a second value of a predictive model beyond anticipating future revenue. Ashwin's team used the model to *ideate*, or come up with, new business initiatives. Without a model, Ashwin might simply have assembled his team and asked them to come up with new ideas—a classic brainstorming session. With a predictive model, the aperture of ideation changes. The factors highly associated with cancellation are now top-of-mind, which leads managers to generate creative ideas inspired by the associations in the predictive model.

Sounds great so far, right? So what's the challenge?

Ashwin's team believed that among all the ideas generated, the best initiative would be to offer a bonus to travel advisors if they bundled airfare with a trip. Notice that the team is suggesting making a change to business as usual because they believe this would lead to better outcomes—in this case, fewer cancellations. But does the predictive model tell us anything about whether this will work?

We saw in OLA's case that for customers who booked air travel on their own, the cancellation rate at time of full payment was 17 percent versus only 9 percent for customers who booked air travel through OLA. Now think about why there might be an association between booking air travel through OLA and less likelihood of canceling the booking.

There are many possible explanations, so let's focus on two that seem most plausible. The first explanation concerns the deposit. That is, when a customer books both airfare and a trip through OLA, they make a 5 percent down payment on the entire bundle. But when they book just a trip, they pay 5 percent down only on the trip—not the airfare, which they purchase separately. Since the deposit is not refunded after a cancellation, it may be that customers who put more money down are less likely to cancel; therefore, bundling airfare with the trip reduces cancellations.

A second explanation has to do with customer commitment. Consumers who are very committed to a planned trip take advantage of the convenience of having OLA book their airfare. In contrast, consumers who are concerned that they may not be able to make the trip will try to minimize their exposure to the cancellation risk by waiting to book their own airfare until closer to the trip date. If true, it's not surprising that less committed customers cancel trips at a higher rate.

Suppose the first explanation is correct—and let's make an even stronger assumption, that it is the *only* plausible explanation. Now ask yourself, would paying travel advisors a $100 bonus to convince customers to bundle the trip with air travel result in a lower cancellation rate? It should, because if more people booked with air travel, the average deposit size would increase, and therefore reduce the likelihood of cancellation. This means that we can use the predictive model to determine how much less likely to cancel are consumers who, because of the travel advisor bonus, now book air travel through OLA. Specifically, the model predicted that for these consumers the cancellation rate will drop from 17 to 9 percent.

Now suppose the second explanation is correct—that it's about commitment to the trip. In this case, it's much less likely that paying a commission to travel advisors will improve the cancellation rate. Why? Because here, booking air travel with OLA isn't the cause of the lower cancellation rate; instead, fewer cancellations was the by-product of consumers' greater commitment to the trip. Paying a bonus to travel advisors is unlikely to make consumers more committed to wanting to go on the trip. Worse, we may end up with customers who are very unhappy because, when they change their plans and have to cancel their trip, they lose their deposit on both the trip and the airfare!

Here is the key point: if the second explanation (or story) is correct, our intervention is unlikely to reduce cancellations, and, moreover, we can't use our predictive model to figure out how booking air travel affects cancellation rates. This is because the predicted difference in cancellation rates is driven by differences in commitment among buyers, rather than the causal effect of bundling air travel with the trip.

So what does all of this mean? It means that if the relationship between any two variables, air-travel booking and cancellations in our example, is not causal, the predictive model will not correctly predict the effect of what-ifs, rendering the model much less useful when you are trying to *influence* future business outcomes. Of course, it may still work for *anticipating* business outcomes. Remember that originally Juan was not trying to influence cancellations; he simply wanted to *anticipate* cancellations and improve the accuracy of his revenue forecast.

Importantly, the idea that there are some types of questions for which you *can* obtain a good answer using a predictive model, and some types of questions for which you *cannot*, is subtle, and therefore leads to considerable confusion among leaders. Part of the confusion is because both predictive analytics and causal analytics create predictions, even though they are used to answer very different business questions. We summarize this in two important statements:

- Predictions for "business as usual" scenarios *don't* require a causal relationship for the prediction to be valid.
- Predictions for "what-if" scenarios *do* require causal relationships for the prediction to be valid.

In the next section we discuss how to prove causality with opportunistic data, or data collected in the normal course of business.

Crossing the Bridge: Proving Causality with Opportunistic Data

At OLA, CFO Juan Rios was successfully using a predictive model to generate more accurate revenue forecasts. Now CMO Ashwin Arora is trying to use the same model to gain insight into how new initiatives would influence the business. To do this, he needs to be confident that he has a causal model—not just a predictive model— to be able to evaluate "what-if" scenarios for specific business ideas.

Nearly every manager we work with has faced this challenge. We refer to it as "crossing the bridge" from predictive to causal analytics. To help tackle the challenge, we put together a four-question "Crossing the Bridge" checklist:

1. Has the business initiative been tried previously?
2. Does this business initiative pass the Causality Checklist?
3. Does the predictive model account for confounds?
4. Can you make use of a natural experiment?

We consider each question below.

Question 1: Has the business initiative been tried previously?

Let's start with the first question, using our ongoing example of the OLA travel business's effort to reduce cancellations. What does OLA's data tell us about the potential effects of paying bonuses to travel advisors for convincing customers to book air travel through OLA? Notice that there are really two questions here:

(a) What does OLA's data tell us about whether paying bonuses to travel advisors will increase the number of customers who book their air travel through OLA?
(b) What does OLA's data tell us about cancellation rates among the customers who were persuaded by travel advisors to book air travel through OLA?

Now ask yourself question (a) above. If you answered, "Nothing," then you're right: the company has never paid these kinds of bonuses before. That means that as much as the data might tell OLA about the relationship between air travel and cancellation rates, OLA has no data regarding the impact of paying bonuses. Is $100 too much, for example? Too little? OLA simply does not know because it has never tried it. In short, if you have no data related to an action you're planning, forget trying to use your predictive model to answer that what-if question. This may seem like a no-brainer, but people violate this principle all the time in the real world. Don't follow their lead. If you choose to offer a $100 bonus to travel advisors and this has never been tried before, it is important to recognize that this recommendation is guided by intuition—not data!

Now let's say, hypothetically, that OLA *did* previously pay bonuses for some trip add-ons, but not for adding airfare to a trip. Moreover, let's assume these bonuses were quite effective at getting travel advisors to push the add-on. Now we have some reason to believe that paying bonuses might work.

Let's move to question (b): What does OLA's data tell us about cancellation rates among the customers who were persuaded by travel advisors to book air travel through OLA? Well, we certainly have data that tells us about cancellation rates for consumers who did and did not book air travel through OLA! But notice that this data captures outcomes under business as usual. Here, in contrast, we are asking a "what-if" question: What if we pay bonuses to travel advisors to get customer to buy air travel through OLA, instead of merely following business as usual? How could we tell?

This brings us to our second question to bridge from a predictive to causal model: Does the effect of this business intervention pass the Causality Checklist?

Question 2: Does this business initiative pass the Causality Checklist?

Hopefully you recall the Causality Checklist from Chapter 4, "Distinguish Good from Bad Analytics" (Figure 8.1), and especially how it helped us recognize that in many example cases we couldn't actually claim a causal relationship between the variables in question. So let's use it again here to avoid making a similar mistake.

As you apply the checklist, recognize that it's a statement of fact that if customers buy airfare through OLA, they're less likely to

Figure 8.1 Causality Checklist

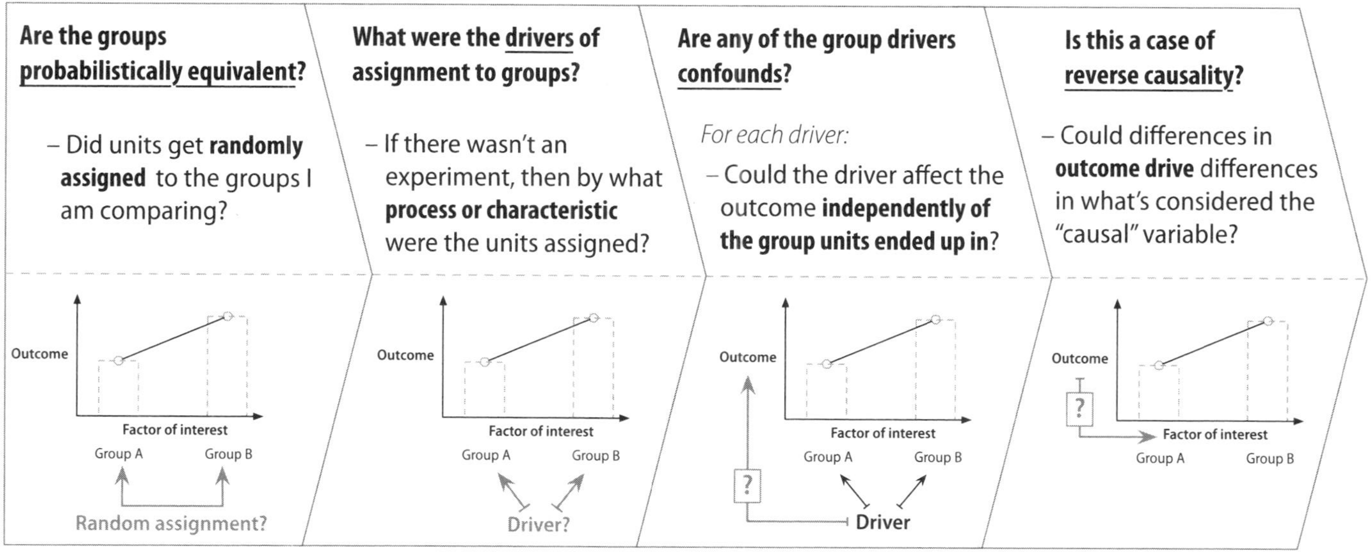

Are the groups probabilistically equivalent?

– Did units get **randomly assigned** to the groups I am comparing?

What were the drivers of assignment to groups?

– If there wasn't an experiment, then by what **process or characteristic** were the units assigned?

Are any of the group drivers confounds?

For each driver:

– Could the driver affect the outcome **independently of the group units ended up in?**

Is this a case of reverse causality?

– Could differences in **outcome drive** differences in what's considered the "causal" variable?

cancel their booking when the full amount is due—nearly twice as unlikely, based on the data. So does this tell us what would happen if OLA travel advisors persuaded consumers to purchase air travel with the booking? To find out, let's apply the checklist.

Step one in the checklist is to ask whether "units" (customers) are randomly assigned to the groups being compared (booked air travel through OLA or not). The answer in our example, of course, is no: customers *chose* whether to reserve air travel with their booking. That means we have to proceed to the other questions.

Our next step is to think about what drivers may have influenced to which group (booked air travel through OLA or not) customers were assigned. We already came up with a possible driver: customer commitment to taking the trip. We considered the possibility that consumers who are very committed to the planned trip take advantage of the convenience of having OLA book their airfare because they don't anticipate having to cancel and lose their deposit. Therefore, "customer commitment" is a driver, or something that influences whether consumers ended up in the "booked air travel through OLA" or "booked air travel themselves" group.

Next, let's think about whether customer commitment is a possible confound. Is it possible that customer commitment to the trip affects the likelihood of cancellation *independent* of whether the customer booked air travel through OLA? Of course! Customer commitment, then, looks highly plausible as a confound.

So, when the model predicts that customers who book air travel through OLA are less likely to cancel than those who do not (17 vs. 9 percent), going through the Causality Checklist suggests that at least some of the difference is due to different levels of customer commitment, not due to the fact that some customers booked air travel through OLA.

What is the implication for what the predictive model tells us might happen when we start paying bonuses to travel advisors? Because customer commitment is a plausible confound, just persuading customers to buy air travel may not yield the decrease in cancellation rates from our predicted model, unless the travel advisor also miraculously manages to increase the customer's commitment to the trip! This is the power of using the Causality Checklist.

To make sure these ideas really stick, let's walk through another example (an anonymized one) of using the Causality Checklist to bridge from a predictive to a causal model. SearchYourRide.com is a website that provides car-related information to consumers, similar to Edmunds.com, Cars.com, and many others. SearchYourRide's business model is to get consumers to submit a lead request that the company then uses to refer consumers to car dealers. Dealers pay SearchYourRide for leads.

One of us attended a presentation at an automotive conference where the president of SearchYourRide shared that the company had successfully used website behavior to predict lead generation. In particular, he said analysts had found that if the consumer visited the pricing page, she was more likely to submit a lead to a dealer in order to be quoted a price on a new vehicle. The difference was pretty dramatic. For example, the predictive model showed that the probability of submitting a lead was 5.2 percent for consumers who had visited a pricing page, but only 2.1 percent for consumers who had not.

Let's say that you saw these findings and had the following thought: "What if we pushed consumers to see pricing earlier in their visit? Could we increase lead submissions by 3.1 percentage points, or from 2.1 percent to 5.2 percent?"

To assess this, let's apply the checklist once more. Answering the first question is easy: clearly consumers don't randomly get shown pricing; they choose to see it. Next, there is a super-obvious driver, which is that someone who is really interested in buying a car is more likely to check out the pricing page. Consumers like to know what things cost before they buy them! Then, is "interest in buying a car" a possible confound? Could it be that consumers who are more interested in buying a car end up being more likely to submit a lead to a dealer than those who are just browsing?

Of course! And as a result, interest in buying a car is a possible confound, calling any assumption of a causal relationship into question. We recount this story because we have seen data like this interpreted in a causal manner with disastrous consequences. High-DSIQ leaders don't fall into this trap. Build your skill at making the right call by systematically applying the Causality Checklist.

In the OLA example, we identified a confound: commitment to the trip. At this point, you should be cautious about using the predictive model in a causal manner. But it's not time to give up on it yet—there is still quite a bit to do! In fact, this is where a good data science team will deliver a lot of value.

Question 3: Does the predictive model account for confounds?

Once you have identified a confound, you need to turn to your data science team and ask the third question on our Crossing the Bridge Checklist: Does the predictive model account for confounds? In the OLA example, the data science team shared the most important explanatory variables for cancellations with Ashwin and the marketing team. But they did not share all the gory details. Is it possible that the data science team had a metric for customer commitment?

Luckily, at the end of each new booking, travel advisors ask consumers, "How important is this trip to your family on a scale of 1 to 3?" OLA leaders think of the answer to this question as a measure of customer commitment. With this data we can "control for" this possible confound in our predictive model. Here is the idea: recall that we did not trust the causal relationship between booking air travel and cancellation behavior because we thought that consumers who booked air travel were, on average, more committed to the trip than those who bought air travel on their own. What if we could ensure that we compared the cancellation rate of OLA air travel and own air travel booking customer only for customers who were similarly committed to taking the trip? In that case, if we still found that OLA air travel customers were less likely to cancel than own air travel booking customers, consumer commitment could no longer be a confound, because all customers were similarly committed! Clever, right?

You might be saying, "But I thought the groups were, on average, *not* similarly committed? If so, how do we compare cancellation rates only for customers who are similarly committed?" Remember we said that we had data on customer commitment to the trip on a scale of 1 to 3. So, instead of comparing the cancellation rates for *all* OLA air travel and *all* own air travel booking customers, we first separate customers into three groups by their commitment to the trip.

Group 1 contains all customers with a commitment level of 1. Group 2 contains all customers with a commitment level of 2, and the same for Group 3. Next, we compare the cancellation rates among OLA air travel versus own air travel booking customers for Group 1 only. Then we do the same for Groups 2 and 3, respectively. Notice that we have now made three comparisons of cancellation rates, each time for customers who were similarly committed. The final step is simply to average our three comparisons (weighted by the number of customers in each group), and, voilà, that is the effect of air travel on cancellations while "controlling for" the possible confounding effect of customer commitment.

Figure 8.2 shows an example of this calculation. The top panel shows our basic finding for a sample of 1,000 customers, namely that consumers with OLA air travel are less likely to cancel than those who booked their own air travel.

Figure 8.2   When Customer Commitment Is a Confound for Trip Cancellation

All Customers	OLA Air Travel	Own Air Travel	Cancellation Rate Difference
Number of customers	384	616	
Cancellation rate	9%	17%	8%
Commitment = 1			
Number of customers	18	242	
Cancellation rate	27%	27%	0%
Commitment = 2			
Number of customers	112	238	
Cancellation rate	14%	14%	0%
Commitment = 3			
Number of customers	254	136	
Cancellation rate	5%	5%	0%

The bottom rows show what happens when we control for customer commitment. Notice that in our example, our suspicion that customer commitment is a confound was correct; once we control for customer commitment, there is no longer a difference in cancellation rates for customers with commitment levels of 1, 2, and 3.

What would these numbers look like if commitment were *not* a confound? We would find that the difference in cancellation rates exists regardless of commitment level. Figure 8.3 offers an illustration.

Figure 8.3   When Customer Commitment Is Not a Confound for Trip Cancellation

All Customers	OLA Air Travel	Own Air Travel	Cancellation Rate Difference
Number of customers	384	616	
Cancellation rate	9%	17%	8%
Commitment = 1			
Number of customers	18	242	
Cancellation rate	9%	17%	8%
Commitment = 2			
Number of customers	112	238	
Cancellation rate	9%	17%	8%
Commitment = 3			
Number of customers	254	136	
Cancellation rate	9%	17%	8%

In practice, we rarely see extreme cases where we can say "commitment is 100 percent a confound" or "commitment is definitely not a confound." Often, part of the effect is explained by the confound but there remains some causal relationship. Consider the example in Figure 8.4.

Figure 8.4   When Customer Commitment Is a Partial Confound for Trip Cancellation

All Customers	OLA Air Travel	Own Air Travel	Cancellation Rate Difference
Number of customers	384	616	
Cancellation rate	9%	17%	8%
Commitment = 1			
Number of customers	18	242	
Cancellation rate	19%	23%	4%
Commitment = 2			
Number of customers	112	238	
Cancellation rate	12%	16%	4%
Commitment = 3			
Number of customers	254	136	
Cancellation rate	7%	10%	3%

Here the confound explains roughly half of the 8-percentage-point difference in cancellation rates. This means that after controlling for commitment, OLA-booked air travel still lowers consumers' cancellation rates, but by less, namely 3 or 4 percent. As you can see, the difference between the basic comparison of cancellation rates and the comparisons after controlling for customer commitment tells us a lot about whether we can interpret our predictive model in a causal way.

We like to use the approach outlined above, with tables and graphs, to explain to managers the concept of controlling for confounds. But if you talk to your data science team, they will have a different approach to control for confounds. They will tackle this problem simply by including confounds in their model. In OLA's case, this would mean including customer commitment along with all other predictor variables in the model. If the difference in cancellation rates remains at 17 percent and 9 percent after we put commitment into the model, then we no longer need to consider customer commitment a confound. But if that effect goes away or becomes smaller, then commitment is a confound that either invalidates or reduces the magnitude of the proposed causal relationship.

Figure 8.5 summarizes our discussion so far, to help you understand whether your predictive analytics can "cross over" into causal analytics—meaning the analytics can predict what-if scenarios and guide you on the intended effect of a business initiative.

You first must ask whether the action has been tried previously, because if it hasn't, your data can't say anything meaningful about causality. If you can answer "yes," then the next question is whether the effect of the action on the outcome passes the causality checklist. A "yes" here means you're all set: your model can predict based on what-if variables, suggesting a causal relationship.

But even if the answer to that last question is "no," you may still be okay. In that case, you have to ask whether the predictive model accounts for confounds, as we discussed above for the OLA example. After you've adjusted the model to do that, then you can use your model to predict what-if scenarios.

But what if you can't control for confounds in your predictive model? Usually this happens because you don't have any data about the possible confound. For example, what if OLA travel advisors did *not* ask the question, "How important is this trip to your family?" and therefore OLA had no measure of customer commitment? Often, this is the end of the road for using a predictive model to answer a "what-if" question, meaning you can't use it predict how a business idea is likely to influence an outcome.

However, there are some situations where you can use a workaround when you have confounds but can't control for them. This is where the last question in our crossing the bridge checklist comes in.

Question 4: Can you make use of a natural experiment?

This question deserves a full, dedicated chapter to answer, so we've done just that. The next chapter dives into the topic of "natural experiments," taking us a bit deeper into the "science" part of data science.

Figure 8.5 Crossing from Predictive to Causal Analytics

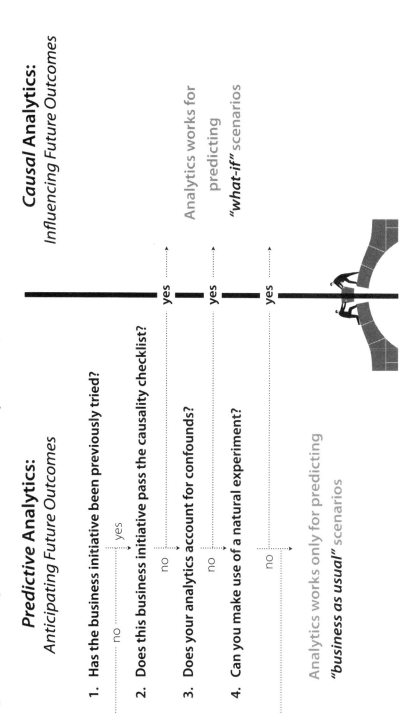

Predictive Analytics:
Anticipating Future Outcomes

Causal Analytics:
Influencing Future Outcomes

1. **Has the business initiative been previously tried?**

2. **Does this business initiative pass the causality checklist?**

3. **Does your analytics account for confounds?**

4. **Can you make use of a natural experiment?**

no

yes

no

yes

no

yes

no

yes

Analytics works for
predicting
"what-if" scenarios

Analytics works only for predicting
"business as usual" scenarios

CHAPTER 9

WORKING WITH DATA YOU HAVE PART 2

Learning from Natural Experiments

As we discussed in Chapter 7, "Designing Your Data for Analytics," it's ideal to design your data by running a planned experiment or quasi-experiment. But in many business situations this simply isn't possible or practical. Moreover, as we learned in the previous chapter, you may not be able to control for confounds—particularly when the confounding variables are things like customer intent or interest, which are hard to measure.

The good news is that across sectors and circumstances, companies and customers unintentionally create situations that mimic experiments. In conducting business as usual you sometimes end up with comparisons that look like they could have come from a planned experiment—but there was no planning involved. Economist Trygve Haavelmo, winner of the Nobel Memorial Prize in Economic Sciences, wrote that we are fortunate to be able to draw on the "stream of experiments that nature is steadily turning out from her own enormous laboratory, and which we merely watch as passive observers."[1] As a leader with high DSIQ, your role is to understand how you can take advantage of these situations—which we call natural quasi-experiments or, more simply, natural experiments.

This chapter will help you identify opportunities for natural experiments in your business and understand how to analyze the data they generate.

WHAT MAKES A NATURAL EXPERIMENT

How do natural experiments arise in a business? In practice, there are many, many naturally occurring factors, such as geographic borders and unplanned events, that are conducive to natural experiments. After we look at a few examples, you will get the hang of it and will likely start spotting them in your business!

Geographic borders often form the basis for natural experiments, with an assumption that such borders—state lines, borders between counties, and others—are placed somewhat arbitrarily. An implication is that in many cases the people who live just on either side of a given border are roughly similar. When we place a somewhat arbitrary geographic border through a similar population, it starts to feel a lot like we randomly allocated customers to one of two groups. In this case, the last ingredient, which creates the natural experiment, is that execution of business practices may be slightly different on one side of the border than the other. For example, firms may spend more on local advertising in one region and less in an adjacent one, which creates a natural experiment of advertising.

In our own research, we have used state borders to determine whether and how a change in US sales tax affects online buying behavior. At the time of our study, the retailer we studied did not collect sales tax in a given state if it did not operate stores there. Since it initially had only a few stores, most customers in most states did not pay sales tax. As the retailer opened up new stores, all customers in the state were required to pay sales tax—for both online and in-store purchases. We focused on zip codes located on either side of a state border, which gives us two groups of customers, both of which were about 100 miles from the new store. So the impact of the new sales tax was on only one side of the border, and it affected only online buying since the new store was too far away for most customers from that side of the border to travel to it. Using this approach, we were able to measure how much online demand decreased when sales tax was charged. The answer was "By a lot!": we saw sales reductions of 10 to 20 percent in some cases.[2]

You can also use geographic boundaries to study how delivery time and other factors affect customer satisfaction levels and other outcomes. Large firms may serve their customers out of different distribution centers, and this may lead some customers who live near each other to experience different service levels. Some get faster delivery than others, for example, due simply to which distribution center serves them.

Another type of natural experiment happens when there are unplanned service disruptions. Imagine that a utility company experiences outages in power delivery that affect some households it serves but not others, including those in similar geographic regions. This, and situations like it, creates the opportunity to examine the impact of unexpected service disruption on customer outcomes including satisfaction, likelihood of service cancellation, and others.

Unplanned shortages in inventory provide another type of natural experiment. Most of us have bought items online, and many of us have ordered an item only to receive a message saying that it is temporarily back-ordered. For a consumer, this is disappointing. But for a data scientist, this is a huge opportunity because it creates a natural experiment. For example, suppose a retailer receives two orders for the same item from two different customers only a few seconds apart, but has only one unit of inventory left. Who gets that last unit of inventory? Well, the customer who clicked on "Buy" a second sooner may get the order, and the other will experience a delay. But if the two orders are very close in time, it's almost as if a coin flip determined who got the last item. This again sets up a natural experiment in which you could examine the impact of different service levels, regular versus back-ordered delivery, on future customer outcomes. In performing such studies, we find that the retailer loses an average of 2 percent of future revenue when a back-order occurs, but the effect can be as much as 10 to 20 percent when an item is severely delayed.[3]

Notice that many of these natural experiments are experiments firms would not run in "real life." For example, a business would normally not intentionally delay delivery of a package or cut service to random households to learn how upset the affected customers become. That's why natural experiments provide such a valuable window into relationships between predictor and outcome variables. The only way to learn about the effectiveness of great service is to occasionally measure what happens when service is not so great, or downright poor. Natural experiments create these valuable windows of opportunity.

How do you find natural experiments like the ones just described? If you start viewing your entire business like a data scientist, you'll likely find that opportunities for these experiments pop up on your radar. And here is why it is critical for you, as a high-DSIQ business leader, to know about natural experiments. Finding them requires knowing a lot about business execution ("How does our ad spending vary across market boundaries?") and business operations ("When was there a service disruption?") in addition to understanding the data science. With data science alone, you are unlikely to find these opportunities to apply AIA in your business.

ANALYZING NATURAL EXPERIMENTS

Let's say you've identified what looks like a valid, naturally occurring comparison in your business. How can you evaluate it? We want to show you three approaches: one you have seen before—*difference-in-differences (DiD)*—and two new methods, *regression discontinuity* and *synthetic controls*. All three methods turn out to be easy to implement and extremely useful for analyzing many business situations.

Difference-in-Differences for Natural Experiments

In Chapter 7, we discussed how to design a quasi-experiment and then use difference-in-differences for the analysis, such as for a gas station on-pump advertising tactic. In a *natural* experiment, where we have to work with the data we have, we can also use DiD for the analysis. But there is a twist: when you design your data, you can ensure that the key assumption of DiD, "floating docks," is likely to hold—specifically, that the outcomes in the test and control group follow the same trend in outcomes of interest over time. We ensured that this assumption held by *matching* test and control groups on historical outcome trends.

With natural experiments, we don't get to pick test and control groups before we execute the test. Instead, we use the data we have and hope we were lucky enough to end up with what seem like matched test and control groups. In these settings, we can still use DiD, but we have to take a slightly different approach.

Suppose a company called PuraSite sells water-treatment technology to municipalities nationwide. Sales had been strong for several years, despite price increases in multiple product categories, so the company wondered whether it could implement another set of price increases. Before doing so, leaders wanted to understand the likely effect on sales. Amy Costa, PuraSite's CMO, asked her team, "How can we leverage existing data to assess the impact of potential price changes, without having to run a planned experiment or quasi-experiment?"

Upon further thinking, the team realized that there was a peculiarity in PuraSite's historic pricing that might have led to a natural experiment. Historically, whenever PuraSite had changed prices, the price change didn't go into effect immediately for all customers. As background, municipalities did not purchase directly from the vendor, but from group purchasing organizations representing specific US regions. Most regions were on a three-year renewal cycle for pricing and contract terms, but New York was on a two-year cycle. On January 1, 2020, the New York region had renewed its contract with new pricing, while the other regions were on their third year of the existing contract and were not set to renew until January 1, 2021, exactly one year later.

Amy realized that the staggering of price changes provided a natural experiment that enabled her to gauge precisely how the market had reacted to the recent price increases. That's because the price increases had been launched in the New York area but had not yet taken effect in all the other municipalities. This created natural variation in prices, approximating an experiment. New York became the test, where the prices were increased, and all regions without price changes became part of the control. Note that Amy did not purposely design the price variation; instead, the price increase was delayed in some regions due to the timing of contract renewals.

Amy's AIA team recognized that a DiD was the right way to analyze this natural experiment. Specifically, the team analyzed the price increase for "chlorinators," a product category designed to chlorinate water pulled directly from municipal and industrial wells. The team organized data in a 2x2 matrix with one column as the test and the other as the control. They then compared sales in the quarters before and after the price increase, as depicted in the table.

	New York ("Test")	Other Regions ("Control")
Q4-2019	Normal Price 489 Units	Normal Price 508 Units
Q1-2020	Price Increase 527 Units	Normal Price 523 Units

The AIA team implemented the idea of DiD to use one region as a test and the other regions as a control. To forecast what would have happened in New York without the price increase, the team computed the trend in the other regions: +3.0 percent. They applied this trend to the Q4-2019 results in New York, which gave them a forecast of 503 units sold for New York. In other words, the DiD suggested that unit sales in New York would have grown by 3 percent (to 503 units) had PuraSite not changed the price. Since the actual unit volume in New York was 527, this suggested that raising the price *increased* unit volume by 24 units, or 4.7 percent.

When Amy met with her AIA team to review the finding, she said, "I would expect that when we raise price, unit volume will decrease. Our analysis suggests the opposite. Let me ask you this: when you ran the DiD, are you sure you used a valid control group? Did you happen to check whether the outcomes in the test and control group followed the same trend over time?"

Notice that Amy's question is informed by the fact that a DiD requires that the outcomes in the test and control group follow the same trend, what we called the floating docks assumption. This means that sales in New York and all other regions should historically be trending the same way.

Following Amy's request, the AIA team produced the chart in Figure 9.1.

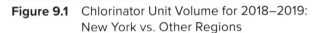

Figure 9.1   Chlorinator Unit Volume for 2018–2019: New York vs. Other Regions

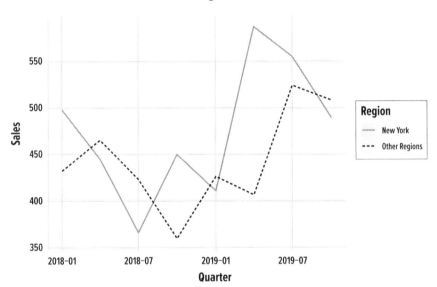

The team noticed that over the past two years, unit sales in New York and other regions *did not* move together. As a result, since the floating docks assumption was violated, the forecast that New York unit sales would have increased by +3 percent had the price change not occurred in that region was most likely incorrect.

At the next meeting with Amy, the AIA team reported the disappointing news that the initial results were most likely invalid. But they also communicated good news: "We noticed that if we look at just a subset of the other regions, namely those in New England, the trends are highly aligned." They showed her Figure 9.2.

Figure 9.2 Chlorinator Unit Volume for 2018–2019:
New York vs. New England

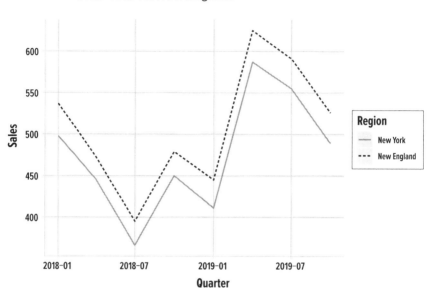

As the graph shows, the New England region mirrors the unit volume of New York every quarter—making the regions "twins" in terms of unit sales trends. While New England consistently sells more units than New York, the gap in sales is relatively constant over time. The DiD approach "doesn't care" if unit sales are at comparable levels for the test and control groups, as long as they trend together. A comparison of New York and New England resulted in the revised DiD analysis below.

	New York ("Test")	New England ("Control")
Q4-2019	Normal Price 489 Units	Normal Price 526 Units
Q1-2020	Price Increase 527 Units	Normal Price 588 Units

Based on the analysis, the AIA team said to Amy, "Notice that chlorinator unit sales in New England grew by 11.8 percent from Q4-2019 to Q1-2020, and when we apply this growth to New York, we forecast that unit volumes, in the absence of a price change, would have grown from 489 to 547. If this is accurate, then the price increase led to a decrease in volume of 20 units, which is the difference between our forecast (547) of what would have happened versus what actually happened (527). In other words, it looks like we lost 3.6 percent in unit volume on our 2 percent price increase."

Now Amy was excited that PuraSite would be able to use this evidence-based insight to understand how price increases generally influence unit volume and other metrics like profit and revenue. In the past, leaders had simply guessed at these relationships, but a natural experiment provided them with hard evidence regarding the price-volume relationship. Once the CMO applied the idea of natural experiments, other managers at PuraSite found similar situations for other products, which led to a knowledge base about how price affected volume for different product types. The business used the growing set of results to build volume forecasts, which helped leadership determine whether to initiate a price increase for a given product or line.

The PuraSite example shows how important it is to understand business execution and operations in addition to the data science. Your AIA team can collect the data and perform the analytics, but it is your job as a business leader to spot potential natural experiments.

Synthetic Controls: Creating "Analytic Twins"

Another popular technique for analyzing natural experiments, one that has been around for only about a decade, is known as "synthetic controls." To understand how it works, let's quickly review how we used DiD for a planned quasi-experiment in the PuraSite example above. Recall that DiD requires the "floating docks," or parallel trends, assumption for the analytics to be correct. Rather than randomly allocating experimental units to test or control, we used matching to create pairs with similar trends over time, one of which was then assigned to the test and the other to the control group.

This works very well in many settings, but what happens if you cannot find a good enough match? Going back to the PuraSite example, what if no single region's unit sales historically trended similarly to New York's? One alternative is just to abandon the analytics project. However, there is a great alternative that might work: synthetic controls.

To make this idea concrete, consider the situation at Canadian Tire, one of Canada's largest retailers. While the business is affectionately known as "The Tire," the company is a general merchant that sells numerous types of products for fixing (e.g., tools), playing (e.g., hockey equipment), living (e.g., kitchen items), and driving (e.g., tires). Managers there wanted to understand the impact of a store-level marketing campaign mailed to customers' homes. With 500 stores across Canada, a subset of 28 stores were identified as test markets, and customers in these markets were to receive the promotional offer. But how might one construct a meaningful control for each store?

Canadian Tire had used matching in the past, but leaders recognized that the matches were never perfect; so it was difficult to find an ideal control store. In this context, the data science team decided to try synthetic controls. The core idea was to use a model to create an "analytic twin," or "synthetic" control store. The analytic twin would be designed to mimic the historical weekly store sales of the test store.

For *each* test store, the data science team built a model that did two things. First, among the 472 locations that were potential candidates as control stores, it identified a small number of stores to use—typically four or five. Second, the model determined the appropriate weights to apply to these stores' historical weekly sales to match test-store sales. In this way, using the appropriate set of stores and the proper weights, the team created an analytic twin for each of the 28 test stores.

The data science team circulated a chart similar to Figure 9.3 internally to illustrate visually how well this process worked on historic data.

Figure 9.3   Using Synthetic Controls at Canadian Tire

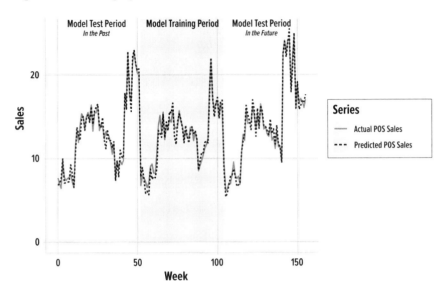

The team undertook the process of choosing stores and weights in the training period, which is shaded. The four or five control stores and their weights were chosen so that the sales of each analytic twin closely mimicked that of its respective test store. The figure shows the results averaged over the 28 actual test stores (solid line) and 28 synthetic control stores (dashed line). The fact that the test and synthetic stores mirror each other in the training region is not a huge surprise—the model is designed to make this happen. However, you can see how well the model works by looking at the past and future testing periods. These periods were not used to create the synthetic control stores. Instead, the dashed line shows the model-forecasted weekly sales for the synthetic stores and evaluates how well they approximate sales in the test stores. We could share the statistics, but the picture sums up the results very nicely: the forecasts are very accurate.

Notice that the movement of sales of synthetic control stores and test stores easily fulfills the floating dock assumption the DiD requires. As a result, the synthetic controls method is a new way to create a valid control group—a synthetic one. Once we determine the synthetic control groups and assign weights to them, we simply use DiD to analyze the results.

Canadian Tire used this approach to launch a new marketing initiative. Figure 9.4 shows the results.

Figure 9.4   Canadian Tire Marketing Initiative Results

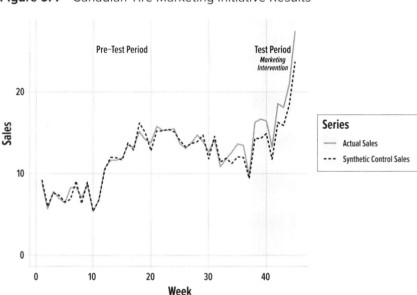

Notice that the solid and dashed lines match well in the pre-test period; this means that the model created excellent synthetic controls by picking the right four to five control stores and weighting them appropriately. The business ran the marketing initiative during the test period, which is shaded. To evaluate the test, we simply sub-tract the solid line (test stores) from the dashed line (synthetic stores), which shows the degree to which the marketing initiative impacted sales. Not only was the marketing effort successful, but the way in which the AIA team communicated the analytics to managers boosted the managers' confidence in the results. Specifically, notice that the figure conveys the DiD approach graphically. Unit sales for the test and control groups are the same in the pre-test period. During the test period, unit sales of the test group are higher than those of the control group. As a result, we know that the marketing initiative causally increases sales.

To summarize, using synthetic controls is a way to ensure that the floating docks assumption holds, which is the core assumption in performing a DiD. When we analyze a natural experiment with DiD, we must identify test and control units with matching trends in the outcome variable: they "float" together. The synthetic controls method deals with the situation where there may not be any such control units. Instead, synthetic controls weights multiple, less-than-perfect controls to form a much better analytic twin or synthetic control for each test unit.

When does this technique work best? First, notice that in the Canadian Tire situation—where there are only 500 stores total and a budget for testing in only 28 stores—a fully randomized A/B test does not work. There are too few stores to ensure probabilistic equivalence. Second, for synthetic controls to work you need considerable amounts of historical data to train and test the model. In the Canadian Tire example, we had weekly sales for several years. Third, you should have pretty good reason to believe that the analytic twins will mimic the behavior of the actual units (stores, factories, etc.). Retail stores represent an excellent application of synthetic controls, as there is good reason to believe that overall store sales may be correlated.

Regression Discontinuity: Looking Through Tiny Windows

When we build a predictive model using historical data, we often throw as much data as possible into the "gears" underlying the prediction. While not every variable may make it into the final model, having more variables is generally better. Similarly, having more rows of data or more observations is generally better. Somewhat counterintuitively, when you apply causal models to the data you have, these models sometimes thrive on tiny windows of data rather than enormous datasets. Let's see why by looking at two case studies.

MexicanVilla: Regression discontinuity using cutoff rules

In many businesses, there are discrete rules with cutoffs related to key decisions, such as whether to offer customers credit financing and at what interest rate. Consider the anonymized example of a Mexican home-furnishings retailer we'll call MexicanVilla, which offers financing for customers to buy sofas, dining tables, bedroom sets, and other big-ticket furniture. To determine the exact interest rate offered, customers are given a numerical score based on their existing credit score (FICO, for example), age, household income, and other factors seen as relevant.

While customer scores vary from 1 to 100, the retailer offers only a small number of different interest rates. For example, customers with scores of 80 or higher receive the lowest interest rate; those with scores between 60 and 79 receive the next best rate.

Now suppose that MexicanVilla wants to understand how interest rates affect whether customers make their loan payments: Do customers with more favorable terms pay their loans on time? Are these customers less likely to default than others because they get better terms? To answer these questions, you might initially be tempted to simply compare customers who have loans with different interest rates. But by now, if you've read the earlier chapters, you should recognize the problem with that approach. Making comparisons among these groups introduces likely confounds such as credit score, income, age, job security, health status, diligence, and trustworthiness, because these can systematically affect both the interest rate consumers were offered and their loan repayment behavior. In other words, simply comparing customers who have loans with different interest rates would most definitely fail the Causality Checklist.

Recall from the last chapter that we suggested controlling for confounds as a possible solution. But what if we don't have data on all of these confounds? For example, MexicanVilla has data on income and age of customers, but no measure of job security or health status. This is where looking through tiny windows of data, rather than a full dataset, can be advantageous. Among data scientists, the approach is known as "regression discontinuity," which sounds a bit complicated but is actually a very simple concept. The basic idea is to compare observations or units that are very close (just on either side) to the threshold used to assign units to different treatments to understand effects of a variable of interest. By narrowing the window, we hope to eliminate the impact of confounds. We know this probably sounds quite abstract. Let's make it more concrete.

For MexicanVilla, using regression discontinuity could mean comparing customers who received a financing score of exactly 80 to those who were given a 79. The former group enjoyed the best-possible interest rate, while the latter was given less optimal terms, despite being so close to the cutoff. Importantly, the proximity in scores means the two groups of customers are likely to look very similar on key variables including credit score, income, and age—the confounds mentioned earlier.

But the real power of this method is that we hope to control for variables we cannot measure. Things like job security, health status, diligence, or trustworthiness might be factors that influence whether any customer repays a loan. It's reasonable to believe that consumers who have similar scores, say 79 and 80, are similar on these unmeasurable variables. If so, it's as if customers were assigned to one interest rate or the other by a coin flip rather than by a meaningful difference in credit score. Because of this, the tiny window of data you have looks just like an experiment—a natural experiment!

In MexicanVilla's case, a comparison of customers with credit scores of 80 versus 79 isolated the impact of payment terms from other variables. Using this natural experiment, the business was able to learn about how payment terms affected whether customers paid on time, and whether they ultimately defaulted. This insight enabled the retailer to improve the design of payment terms for different product categories.

Pass-Through of Automaker Incentives: Regression discontinuity using time

Regression discontinuity is also powerful because it can use time as a threshold. Let us illustrate this idea using an example you became familiar with in Chapter 4. To refresh your memory: Auto manufacturers spend *a lot* on purchase incentives. Manufacturers want to understand the *pass-through* of cash incentives, or put differently, the amount of the incentive that is being passed to customers rather than kept by dealers. In that earlier chapter we analyzed transaction data for the Toyota Prius model that showed that, on average, incentive amounts were approximately $2,000. For cars sold with no incentive, the average purchase price was about $25,000. In contrast, Priuses for which there was an incentive sold for about $23,000. At first glance it looked like 100 percent of the dealer incentive was passed through to the customer: the dealer incentive of $2,000 reduced the price paid by the consumer by more or less that exact amount.

Applying the Causality Checklist quickly uncovered a confound, namely *demand conditions*. Promotional incentives are generally offered only in periods of weak demand (meaning demand conditions are a driver). In addition, weaker demand will result in lower negotiated prices because dealers want to get rid of cars that are not selling as expected, regardless of whether manufacturers offer promotions—meaning demand conditions are a confound! We concluded from this that we cannot tell how much of the $25,000 versus $23,000 price difference is due to different demand conditions, and how much is driven by the $2,000 promotion. Therefore, we rejected that the analytics provides evidence for a 100 percent pass-through. Figure 9.5 summarizes the finding.

Figure 9.5 Toyota Prius Pass-Through Confound

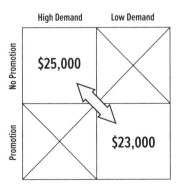

In summary, during periods of high demand, automakers typically do not promote cars. During low-demand periods, promotions are more likely. As a result, when we compare $25,000 with $23,000, we are not comparing just the effect of promotions but also that of different demand conditions.

Having failed the Causality Checklist, how can we then determine the true pass-through without running a (costly) planned experiment? How can we make do with the data we have? The key—as is often the case to succeed with AIA—is to understand the business. It turns out that most auto manufacturers have promotion teams that conduct weekly reviews to determine which vehicles to promote. The key industry fact that now helps us is that it takes one to three weeks for the promotion to be implemented. For example, let's say that the Toyota promotion teams decided on October 14 to implement a $2,000 promotion on a Toyota Prius. It may take until October 28 for the promotion to be rolled out to dealers (dealers are not typically told that a promotion is forthcoming).

How does this help us? The key here is that from October 14 to October 27, demand was weak (which is why the promotions team acted) *and* there was no promotion in place. On October 28, however, demand was still weak (demand does not change that quickly) and the promotion was in place. Can you see where regression discontinuity comes in? Declare the threshold to be midnight of October 27. Now use October 27 as the control and October 28 as the test. Are demand conditions still a confound? Very unlikely, since demand does not usually change over the course of two days; however, the available promotion *did* change by a lot, namely $2,000. How about a slightly bigger window? Say, the week leading up to October 27 as control and the week starting October 28 as test. Again, demand conditions are unlikely to be very different. However, as the window expands, we should keep in mind that demand conditions could be different before and after the threshold. Hence our conclusion at the beginning of this section that this approach thrives on tiny windows of data rather than enormous datasets.

Let's implement this idea using one-week windows around not just one but many Prius promotion starts. The data using that approach shows that the average price for a Prius purchased during the nonpromotional period just before an incentive is implemented is not $25,000 but closer to $24,000 (see Figure 9.6). That means that dealers have already lowered the price of Priuses in reaction to weak demand, even though the manufacturer did not offer an incentive. When the promotion starts, we see that the price drops another $1,000, to get to a final average price of $23,000 in the promotional period.

Figure 9.6 Toyota Prius Pass-Through Calculation

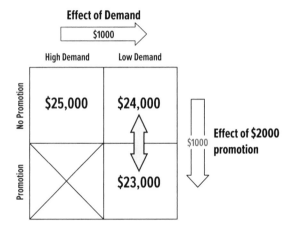

Bottom line: the dealer pass-through in this example is about half of what we thought: 50 percent versus the full 100 percent (about $1,000 of the $2,000 difference between promotion and nonpromotion prices).[4]

In summary, you have just learned three powerful, easy-to-implement methods for taking advantage of data you have through a natural experiment. As a leader with high DSIQ, you will see lots of applications for these methods. We think of them as "jerry-rigging" an experiment from nonexperimental data!

CHAPTER 10

OPTIMIZING AND SCALING YOUR DECISIONS

Suppose that your AIA team has just finished building a high-performing predictive model, or wrapped up a great experiment to build a sophisticated causal model. The AIA is done, and it's time for you, as a business leader, to make decisions. You want to make the best decision—or optimize—and on top of that you are interested in scaling your investments across the organization and growing your returns from AIA over time. What are your challenges?

Business leaders who are new to AIA often have the naive view that the role of business leaders and managers is minimal when you move to evidence-based decision-making. After all, you poured millions of dollars into data, systems, and people; you've been working on AIA for months; surely these investments will pay off and deliver the promised business outcomes. The reality is there is still tremendous hard work ahead. You may have finished the "science," but your business needs to interpret and act upon recommendations generated by AIA. That means your role as a business leader is more important than ever.

In this chapter, we first review common challenges in decision-making with AIA. For each challenge, we provide practical advice on making better decisions. Then we turn to three issues with scaling AIA decisions, with some practical guidance there as well, to help prepare you as a decision-maker. In Chapter 13, "Organizing for

Success," we will turn to how you can transform your organization to better support AIA.

MAKING GOOD DECISIONS WITH AIA

There are many situations where making evidence-driven decisions is easy. This is the case, for example, when you run an advertising experiment that tests two different ad copies, and then calculate the projected ROI from a rollout. You look at the ROI of each option and pick the winner—sounds simple enough. Thus, it's tempting to make the leap from this simple example to assuming that all AIA decisions can be handled in such a straightforward manner: look at the numbers and the results will be self-evident. Indeed, when decisions based on AIA are easy, you should get out of the way, automate the models, and let AIA do its thing. Such decisions have several features in common, as we discuss below.

Identifying the Easy Situations

The first indicator of an easy decision-making situation is that you are evaluating a well-defined and usually small set of options, rather than large and multidimensional ones. When the number of decisions is relatively small and well-defined (such as "Should we accept or reject a loan application?" or "Which of five homepage designs should each customer be served upon visiting our website?") AIA lends itself to automated decision-making.

Second, such decisions need to be made many times over, and each decision is very similar to the previous one. Facial recognition falls in this category ("Is this person X?"), as does warehouse robotics ("Should a bot turn left, straight, or right?") and credit scoring ("On a scale of 0–100, what is this customer's risk of default?"). In these examples, AIA lends itself to, in fact requires, automated decision-making without managerial intervention.

Third, you need a clear, unambiguous link from analytics to business KPIs, which is how your business outcomes model connects with

AIA. If this is not clearly pinned down, decisions are more difficult and you, as a business leader, need to be more involved. For example, if there is a clear link from customer churn to profit, decisions may be easy. But what if business units cannot agree on whether profit should be measured over a one-year or three-year horizon? Then, decisions are more complex.

Fourth, the data used for AIA must be complete. By this, we mean that most relevant pieces of data on your wish list are in the analysis. If so, the decisions become much easier. But recall all of our examples where we had difficulty measuring fuzzy concepts like "interest" or "commitment." Moreover, you may be missing critical information about your competitors' sales, prices, and offers. When these types of variables are not in your analysis, your role in decision-making is much more important.

Fifth, consider whether the market conditions under which your data was collected and analyzed are comparable to the market conditions you face today. If today's situation is very different from the time period in which the data was collected and models were built, you need to lean more into your judgment and intuition. This is the "situational invariance" requirement we discussed earlier in the book.

Finally, and perhaps most critically, you need to understand the business assumptions behind the AIA, and whether they hold. When you are confident that these assumptions hold, you can be more comfortable drawing a direct link between AIA and decision-making. If not, your ongoing judgment is required.

What's an example of AIA-based decisions that are straightforward from a decision-making point of view (though the AIA can be very complicated) and usually don't require managerial intervention? US Customs and Border Protection (CBP) has recently started using AIA-based facial recognition to screen entry into the United States. The system uses photos collected from CBP-owned cameras and equipment provided by airlines, airports, and cruise lines with photos in the Department of Homeland Security's IDENT database. This includes passport and visa application photos, and photos from prior US entries and exits. According to CBP, this system is more accurate than having humans check passport photos against a person's face.[1] This type of system meets all six of our criteria for easy decisions and, as a result, can be automated since there is little need for managerial judgment.

Regrettably, most business decision don't meet our six criteria. They are what we think of as hard decisions. The challenges, or "optimization traps," we describe next help make them that way.

Optimization Traps

To a data scientist, optimization is simply the process of finding the best answer from a set of many possible answers. In performing AIA, we optimize at many stages. For example, to arrive at the best analytics model, we optimize how the model fits the data. In a regression model we estimate its coefficients, and in a neural network we determine its weights, as we saw in the examples of BrightStar Mobile and Level Up Games presented earlier in the book.

Optimizing business decisions ("Given the results of AIA, what's the best business decision?") is very different from optimizing AIA. Answering this question involves weighing costs and benefits with an eye toward a specific business outcome, such as profit, again as we illustrated in previous examples such as Level Up Games.

We see two common traps when it comes to optimization. The first relates to optimizing AIA, and the second relates to optimizing AIA-based business decisions. First, managers underestimate *how difficult AIA optimization is.* That is, if you aren't an expert in data science, it may be difficult to appreciate how hard it is to optimize a model. It's easy for business managers to read about amazing, innovative applications of machine learning or AI and imagine that these models can readily be applied to their own data. The reality is that such models often required highly specialized data scientists and considerable time to optimize. Thus, business leaders who are new to AIA often underestimate the time and resources required. For example, one of us was asked to help a CEO with an analytics project and had about one week to pull together some analysis before we met. At the start of the meeting, we cautioned the CEO that our progress was constrained by only having one week of time to prepare. His response: "A week? That's a lot of time!" In general, analytics projects often operate on a much slower timescale and are much more complex than most senior leaders realize.

The second pitfall relating to optimization is perhaps even more common and relevant for business managers. Let's call this the *turn-key illusion*, which is the misguided belief that decisions based on AIA are by definition easy because they require no managerial judgment. Indeed, the hard work often begins—or continues—once you have an AIA model in hand. That's the point at which you need to measure costs, benefits, and myriad other factors that were specified previously in your business outcomes model. You also need to understand the full set of options under consideration, and their pros and cons. It is naive to think that models inherently incorporate this complexity and readily deliver the best answers to you. Models usually are just an *input* to your decision-making, not a replacement for it.

In fact, many real-world business problems are highly complex, which makes finding the best answer a challenge at best and ridiculously difficult at worst. Our colleague Duncan Simester at MIT codeveloped a simulation where managers are asked to design a messenger bag like the ones that bicyclists carry over their shoulders in major cities. Design options include things like a handle, water-bottle holder, color, size, and price. While the problem seems simple enough, even having a relatively small set of options results in more than 4,000 possible bags! In our executive workshops, we run an exercise in which we ask participants to optimize the best assortment of just five possible bags from all these combinations to sell in a retail store. We've asked the head merchant of a large retailer how long this decision would take using intuition alone. The senior merchant told us, "I'd spend about five minutes on this. Any more than that means I am wasting my time."

It seems reasonable to assume that if a human could pick the best five bags in less than five minutes, surely AIA could do that more quickly. Notice that to fully optimize the bag assortment, we need to evaluate the performance of all possible combinations of five messenger bags. It turns out there are *4.9 quadrillion* such possible combinations. That is an enormous number! Even if we could use AIA to run 1,000 experiments (scenarios) per second, it would take 155,000 *years* to finish the job. And if we could run one million experiments (scenarios) a second, it would still take 155 years! In Boston speak, this optimization problem is "wickedly difficult!"

And it gets worse. In our simulation, we give managers about 10 minutes to use a spreadsheet to find the optimal answer. The spreadsheet automatically computes profits and market share for any combination of messenger bags (i.e., it simulates the results of any assortment experiment that participants want to run). What typically happens is that managers start with a ton of intuition about the best assortment and evaluate the resultant assortments. And then things go wrong. After one or two minutes, our participants start looking for options that increase profit, since that is the objective we gave them. We have found that this quickly displaces their intuition, and they move to fishing for the best answer using trial and error—a futile approach given that there are 4.9 quadrillion fish in the pond!

When the simulation ends, we identify the manager who managed to create a combination of five messenger bags that yielded the highest profit. We display this "optimal" solution to all the participants and ask the winner to explain inconsistencies in the final assortment. For example, a winning answer often has a large bag selling for a lower price than a small bag, which is at odds with usual pricing practices. Inevitably, the best answer is very hard to rationalize. Nonetheless, the winning participant defends his or her choice by saying, "The model said that this was the best assortment to offer!"

This example fails at least two of our criteria enabling easy AIA-based decision-making. First, we had many options to consider (4.9 quadrillion!). Second, our simulation model, by necessity, was missing a lot of important information, such as competitor sales, advertising, and in-store marketing. Participants knew this; nonetheless, they took the results of the model as truth. These are situations where blindly using a model can lead to poor decisions. This is what we think of as an optimization trap. Given the growth of tools and systems from vendors that promise easy optimization, such optimization traps are everywhere.

What can you do about optimization traps? First, recognize the limitations of optimization in complex, real-world settings. In most cases, both AIA and business optimization are much more difficult than they may appear, and there are simply no turnkey solutions. It's difficult to evaluate options expediently when there are too many of them, as the messenger bag example shows.

Second, move your AIA process to scenario analysis. In the messenger bag example, a reasonable approach might be to generate 10 different combinations of bags that make intuitive sense. These are business scenarios that you can rationalize, explain to others, and justify. Now the question is: Which of these scenarios is best? This is where you want to use AIA to evaluate the scenarios. In the messenger bag example, your intuition may not be a very good tool for generating a demand forecast for each scenario—and this is why you should use AIA for scenario analysis. Use the experiments (scenarios) to predict demand, and then use the predicted demand in your business outcomes model to compute profit, market share, and other important measures. Finally, choose the option that yields the best business outcome.

Sandra Dawson, CMO of an online-only retailer, shared with us how her company fell into an optimization trap.[2] She said (we paraphrase): "When I came in as CMO, I was completely new to the business. So I started trying to understand everything from operations, supply chain, and marketing. I really wanted to understand the whole business. When I reviewed our website, I found pages where we would push discount messages in the lower left corner and then new product innovations in the banner. I wanted to know why we did that."

Sandra's question led her to the head of data science, who provided an explanation: "We use A/B testing on every page, and it is very detailed. Think of each page as a grid with multiple sections; we run A/B tests on each section of a page and then implement the winning solution. On the page you are referring to, the discount message was best for the left corner, and the new product message was best in the banner." Sandra replied, "But did anyone ever A/B test the entire page against alternatives?"

The head of data science had no answer. The company had fallen into an optimization trap. What was missing in the data were the connections among sections, or what Sandra thought of as the overall marketing message or strategy. As a brand, are we pushing discounts? Or is our brand strategy about quality and innovation?

The analytics were simply too narrow and not focused on the big picture. So Sandra made changes: while A/B testing remained the norm at the business, she adjusted how testing was implemented to align with the company's brand strategy. This included use of full-page A/B tests instead of just testing page elements, and removing options from A/B tests if they were deemed inconsistent with overall brand strategy.

Eclipse Moments

Imagine you are having dinner at a new restaurant and need directions: how would you get there? For nearly all of us, the answer is obvious. We use our phone or vehicle GPS, enter an address, and off we go! Pretty easy. Notice that your GPS is probably going to provide you with predictive analytics: "You will arrive at the restaurant in 11 minutes." And along the way you might get recommendations like "I have found a faster route. Your new arrival time is 10 minutes." This is a causal recommendation: if you change your route then you are likely to arrive in less time.

It's tempting to think that all AIA systems operate with this precision. The reality is that many simply don't have this degree of accuracy. As a result, our advice to every business leader is that you need to use a combination of intuition plus AIA to make good decisions. In the driving example, think of the GPS as getting you to the neighborhood of the restaurant, and from there you use your intuition to find the establishment's front door. In other words, think of your GPS system as much more like an old-fashioned Boy Scout compass, which is informative but not precise. Indeed, many AIA systems are the same way: they ultimately function more like a compass.

To underscore this point, we want to share a story that one of us experienced some time ago. On August 20, 2017, a Sunday, Anderson and family were invited to a big party to celebrate and view the solar eclipse. That night, 40 friends and family gathered in southern Indiana for a barbeque that included a live band, great food, and wonderful company. On Monday morning, the group caravanned to Golconda, a small town in southern Illinois, to have a picnic, continue the celebration, and watch the solar eclipse. As they were in the "zone of totality," the eclipse started around 1:30 p.m. and lasted a total of two minutes and 40 seconds. It was magical!

But it was Monday, and Tuesday was a workday for everyone. The Andersons packed up their gear, got back to the car around 2:00 p.m., and started the drive back to Chicago. Anderson opened up his favorite map software, selected his home address, and a kind voice that the Andersons call "Effie" said, "You will arrive at your destination at 8:00 p.m. You are on the fastest route." Six hours of driving. No problem. Generally, the drive was around five hours without traffic.

After 15 minutes of driving on winding country roads, they arrived at the I-57 highway. They eased onto the highway with all the other cars, but soon traffic was at a standstill. After 30 minutes of that, Effie piped up: "There is a traffic delay ahead. Your new arrival time is 9:00 p.m. You are still on the fastest route!"

Two hours later, progress was minimal. Everyone in the car was growing antsy. And then Effie proudly announced, "I have found a faster route." The excitement in the car was palpable: the Andersons were going to get home 15 minutes faster. Thank you, Effie! They exited the freeway and began navigating myriad twists and turns. Progress was self-evident because the car was finally moving. But then traffic came to a halt in the middle of a country road surrounded by cornfields.

A few minutes later Effie returned: "There is a traffic delay ahead. Your new arrival time is 10:00 p.m." What happened? The Andersons weren't the only ones getting great advice from Effie; versions of her were telling every other car to get off the highway and take the new route. Now there was a traffic jam several miles long as cars tried to get back on the highway—the same place they'd all started!

An hour later, the Andersons were back on the highway and slowly grinding their way toward home. At 8:00 p.m., six hours into the journey, they had traveled less than 100 miles and still had 250 miles to go. As they neared the next freeway exit, Effie announced, "There is a construction delay ahead. Your new arrival time is 12:00 a.m. You are still on the fastest route!" Exhausted, deflated, and low on gas, they pulled off the freeway into a gas station. Team huddle.

Time to regroup and reconsider the options. Effie was no longer the family friend; she was turned off unceremoniously.

Now, no longer relying on GPS guidance, the Andersons looked north on I-57 to see that traffic was going nowhere, with every on-ramp clogged with cars trying to enter the highway. But nobody was going east. They had no idea where they were, but how bad could it get, they figured, if they just started driving east. After about an hour of driving east, it was 9:00 p.m. and the sun was fading into the horizon. "Let's turn north to Chicago," they agreed. They found a small country road, the kind with no dividing line, and headed toward Chicago. As the moon rose, there were only cows, cornfields, and most important . . . no cars.

Around 12:30 p.m., an exhausted Anderson family pulled into their driveway. Everyone went straight to bed. The next morning, they learned that friends in the caravan who had stayed on the highway—as instructed by their GPS systems—reached Chicago around 5:00 a.m.! Zettelmeyer likes to point out that he and his family saw the eclipse in Jackson, Wyoming, took a flight home to Chicago, and were home by 7 p.m., five hours before the Andersons arrived!

Here is why we love this story. As a business leader, you should always think about whether you're in the midst of an "eclipse moment" in your business. Effie is an AIA system that provides recommendations based on predictive models and causal models—it is trying to anticipate and influence travel time. The system has observed car travel times for years and built a highly reliable model that works well in most situations. So why did Effie fail the Andersons that day?

The system had never experienced a situation like the solar eclipse. At the time, southern Illinois had more than 100,000 visitors scattered throughout the region, all viewing the same event. Many of them had the same objective when the eclipse ended: returning home as quickly as possible. On most Monday afternoons, the highway is empty. On that particular day, the volume of traffic was well beyond what had ever been seen historically. If you think of this as a business situation, it would be one the AIA had never encountered. As a result, the recommendations the system generated were fundamentally flawed; there was no situational invariance—it was uncharted territory.

But notice that Effie did not call this out to the Andersons. She did not say that her predictions and recommendations were highly uncertain and should be followed with caution, that there were unusual patterns of data she had never seen before. Instead, she did her best to provide her usual advice. Today, many systems operate this way; they always generate answers and recommendations, no matter the situation. Because of this, your challenge as a manager is to learn when to trust the analytics, and when to lean more on your intuition. That means asking whether you're facing an "eclipse moment" that could invalidate the recommendations produced by your AIA. Is there a sudden change in competition from a large player in your market? Has there been a huge, unexpected shift in the economy, such as that caused by a global pandemic? Have you launched new initiatives the system is not aware of? At such times you may need to blend judgment with models or to switch entirely to instinct and intuition, like the Andersons did that day. Good analytics always requires good judgment, so keep yours close at hand, ready for deployment as needed.

Last, you should appreciate that this is very, very hard to do—particularly when you have come to trust a system like Effie. For example, it took Anderson, an AIA expert, six hours to shut off the predictive and causal recommendations from Effie and start using his intuition!

The Confidence Conundrum: Business Versus Technical Assumptions

To maximize success when decisions are hard, business managers and data scientists must collaborate effectively. To illustrate this challenge, we want to put you through a short simulation.

Imagine you are a consultant who specializes in retail pricing and you have been hired by an office supply chain, Total Office Supplies. At a recent meeting, the firm's SVP of Strategy Josh Goens said, "I believe the online marketplace is now more competitive than the offline environment, and I don't think our everyday, regular online prices and in-store prices are aligned with this reality. Can you review the prices on our website and in our stores and help us optimize the gap in online prices versus in-store price?"

To answer this question, Total Office Supplies' data science team decided to analyze 52 weeks of data for two categories: inkjet cartridges and markers. The weekly data included price paid, cost, and units sold at more than 1,000 physical stores and the online store, along with information on whether any given item was promoted on Total Office Supplies' weekly flyer. The company had been scraping the prices on competitive websites for other projects, and this information was also merged into the dataset. This allowed the data science team to build a model to predict weekly sales volume for the two categories in the physical stores and the online store. Next, the data science team used the model to analyze hundreds of "what-if" prices to optimize the prices that maximized profits for all stores and the online channel. The analysis suggested that online prices should be 10 percent lower than offline prices for inkjet cartridges, and 5 percent lower for markers.

Take a moment to assess Total Office Supplies' AIA approach from a business perspective. How might you be able to have confidence in these recommendations? If you were Josh Goens, what questions would you ask your data science team to develop the confidence that their AIA approach solves your pricing problem?

In our experience, business leaders often don't know what questions they should ask data scientists. Sometimes business leaders ask no probing questions, thereby accepting and implementing the recommendations of the data science team blindly. ("After all, they are the experts!") More commonly, a curious business leader starts to ask questions, but the communication becomes an exercise in frustration: "I have no idea how you arrived at this answer!" the leader often concludes. In trying to explain what they did more clearly, data science teams lean heavily on the technical details, which simply adds to the frustration because these seem irrelevant to business leaders.

Asking the right questions of data scientists is a critical skill for business managers who want to drive value with analytics. In fact, in this case, it turns out that if Josh Goens didn't ask the right questions of his data scientists, Total Office Supplies would end up failing miserably on the price-optimization initiative. As will be obvious in a moment, the recommendations of Total Office Supplies' data science team are deeply flawed. First, however, we want to make some recommendations about the role that data scientists and business leaders should play when making AIA-based decisions.

Business leaders and data scientists each have a primary role, or what you can think of as a "swim lane." Business leaders own business decisions; data scientists own the science. The key to success is to combine the concept of "staying in your lane" with effective collaboration among business managers and data scientists. "Staying in your lane" means that data scientists should not question managerial judgment or business decisions, and managers should not question the science. Effective collaboration means that business leaders must be able to understand what drives the results from the AIA and what business assumptions went into performing the analysis, in order to make decisions confidently. It also means that data scientists understand the business problem they have been asked to solve and are given enough information about the business context to inform their analytics.

To achieve this goal, we believe there are four questions you should ask your data science team. We illustrate the power of these questions in the context of the Total Office Supplies example.

Data Variation: What is the variation in the data that feeds the AIA?

As we've emphasized throughout this book, variation in data is paramount for effective AIA. To be confident in the AIA, you need to have confidence in the source of variation that feeds AIA. You also need to understand the rules and processes that limit the variation of your data.

Had you asked about data variation in the Total Office Supply case, you would have learned that the company historically had a "one price" policy: the online and in-store prices were always the same. As a result, the historical data included *no price gaps whatsoever* between those channels. This means that the predictive model had no way of assessing how a gap in online and offline prices was likely to affect people's purchasing behavior in either channel, which was the project's central goal! You might wonder: If there was no variation in the price gap, how did the data science team make a recommendation in the first place? We will explain that in the next section.

Comparisons: What comparisons does the AIA rely on? Are these comparisons valid?

Comparisons are the beating heart of analytics. In the Total Office Supply case, the model assesses price sensitivity or price elasticity by comparing situations with high prices to those with low prices. Here, the model compared situations where items were sold at the regular price with situations where they were sold on temporary price promotions (e.g., "20 percent off this week!") in both the online and offline channels (since prices across channels were always the same). Because the online volume was more responsive to these promotions, the model found that online demand was more price-sensitive, leading to the recommendation that online prices should be lower.

But is this the comparison the business wanted? Remember: leadership wanted to understand the optimal *regular* prices to set for each channel. But the model compared regular versus promoted prices—say 20 percent off one week versus full price the prior week. From this comparison, the model learned and generated a price recommendation. If you are in the retail business, you know that regular and promoted prices are often very different beasts, even if the dollar value associated with each price is the same. As a result, the data science team would have been much better served by designing experimental variation in the price gap between online and offline channels—this was the ideal comparison. The resulting data would have answered the intended business question.

Marketplace: What assumptions about the business marketplace did you make in the AIA? Why do you think they are valid?

Every AIA finding relies on a set of assumptions about the business (e.g., "Next year's growth will be similar to this year's growth" or "Consumer preferences for our new tablet in Germany can be approximated by consumer preferences in France"). Your goal as a business leader should be to understand these assumptions and then assess whether you believe them.

Even randomized experiments, which are the least assumption-dependent AIA approach, require assumptions to be valid—specifically, that the randomization was properly executed and that experimental groups don't bleed into one another. All other AIA methods make *more* assumptions, and many of these are business assumptions, not technical ones—like the ones presented parenthetically above.

As a leader, you must find out what assumptions your data science team made about the business marketplace and how they justify those assumptions. For example, the Total Office Supplies project used 52 weeks of data from the prior year to forecast next year's results. This requires an assumption that the market Total Office Supply faced in the past year is similar to the one the business will encounter next year. Moreover, the analysis implicitly assumes that major competitors, like Amazon, would not change their prices in response to the pricing recommendations. As you can imagine, that's a very problematic assumption since a large competitor is likely to lower its price if you permanently lower yours! Most important, while all AIA approaches require some assumptions to work, these are assumptions you, a business leader, should assess, not the data science team.

Business Intuition: Here is my business intuition. Can you explain how the analytics reflect my intuition?

Last, you should always ask enough questions to ensure that the analytics reflect your business intuition accurately. In the case of Total Office Supplies, for example, you may have had an intuition about how physical-store shoppers cross-shop the physical and online stores. Asking about how the model captures this switching behavior would have quickly uncovered a major limitation of the analytics: based on the historical data, you can't forecast how customer behavior will change if there is a price gap between online and offline.

Moreover, the intuition that spurred this project in the first place was that the online channel is more competitive than the offline one. The implication is that the business could lose price-sensitive online shoppers to competitors. This intuition may be correct, but the data contains no information on migration to competitors. As a result, the AIA simply can't speak to the core business intuition that Total Office Supplies started out with.

Now, please step back and take another look at the four questions. Do you notice that they all tackle *business* assumptions rather than technical assumptions? As the example suggests, when you need to make complex decisions with AIA, you must ask the four questions above to take ownership of these business assumptions. This will give you confidence that the business assumptions supporting the analytics are reasonable, so that you can trust the AIA required to make the best-informed decisions. If you don't take ownership of business assumptions, data scientists, for better or worse, will make those business assumptions for you. After all, data scientists are expected to produce answers, and getting to answers requires assumptions.

In general, to gain confidence in results, business leaders and data scientists need to understand their roles and how to communicate more effectively. Success with analytics requires confidence in both business assumptions and data science assumptions. Business leaders need to trust that they have hired top-notch data scientists who produce high-quality work—that the science is technically correct. And business leaders must understand (and ideally make) the business assumptions that go into the science, so that they can have confidence in the AIA-based decisions they are asked to make.

Finally, everyone needs to trust the data. This doesn't mean that the data is perfect, but rather that everyone must be willing to make decisions using the imperfect data available—a cultural norm any organization should have. Once you have trust in the data and science, then data scientists and managers can collaborate to understand what they need to believe about the business to have confidence in analytic results.

In the Total Office Supply example, the answers to *any* of our four questions would have made you, as a business leader, question the recommendations. Managers new to data science are typically blown away that data and a model can lead to precise recommendations—it is liberating when you feel like you are doing science rather than simply using intuition. As business professors, it is akin to us wandering through a medical laboratory with a white lab coat and feeling like we are doing hard-core science. Simply tossing on a lab coat doesn't make a business professor a medical scientist. Remember, every model generates a recommendation, and your job is to assess the science from a business perspective. Your ability to trust the recommendations depends on your belief that the business assumptions that support the AIA are valid.

SCALING AIA ENTERPRISEWIDE

We have talked at length about what it takes to make good decisions with AIA. But making a few good decisions is not enough. To deliver business value, AIA needs to be scaled throughout the enterprise. This starts with turning a one-time project into a "system," nurturing this system over time, and then deploying the system through multiple business units. The next sections provide practical tips for doing that.

Projects, Systems, and Humans

Many analytics projects start as one-off initiatives. Successful projects are subsequently reviewed for whether they can be turned into a full-blown system that is embedded into day-to-day operations. For example, Tom O'Toole, the former CMO of United Airlines, told us how the enterprisewide analytics team he started used analytics to predict when luggage would get lost. One task is to build such a model. An entirely different task is to put such a model into production, to turn it into a "system." Now, baggage handlers and operations personnel have to be able to interpret and act on the predictions. Not surprisingly, the process of going from a one-off project to a system can be extremely challenging. What works in a small-scale proof-of-concept project requires considerable effort to scale. Aside from technical challenges, one of the largest challenges is that systems need to interface with humans and existing business processes.

Human behavior can be challenging if you want to create a scalable system. To illustrate how difficult it can be, consider an example provided by an analytics consultant we spoke to. He described an AI project for an insurance-industry client, and said that the efficacy of the AI had been proven out via simulation and several successful pilots. When the client decided to scale the AI project into an AI system, an employee in the target business unit was asked to work with the consulting firm and the client's data science team to improve and then implement the model. For example, the system was initially designed to handle simple, less complex cases, leaving more complicated cases to humans. Before turning the AI project into an operational system, the client decided to improve the model by incorporating so-called "edge cases" or moderate-difficulty cases. This would scale the number of cases the model could handle and improve the ROI of the AI system. Incorporating these edge cases— cases the model did not know how to handle—required input from employees. However, realizing that their jobs were at stake, some of the employees worked actively to sabotage the model. Such resistance is not uncommon. As you scale AIA, employees need to participate, but they may also be affected; you need to anticipate and plan for how your organization will approach this tricky challenge.

A related challenge the insurance example illustrates is that an AIA-based system may change the mix of skills you need in employees. For example, carrying the illustration above further, suppose the end-state of the AIA system for the insurance client was that 50 percent of cases could be handled by the system, and employees needed to handle the remainder. The implication is that employees are now handling only complex cases. But you may have started with a team with a mix of skills, or employees who can handle a combination of simple cases and the occasional harder ones. This may no longer be the right skill set in a world where all cases handled by employees are complex.

Finally, suppose an AIA system is designed to complement the work of employees by enhancing their productivity. Your vision may be that an employee needs to interface with the system on a regular basis by reviewing results and asking questions. This may be straightforward if you have highly trained employees who can interface with the system through what look like a series of SQL queries (database commands). But most likely you may also need a conversational interface where a nontechnical person can interact with the AIA system through spoken language. As you can imagine, transitioning from a pilot to a concept and finally to a full-blown system with a conversational interface is a large-scale undertaking. You will need to understand intent, derive meaning, interpret, and make recommendations that may be highly specific to the user and business context. In other words, scaling such a system is a large endeavor.

Our advice: take it one small step at a time. To illustrate, think of the well-known Apple interface Siri. When Siri was first introduced on the iPhone, it seemed magical. You could ask Siri all sorts of questions like: "What was the score in last night's Cubs game?" or "Where is the nearest Starbucks?" and Siri would instantly generate answers. However, was Siri truly capable of interpreting nuanced questions and understanding intent? It was not. As recounted to us by Siri's cocreator Dag Kittlaus, the system was focused on answering consumers' questions related to entertainment and geographic directions. Siri could capture a human voice, translate, and provide fairly basic responses by looking up game scores or entering locations into mapping software. Complex questions, in contrast, typically generated no response or a humorous answer. We think that this was the right approach. A complex, fully functional interface would have been impossible when Siri was first launched. Over time you can improve a system, but the idea as you scale is to start simple and don't overpromise.

Scaling Across Business Units: Context Matters

To scale AIA, you may want to take models and systems that work in one business unit and apply them in another business. Pat Connolly, former chief strategy and business development officer at Williams Sonoma, explained to us how the company successfully scaled analytics across its portfolio of related brands, which includes Pottery Barn, West Elm, Rejuvenation, and Mark & Graham. This works well when you have a well-integrated company with a common IT infrastructure and similar types of businesses—in this case, home furnishings. But scaling across more varied business units is often quite complex.

To illustrate this point, one of the functions we take on with our business clients is to help them assess new AIA technology. This may involve joining conference calls or participating in live demos of the new technology. Many of the vendors we evaluate are smaller players that have had success in a single vertical such as insurance, banking, or retail. When asked to explain their technology, the pitch usually starts with a focus on technical functions like matching algorithms, predictive models, and causal models, along with cool visualizations of past projects.

But clients usually want to see examples from their own industry. When pressed for these use cases, the presenters usually pause and eventually say something like, "We have a lot of experience in banking. We have a proven track record and many satisfied clients. We're confident we can apply the same models to your industry and deliver value." At such moments, we do our best not to cringe. The reason that the vendor had prior success most likely had a lot to do with the fact that there was collaboration between data scientists and business leaders to solve a specific problem. Adapting an AIA model to new problems in a new business domain, then, can be a huge undertaking.

Yes, it is technically possible that the models will work well on data from a completely different context. For example, CMO Tom O'Toole's analytics team at United Airlines viewed the problem of predicting customer churn (a lost customer) as analogous to the problem of predicting whether a bag would be lost, and developed effective analytics with that viewpoint. The Chicago-based data analytics firm Uptake, a multibillion-dollar unicorn as of this writing, built its business model on the premise that expertise in building and operating analytics models would transfer easily across industries. It reasoned, for example, that models that help deploy locomotives and engineers could be applied to the allocation of doctors, nurses, and equipment in a large hospital—they are both systems with people and equipment.

But exceptions help reinforce the rule: analytics models require integration of key contextual features to be most effective. When business problems are different, this often requires changes to assumptions, and therefore to how the AIA models work. When data is different, you need to understand the data and to perform "feature engineering," a potentially huge task.

Feature engineering is a computer science term and refers to the process of transforming raw data into meaningful variables that enable the models to perform better. Here is a simple example: You may have variables like latitude and longitude in your data. On their own, they are not terribly useful. But in an application where you want to predict the productivity of a salesperson, you may have an idea—or hypothesis—about how the distance between client locations matters. In particular, if clients are geographically clustered, a salesperson is likely to spend more time selling and less time traveling. Latitude and longitude can be used to compute distance and create meaningful variables that are relevant for this context. In the well-known Kaggle analytics competitions—which cover everything from predicting final home sale prices to forecasting which passengers would have survived the *Titanic*'s sinking—the winning entries almost always include significant amounts of feature engineering.

In general, simply applying a generic model, or one from another domain, rarely leads to success. In a recent conversation with an AI startup, a senior leader told us, "We have built really strong forecasting models for many companies, but with every client engagement we need to customize our models to their context." The takeaway here: don't think of analytics models as one-size-fits-all superheroes. For best results, customize them carefully to your business context.

Scaling Over Time: The Capabilities Paradox

Another way to scale AIA is to improve a model over time. This poses its own challenges. As we discussed earlier in the book, most firms that get started with analytics rely on data they have in hand, or opportunistic data. What they typically don't realize is that AIA success today may cause unintended difficulties with scaling future analytics work. We call this the "capabilities paradox."

Let's take a closer look. Imagine that you are a retailer who determines through AIA the best price to charge for a popular sweater: $24.99. For six months, sales of that item (at that price) meet expectations; but over the last few weeks revenue from the sweater have stagnated. Can AIA help you determine whether to adjust the sweater price using just your historical data? No. You can't build a causal model to help you adjust price with this data from the last six months. The reason is that the price for the sweater has always been $24.99 in that period; there is no variation in your data.

In a B2B context, suppose you use historical data from sensors in an aluminum manufacturing plant to optimize the production process. Since there was a lack of standards among machine operators, the plant operated each week with slightly different inputs and factory settings, like speed and temperature. Using historical data, a model was built that provided recommendations that would yield maximum plant efficiency. Managers relied on the model to make decisions and believed that this eliminated many poor choices that had occurred in the past. But over time, managers were convinced that the model was becoming less and less effective and unable to respond to changes in the business—but they weren't sure how to test this, as there was less variation in inputs now.

Finally, suppose that a young, fast-growing retail business begins to use opportunistic data to build predictive and causal models to understand the impact of promotional campaigns and other business initiatives. Early on, the models "feed" off variation in both input and outcome variables that occurs naturally because the young firm does not know what will work best to improve profits. Over time, growing its AIA skill enables the business to find the best answers and implement profit-driving initiatives with great precision. In this way, the firm evolves into a mature firm with exemplary AIA capability. Then one day the "proven" models stop working: the predictive and causal models stop delivering many actionable findings and insights. Business leaders eventually recognize that their analytics models are starved; available data simply lacks the variation that fueled previous AIA efforts.

What's happening in all of these situations is the same simple problem: by focusing on consistent execution, business practice squeezes out variability, the exact thing needed for comparisons that inform predictive and causal models. While these are specific examples, they reflect the natural evolution that comes with AIA. The problem becomes particularly severe when AIA projects become systems. Remember our early discussion about data, learning, and knowledge. The only way to learn from data is to have the right data. And systems that make good recommendations squeeze out precisely the information you need to learn. This is the paradox.

So what can you do to escape the capabilities paradox?

The solution focuses on long-term planning and the careful development of designed data. The firms most capable with AIA often invest heavily in experimentation abilities to escape the paradox. They recognize that fueling predictive and causal models may require the thoughtful creation of new data, and they work to develop the skills and capabilities to do that. Hence, building experimental capability and experimentation platforms is a long-run imperative for many firms.

Another solution rests in designing systems that explicitly incorporate learning as one of their objectives. The type of machine learning that does this is called reinforcement learning, which we briefly discussed in Chapter 6, "A Smarter Crystal Ball." Think of this as a system that makes calculated mistakes with the goal of creating the variation in the data needed for learning. For example, how might a retailer learn over time whether it has the best price for a given item? The system periodically offers a few wrong prices for a very short period of time (calculated risk), measures sales, and learns. If it turns out that one of the wrong prices is a winner, there may be more investigation—such as a larger A/B test. If, as expected, the prices are wrong, the system learns that it is on track and making the best decision. Learning that you are doing the right thing means that you occasionally need to do the wrong thing.

In sum, to improve a system over time, watch out for the capability paradox. Systems may not naturally improve on their own—they may actually get worse. With care, feeding, and nurturing you can go from an AIA project to a system, but you may need ongoing experimentation, A/B testing, and reinforcement learning. This won't happen overnight. It can take many years to build a high level of AIA capabilities. But we can assure you that it will be well worth it.

SECTION 4

Executing on AI
and Analytics

You now know how to use the AIA framework to link your
business objectives with AIA, and how to make AIA-based
decisions. In Section 4, we turn to your role as a leader
who wants to create business value. This starts with
identifying, prioritizing, and planning for AIA opportunities in your
business, which we cover in Chapter 11. Next, we turn to your role
in transforming the organization so that these AIA-driven projects
can succeed. This requires you to identify barriers within your
existing organization (Chapter 12). Finally, we discuss how your
organization may need to adapt in terms of people, data and systems,
organizational structure, and culture to support AIA (Chapter 13).

CHAPTER 11

IDENTIFYING OPPORTUNITIES AND PLANNING FOR AIA

So far we have shared stories about how businesses have succeeded or failed in using AIA to drive business value. Now we want to help you answer the question: "How do *I* come up with ideas that will help my business utilize AIA to achieve business success?"

When we first started advising firms on AIA, we thought that their hardest problems would be in developing the expertise needed to execute AIA-driven business initiatives, such as building a ML-based model or fine-tuning an AI system. Indeed, this expertise is crucial and not easy to build; however, the expertise is wasted if you are not working on the right *business problem* in the first place. So it was something of a surprise to us that managers who were not very familiar with AIA found it very difficult to even begin to generate high-impact initiatives. In some of our early workshops, for example, we would put managers into brainstorming sessions to develop new, AIA-supported business ideas. This worked for those managers who had a "sixth sense" about AIA, but many experienced something akin to writer's block: they simply couldn't generate ideas for how AIA could create value. Once we recognized this, we worked hard to develop a systematic process for developing and planning for AIA.

Indeed, we realized the importance of planning for AIA while preparing a training session for a Fortune 500 firm that asked us to help its leaders make better decisions with data. In preparing for the meeting we were told something like this: "We have massive amounts of data, with more coming in daily. Our leaders need new skills to understand the latest techniques for dealing with complex data-driven decisions." In the weeks leading up to the meeting, the client seemed concerned that we were not delivering on this request. And then we had our "aha!" moment. The client viewed their problem as getting business leaders to use existing data (as opposed to using intuition) to make decisions—clearly a legitimate goal. But in our experience, a more fundamental problem is that managers often work on the wrong problems with the wrong approach. And the root cause is that there is no process of planning for AIA. Our view is that business leaders should focus on creating, implementing, and supporting the processes that support AIA-driven business initiatives. Then, *once you have a rock-solid plan for AIA, you will work on the right problems with the right approach, and decision-making will become much easier.* Once we communicated this to the client, the leadership team was sold on our view.

We have implemented our framework for identifying opportunities with AIA and planning for AIA with many, many executives at many companies. The benefit of following a systematic process is that decisions are easier and success is more likely. This chapter is about how to create that identification and planning process. What we cover next is hard, time-consuming work, but we promise that it's worth it.

So let's dig in!

IDENTIFYING OPPORTUNITIES TO APPLY AIA

Follow the steps in this section to develop a systematic process for identifying opportunities to apply AIA, as based on our AIA Framework, first introduced in Chapter 2.

Start with Business Problems and Objectives

We want you to start with the first item in the AIA Framework. As we have said throughout this book, analytics must start with your business objectives and business problems. What are you trying to achieve? Why are you having difficulty?

When we conduct workshops with clients, we never start with data, models, or analytics tools. From the outset, we always try to understand the top three to five business problems managers face. Often, it's easiest to focus on the parts of the business that are not meeting expectations. This generates ideas about how AIA can help.

Moreover, AIA has the greatest impact if applied to problems that you care most about. Suppose that a wealth management firm finds that revenues from financial advisors have fallen below business plan expectations. Here is how the CEO summarizes his priorities to his team, in this hypothetical: "Look, if you can solve my revenue problem then I will hit my numbers for the year. Yes, there are other priorities in the strategic plan, like lowering our cost structure and enhancing our use of digital technology. But if we don't hit our revenue target, none of that really matters." Similarly, while nearly every business leader has multiple objectives for the year, a key to success with AIA is to identify what leaders care most about. While this may seem obvious, we have seen organizations spend considerable effort using AIA to solve problems that ultimately turned out to be low-priority for the leadership.

Indeed, at the end of this part of the process, we urge you to focus on the single most important problem you face. If you are thinking of trying to address multiple problems at once, the ideation process becomes unfocused and less impactful. That's largely because you are more likely to generate fewer ideas per problem—making each one less likely to be a blockbuster idea. It's better to focus on a single problem and then brainstorm lots of ideas to address it. Hopefully one of your ideas is a home run!

Generate Multiple Ideas That Address Your Most Important Problems

As you generate ideas, we advise that you focus on business ideas rather than jumping right away to analytics ideas or technical ones. If you start directly with questions like "How could AIA help solve my business problem?" you are unlikely to have success generating a viable AIA-driven business initiative. For someone new to AIA, this "ask" can understandably be daunting.

Instead, we ask managers to first think about their business, their business problems, and their existing processes. We probe using questions like "Can you tell me more about why you believe your business is not operating at its full potential?" and "What seems to be broken?" Once you have unpacked the primary problem and understand what is potentially broken, then you can start to brainstorm about how AIA might help—ideally, this is a collaboration of business leaders and data scientists.

If we return to our wealth management example from above, recall that revenue was falling short of expectations. When asked "Why?", managers offered the following ideas:

- Financial advisors believe they are not receiving enough high-quality leads from the marketing department.
- Advisors are spending too much time on the phone answering administrative questions from clients—questions that could easily be answered by non-advisor employees or by online resources such as the company website.
- Clients are leaving at an unexpectedly high rate, and advisors are spending significant time and resources trying to get them back, with little luck.

At this point, we understand the core problem (revenues are below expectations) and different possible explanations for it. Notice that we have avoided all AIA jargon and stayed in leaders' comfort zone by asking them to articulate their business problem and explanations for what might be going on.

Along the way, we have identified a set of existing business practices we ought to examine more closely. In this case, leaders identified lead generation, answering administrative questions from clients, and time spent on customer retention as potential targets. Next, we want to start generating ideas related to each business practice. For example, can we think of a way that AIA may be used to generate better leads?

You spent the majority of this book increasing your DSIQ. This is where it pays off: because you have a working knowledge of data science, you are now better able to link your business issues with AIA. For example, in this wealth management example, you may come up with the idea of building a predictive model to determine which factors are associated with lead conversion. Or you might generate ideas for running experiments to test the effectiveness of existing approaches for lead generation.

A high DSIQ makes it easy (and fun!) to come up with lots and lots of ideas. What about the problem that advisors are spending too much time on the phone answering administrative questions? One idea is to experiment with different nudges to get customers to use online resources for simple administrative tasks. To address the problem of advisors spending their time trying to win back clients, you could build a proactive retention program where you reach out to customers who are predicted to leave *in the future*. Clearly, this must be powered by predictive analytics.

So far we have examined existing business practices that we hypothesized were broken. A second great way to generate ideas for adding value with AIA is to identify business practices that are not fundamentally broken, but may never have been evaluated using an evidence-based approach. For example, what evidence do you have that your practice for setting advertising budgets is best? Do you know whether your salesforce compensation system works well or could be improved? Many companies are full of so-called truths and best practices that have been anointed by a set of legacy cultural norms but that have never been proven using hard evidence. As former Harrah's CEO Gary Loveman often points out, people *believe* these practices are best but do not *know* they are best. One great way to come up with AIA-driven business initiatives is to test current best practices using a planned experiment or quasi-experiment.

A third way to generate ideas is to figure out what new business opportunities could be unlocked using AIA. In the wealth management example, can you generate new ideas about how financial advisors can attract younger clients, like millennials? Perhaps some financial advisors are interested in building their digital presence through podcasts directed to younger consumers. This would be a very new approach to lead generation. The ultimate role of AIA might be to predict, for each customer, which approach works best. But since we currently have no data on how people react to podcasts, we may need to run several experiments that generate new data for our predictive model.

The process of identifying opportunities for AIA in your business leads to a set of ideas to improve existing business processes and, potentially, to find new business opportunities using AIA.

Prioritize Your Ideas

How do you prioritize your ideas? First, we recommend asking: "Can I easily explain to others how this initiative is linked to the business?" Several ideas are likely to fail when put through this lens. The best ideas satisfy the elevator-pitch standard: you can explain the idea in the 30 seconds a short elevator ride takes.

The second consideration is the scale and scope of the initiative. Is this a too-small idea or a boil-the-ocean idea? With AIA-driven business initiatives, you need to be careful to avoid either extreme. Very small ideas are easy to execute and likely to succeed, but may have low business impact. Huge ideas will have tremendous impact if they succeed—but these are often long shots that may take significant time and resources. The best ideas are those that are big enough to have impact, but not so large that they overwhelm the organization.

Third, do you have a strong belief that this idea, if successful, will have meaningful business impact and help you achieve your business objectives? If the answer is a definitive *yes*, then the idea should have high priority. Notice that this question presumes that the idea works. Later in the process, we will ask probing questions to assess whether an idea is likely to be successful.

When you are done with this process, you should have a prioritized list of ideas regarding where AIA can be deployed to improve your business. Next, we illustrate how you can flesh out a detailed plan to bring such ideas to life.

CREATING AN AIA BUSINESS PLAN

Every company is familiar with generating business plans. These spell out opportunities to improve the business and are used for many purposes, including capital allocation and annual strategic planning. When it comes to AIA, we want you to develop an analogous type of document that we call an *AIA business plan*. Today, your company almost surely has a process for developing and evaluating business plans; to support data science you need a comparable process for AIA business plans.

An AIA business plan ensures that an AIA-driven business initiative is:

- Linked to the business
- Resourced correctly
- Impactful

Just like a typical business plan, an AIA business plan does not dive deep into the details of execution, which is likely to involve collecting data and building models. Instead, an AIA business plan specifies the business objective, resource requirements, and likely impact of a specific AIA-driven business initiative. In our experience, these plans foster consensus and trust among business leaders that the investments of time and resources to support the AIA-driven business initiative are likely to pay off—a prerequisite for ensuring AIA thrives. If you carefully plan an AIA-driven business initiative and build organizational support (more on this in the next two chapters), then such projects are much more likely to succeed.

The process we outline below can be used to either *create* or *evaluate* an AIA business plan. If you are responsible for AIA projects, you can use the process to develop your AIA business plan. But you might be more likely to evaluate rather than create an AIA business plan—looking at a proposal through the lens of "Should I support and fund this AIA-driven business initiative?" We wrote this section with that question in mind. Consider a situation where your team has finished a brainstorming session, identified their best idea, and come up with an AIA-driven business initiative. Now they want you to support and approve the initiative. What questions should you ask to ensure that this AIA initiative will lead to a successful business outcome? What should you be listening for when its owners describe what they plan to do? Here are eight questions to guide you in evaluating an AIA-driven business initiative for your business.

EIGHT CRITICAL QUESTIONS FOR AIA PLANNING

In this section we present three sets of questions. The first is intended to make sure that AIA is linked to the business. The second is aimed at ensuring that AIA is resourced correctly. The last set deals with the impact of the proposed AIA-driven business initiative. For each question we describe what you want to hear, followed by what to watch out for.

Making Sure AIA Is Linked to the Business

As you think about the Questions below, imagine that your team has just pitched you their idea for an AIA-based business initiative.

Question 1: Can you tell me how data analytics and AI will enable better decisions and business outcomes?

What You Want to Hear

We have shown you that AIA can generate value in three broad ways: it can help you ideate business initiatives, it can enable business initiatives, or it can help you evaluate the success of business initiatives. In Chapter 2, we illustrated ideating through the example of El Camino Hospital, which used a predictive model to come up with new ideas for improving patient length of stay. Enabling refers to the situations where AIA is a key component of executing a business initiative. For example, in marketing, AIA enables hyper-personalized offers. Finally, you may want to use AIA to evaluate different options through experiments and A/B tests.

If your team built their proposed AIA-driven business initiative around a clear business problem, answering your question should be straightforward. Using our wealth management example, if your team had proposed to improve lead generation, they should be able to explain how AIA could be used to identify higher-quality leads and how this is likely to improve revenue.

What to Watch Out For

One of us worked with a large aerospace company. This business had placed a big bet on using AIA as part of its brand. This meant making sure that everything it built (jet engines, for example) was instrumented and generated data that could be used by analytics. As a result, the company narrowly thought of data through the lens of monetization, or how AIA could enable a new business initiative, which consisted of making money by selling AIA-based services powered by its Internet of Things (IoT) sensors to airline customers.

We admired the company's laserlike focus. However, this meant that the art of the possible was lost. When we asked them to think of other uses for AIA, they noticed with surprise that AIA could also be used to improve marketing, make the product development cycle more efficient, evaluate new security protocols, and so on.

There are many uses for analytics. Listen for "ideate, enable, evaluate," and if you don't hear all three of them, *ask* about them.

Question 2: What do you plan to do differently depending on the results of the AIA?

What You Want to Hear

We love this question, but it is rarely asked and often ignored. The sad reality is that some business leaders don't like to answer this question because they use data science as a political tool. When the data science confirms a truth they hold dear or advances a business position they support, they tout the results widely throughout the organization. But when the opposite happens, the data science is dismissed and buried. To move toward a culture of evidence-based decision-making, you must act upon results objectively and, ideally, precommit to taking action—even when it goes against historical norms.

Our colleague's experience at eBay is a great example of this. For years, eBay had invested substantial marketing dollars in paid brand search with the three major search engines: Google, Bing, and Yahoo. When a consumer searched for "eBay," eBay paid the search engines to show its link at the top of the search results—this is called "brand-keyword paid search." These links are typically labeled by the search engine as paid by the advertiser—that small "Ad" notation you see on the link. Below these links, consumer see the results of "organic search." In contrast to paid search, eBay pays nothing when a consumer clicks on an organic search link.

Our colleague, UC Berkeley economist Steve Tadelis, while on leave from the university to build eBay's economics research group, asked a simple question: "What is the ROI on these investments in paid search?" After a bit of investigation, it became clear to Steve that nobody at eBay or the search engines had a good answer. The related analytics were simply not sound. So Steve proposed running a planned quasi-experiment. Some managers worried that if eBay stopped buying paid search for terms like "eBay," competitors would swoop in and steal customers. As described above, these might be precisely the managers who are predisposed to dismiss AIA results if they were to suggest reducing or discontinuing paid search: the results would go against their long-held beliefs.

This raised the question of whether managers would go along with what the data science found. It was put to the test when the data science team found that eBay would be better off discontinuing paid brand search and pursuing other marketing investments. The managers stepped up to support the new direction, and the experiment helped to redirect millions of dollars in ad spend.

While we admire that eBay followed the recommendation of the experiment, ideally we recommend *up-front* buy-in into decisions when planning an AIA-driven business initiative.

What to Watch Out For

Not committing to doing something differently ahead of time creates waste and can be very frustrating for those performing the AIA. Recall the amusement park example we mentioned in Chapter 7, where a manager had collaborated on an experiment to learn the best price for photos consumers can buy as they exit each major attraction. The results proved that a new price was better than the existing price, but the company never implemented a price change. Why? It's hard to know exactly, but our guess is that this was not a top business priority of senior leaders and there was no up-front commitment to act on the results. Better planning would have led to greater buy-in and might have avoided this outcome.

Question 3: What are the most important metrics that will be influenced by this business initiative?

What You Want to Hear

You want to hear two things from your team. First, you want them to be able to articulate that the AIA metrics (e.g., "churn") are clearly linked with the business outcome KPIs (e.g., "customer lifetime value"). This requires that the team has defined a detailed set of AIA and business outcome metrics. Also, there needs to be a scoreboard that explains how AIA metrics translate into business metrics. Business and data science leaders need to agree on this scoreboard before the initiative is launched.

Second, if the intent of the AIA-driven business initiative is to influence multiple business KPIs, these measures must be weighed and prioritized. Are they equally important, or do some KPIs matter more than others? Ideally, you want to have a single business outcome metric, or at most a few. And if the metrics are in conflict, you need to define trade-offs in advance. For example, suppose you are considering an AIA-driven business initiative to create targeted, personalized offers that will improve net promoter score (NPS) and boost profits. But you are also under scrutiny to minimize costs. Tackling this problem requires a model that predicts the probability that each customer is likely to respond to the personalized offer. You need to make sure that the AIA metric "response probability" is clearly connected to the relevant business KPIs: NPS, profit, and cost.

As an example, the AIA business plan would state that there is agreement that profit will be calculated over a 12-month horizon and that costs will include marketing, product, and operations expenses. The plan should include an example of the profit calculation and a list of costs. Finally, the plan should contain an agreed-upon balanced scorecard that spells out how NPS and profits will be traded off. Finally, the plan may address cost concerns by stating that up-front costs will not increase by more than 2 percent and explain how the team will pursue ongoing cost reductions in the future. If your team has discussed and aligned on these issues up front, the AIA process is much more likely to succeed!

What to Watch Out For

We have noticed that in many AIA-driven business initiatives, the creation of a business outcomes model is typically an afterthought. Often, a business leader sponsors a project. Next, a data science team does the heavy lifting of collecting, cleaning, and integrating data. The team then trains, tests, and optimizes models and shares the final results with the management team. At this point, the science is done and managers need to make business decisions. There are often multiple business KPIs, such as profit, revenue share, and costs. But how the AIA metrics are translated into each KPI is up for debate. For example, should you look at one-year or three-year cash flows? What discount rate is appropriate?

The AIA process falls apart when leaders advocate for assumptions that tilt results in favor of their preferred outcome. The problem is that at this point the data science results are known. So it becomes very easy to see how assumptions regarding how to translate AIA metrics into business KPIs create winners and losers. The scientific process has turned into a political process.

A further watch-out is that KPIs are not prioritized and trade-offs are not discussed in advance. It's fine to have multiple KPIs, but you need to both prioritize and weigh them. Are all metrics equally important? Or is one metric more critical than the other? For example, perhaps you are focused on revenue as the key KPI metric, but have two business units: one large, established unit and another that is just starting up. Do you want to prioritize revenue from the larger unit? The smaller unit? Or are both equally valuable? This decision needs to be made up front.

With two or three outcome metrics, the KPIs may not be easy to compare or may even conflict. Suppose, for example, that your top priorities are to grow market share and operating profit. The challenge is that these metrics may simultaneously move in dramatically different directions: market share can be maximized with low prices, but that would likely impact profit negatively. When outcome metrics are inherently difficult to compare, managers need to discuss how they will balance trade-offs in advance rather than after the results appear. If not, we are back to politics.

Making Sure That AIA Is Resourced Appropriately

If your team has been able to answer each of the first three questions to your satisfaction, it suggests they have proposed a viable idea for an AIA-driven business initiative, and one that is connected to your business goals. Now it is time to think through the AIA resources you will need to support the data science.

Question 4: What types of analytics will this project utilize: exploratory, predictive, or causal?

What You Want to Hear

This question speaks directly to one of the main points of this book: managers need a way to speak to one another about data science. What you want to hear back from your team is that there is a clear understanding of the types of analytics to be used for the AIA-driven business initiative. To understand whether projects are resourced correctly, you first need to understand what type of AIA is required.

Recall the example of Once-in-a-Lifetime Adventures (OLA), an adventure trip provider, from Chapter 8. OLA was concerned about the customer cancellation rate when payment for a previously booked trip is due. The customer engagement team may propose a project to gather historical data and describe how customer cancellations are currently handled. They propose benchmarking current practice against a set of industry benchmarks to identify opportunities for improvement. If this project is approved, it falls squarely into the domain of exploratory analytics. In contrast, the finance team may propose an AIA-driven business initiative to improve revenue forecasting by better predicting customer cancellations. This is pre-dictive analytics. Alternatively, the marketing team may be looking at initiatives to reduce cancellations by running a planned quasi-experiment with travel agents, which is causal analytics. As you know, the data and skill sets required to support each type of AIA differ—and this is why you need to understand the type of analytics a project will utilize. Our subsequent questions about data and peo-ple will link back to this question.

What to Watch Out For

There is a good chance that your team will not know the distinction between exploratory, predictive, and causal analytics. If so, ask them to work more closely with the data science team to understand what type of analytics the initiative will require.

Sometimes this collaboration will reveal that your company does not have a shared language for talking about AIA. For example, does everyone agree on the distinction between opportunistic and designed data, and what it implies? If not, it will be difficult to collab-orate on AIA. We don't think that it is important to use our specific terminology, but make sure you have terms that everyone agrees on.

Question 5: What data do you need for the analytics?

What You Want to Hear

Remember that there are two broad types of data: opportunistic data (historical) and designed data (experimental or quasi-experimental). The AIA business plan needs to align the proposed AIA methods with the data requirements. For example, if the project is going to be largely a reporting and backward-looking exercise involving explor-atory analytics, then historical data will suffice. If the project involves a predictive model, then historical data may also be sufficient. But when the project is going to involve causal models, you need to con-sider whether you require only opportunistic data or need designed data. If you are going to rely on natural experiments (see Chapter 9), then opportunistic data may be enough. But if you plan to design an A/B test or conduct a planned quasi-experiment, then you are in the world of designed data.

Of course, you may very well need both opportunistic and designed data. It is fairly common to start a project with opportunistic data and score some quick wins. This is often done with exploratory analytics and some simple predictive modeling. Then, as the project progresses, you may conduct an experiment or quasi-experiment to learn about a specific relationship or prove out an idea. With more sophisticated experimental data, you can then go back and try to improve your predictive model.

For example, a large retailer one of us worked with wanted to customize catalog mailings to households, and began the AIA process with a sophisticated predictive model. The model generated some improvements in existing practice, but the next step was to run a few experiments where customer mailings were randomized among households. The experimental data was then used to enhance the predictive model and personalize catalog mailing decisions, which generated even larger performance improvements for the business. Overall, the project utilized a combination of historical and designed data.

What to Watch Out For

The main watch-out here is that your team may mistake "lots of data" for "the right data." Remember that variation in data is the rocket fuel for all types of AIA. Watch out for smokescreen comments like: "We have exabytes of data . . . so we're all set!" As we discussed in the car ads example in the introduction to this book, having large volumes of historical data could not answer a fundamental question about ad effectiveness. If a project requires historical data, make sure you have the intuition for *whether* and *how* existing data will answer your business question. Your team should be able to explain clearly how existing data will be informative. It's pointless to start a project unless you have a pretty good sense that you have the data needed to deliver a successful outcome.

Similarly, if your team has proposed any experiments or quasi-experiments, dig a little into their proposal for clear evidence that they will succeed. Simply saying that they plan to run an experiment is not enough. Please refer to Chapter 7 for some guidance, and ensure that your team has used the five-step checklist for experiments. Or, if they are proposing a planned quasi-experiment, make sure they articulate exactly how they plan to use matching or DiD.

Here is a story of what can go wrong. We know of a B2B firm that planned an A/B test to learn about best practices in pricing. In the final experimental design, they adjusted prices by less than 2 percent. When the AIA team circulated the final plan among leaders for approval, one manager emailed: "I feel comfortable that the price changes won't jeopardize any of my business. Our livelihoods are at stake here!" While everyone felt comfortable with the experimental design, the A/B test failed because the price changes were simply too small to learn from.

Your role as a leader with high DSIQ is to help your team avoid situations like this. If your organization has a strong fear of failure— like the B2B firm in the example above—your experiments may not yield data that helps you learn how to improve the business. You need to guide others to the insight that small losses today may yield big payoffs in the future.

Question 6: What are your people requirements for the analytics?

What You Want to Hear

Ask your team—in some detail—who is going to do the work. For starters, you want to see a clear plan for who will collect, clean, and process the data. In nearly every company we have advised, IT resources represent a bottleneck that limits the success of AIA-driven business initiatives. Ask your team: How long will it take to assemble the data? Who in IT is capable of doing the work? Who is available to do the work? IT resources are critical. And you need to know as much as possible about the data and IT requirements of the proposed AIA-driven business initiatives so that you can help your team marshal the appropriate resources.

Your team should also draw a clear link between the proposed types of analytics (exploratory, predictive, causal) and people require-ments. If the team proposes using exploratory analytics, then business analysts may be sufficient. If the team proposes sophisticated predic-tive analytics, they probably need computer scientists with expertise in ML and AI. But if the team suggests causal analytics, they may need a statistician or econometrician. Finally, if your team proposes experiments, they will need someone with expertise in experimental design; data scientists trained in psychology, political science, statistics, or economics are most likely to have those skills.

What to Watch Out For

If your team plans to conduct an experiment, make sure they have a good process for the data science team to coordinate with the business team in whose domain the experiment falls. Experiments on a website, for example, require coordination with the business team that runs the digital platform. Experiments in a physical environment, like a retail store, need to be coordinated with operations and logistics teams. Experiments fail when they are simply ideas that have not been vetted through the lens of the business. You need to ask your team: Can we actually implement the ideal experiment? What are the business constraints and considerations you face, and how does the experimental design address these? In general, successful experiments must be tightly planned and coordinated with integrated teams of data scientists and business leaders.

A second watch-out is the belief that all data scientists that could be assigned to the AIA-driven business initiatives are equal. For example, suppose the AIA work is proposed to be done by a centralized AIA group, which includes a mix of experts from different disciplines. Given your high DSIQ, do you want your team to be assigned a random data scientist? You will be much better off having a say in which data scientist you work with, to make sure the person has the specific skills and expertise the initiative requires. For sophisticated AIA-driven business initiatives, for example, you may push your team to be very specific about the set of data scientists they need and to make sure that those individuals are available to do the work. In general, digging a bit deeper on who is going to do the work is critical.

Making Sure That AIA Has Impact

Once you have the data and people to execute the AIA in your AIA-driven business initiatives, data scientists will start to analyze data, build cool models, and deliver findings. In some cases, the work can be done in just a few days. But often, such initiatives will take weeks or months to complete. Once the technical work is complete, it will be time to make a business decision. To make sure your team is ready when that time comes, ask them the next questions.

Question 7: What is your process for going from the analytics to a business action in a timely manner?

What You Want to Hear

You want to hear that business leaders and the AIA organization are tightly coordinated. Ideally, your team's proposal spells out the process of going from AIA results to business decisions.

An example of how to do this right is how search-engine Microsoft Bing tests on its website.[1] There is a planned process where tests occur for exactly seven days and the same outcome metric (sessions per user) is used to evaluate success or failure. If a test succeeds, there is a review to ensure there are no execution errors, and winning tests are repeated for seven more days. If a test wins twice, the results are implemented. This is a tightly coordinated plan that integrates A/B testing and business implementation.

You also want to hear that the time frame of the AIA-driven business initiative aligns with broader business goals. Short projects with clear milestones at each interval rarely raise concerns. Larger projects with more uncertainty, longer horizons, and ill-defined go/no-go points should raise concerns. If the AIA-driven business initiative takes an unexpected turn, what is the contingency plan? Will the project stop or proceed? You should be wary of proposals with long time frames and no clear plan to course-correct during the initiative.

What to Watch Out For

A big watch-out for AIA-driven business initiatives is that your organization may not be set up well for implementation and scaling. What works as a one-off project in an analytics sandbox may not be feasible at scale. For example, we witnessed when a large company used a consultant to do a pilot project to personalize marketing offers to consumers. The pilot worked well and demonstrated clear value to the business. But the problem was that IT was not capable of implementing mass-scale personalization of the e-commerce site where the pilot would have to be scaled. So, while the pilot proved successful, the AIA-driven business initiative failed. Asking the simple question above might have uncovered this limitation before the company pursued the AIA-driven business initiative.

Question 8: How do you balance agile analytics-based decision-making with scaling decisions across the enterprise?

What You Want to Hear

This question addresses a common challenge in nearly every AIA-driven business initiative we have seen in large companies. In the process of proposing an AIA-driven business initiative, leaders are wary of large-scale projects. At the same time, there is often a desire to grow projects from a one-off initiative to an enterprisewide system. So how can you help your team get there?

First, encourage your team to think in multiple stages of execution right from the get-go. For example, we observed a large manufacturer's attempt to apply AIA throughout the manufacturing process enterprisewide. This manufacturer operated multiple huge manufacturing plants. The team responsible for the initiative decided to start small but keep scalability in mind. To this end they identified a small part of the manufacturing process where they believed AIA was an opportunity. Importantly, while the focus was on only a small part of the plant's manufacturing process, it was a process that existed at all other plants as well. The team initially focused on a single plant and built a model that established proof of concept. After successful implementation of AIA-based changes at one location, the company rolled the approach out to other factories.

By keeping the scope of the project small (one specific part of the factory), the initial AIA approach was agile—the first project was completed in a few months. Then the team worked to scale the AIA at other factories. In the process of scaling the model, the team added new "edge cases" and improved the model. Good AIA business plans have a clear explanation of not only the initial project but projects that may follow.

What to Watch Out For

The right scale and scope of an AIA project will depend upon your resources. As a business leader, you need to ensure that your team's proposal meets your business needs but is also aligned with the resources you have in your business and AIA groups. If your company is new to AIA, keep projects in a one-month to three-month time frame—shorter projects are much easier to sell, and more likely to succeed. Finally, have realistic expectations for scaling these initiatives—it takes a lot of work!

Avoid the situation one of our workshop participants shared: A business leader in his company promised the senior leadership team that he would deliver $30 million in incremental value from data science if the senior team approved a budget to hire 30 data scientists. One million dollars in value per data scientist sounds impressive! Moreover, he promised that the value would be realized in a 12-month time frame. The perhaps-not-surprising result: the leader was fired after one year.

We know this chapter has provided a lot for you to digest. But the ideas here are immediately actionable. You probably have an existing approach to ideation and brainstorming new ideas in your business, and we have shown you how this process can be nudged so that you can generate ideas for AIA-driven business initiatives. Once you have a new idea, our eight questions provide you with a thoughtful way to guide the development of an AIA business plan. Or you can use them to evaluate a proposed business plan. A good plan will link AIA with your business problem, resource the AIA correctly, and enable you to think through implementation and scaling. Doing all this hard, up-front work makes your AIA initiatives much more likely to succeed!

CHAPTER 12

UNDERSTANDING BARRIERS TO SUCCESS

Thus far, we have emphasized your role as a leader in executing effectively on AI and analytics (AIA). Having enhanced your DSIQ, you now understand terminology, have a growing intuition for models and methods, and can better envision your ideal role in planning and decision-making. Now you won't be surprised to learn that to use AIA to maximum benefit also means that you must understand and address *barriers* to success. That's the focus of this chapter.

As context, understand that nearly every company today has pockets of AIA located in areas where such capabilities are critical to the business's survival. In airlines, for example, AIA has been a key part of revenue management for many years, and more recently became important for business functions like baggage handling. For insurance businesses, AIA abilities have historically been central to the actuarial division but now are taking center stage for the marketing group. Typically, when and how AIA became important to a part of the business didn't happen by design, but arose organically out of the organization's need.

Regardless of how it came to be, the organizational reality of AIA in many companies makes it difficult for leaders to determine how to make the best use of the related resources and talent they have today *and* grow and scale AIA for the future. Indeed, many potential barriers stand in the way of maximizing and scaling the use of AIA.

The good news is that you can empower yourself by understanding the most common barriers and taking practical steps to address them. To grasp these areas fully, we've talked to hundreds of executives about the biggest challenges they face in scaling and succeeding with AIA. Here, we summarize the four typical, interrelated barriers firms deal with in this area. The next chapter—"Organizing for Success"—shows you how successful firms break down these barriers through investments in organizational structure, people, data and systems, and culture.

Here are four of the most common barriers to maximizing AIA we have observed:

- AIA groups are not set up to solve the most critical business problems.
- AIA and business groups don't know how to collaborate.
- There is no shared view of the truth.
- There is no culture of evidence-based decision-making.

The remainder of this chapter explains each in more detail.

AIA GROUPS ARE NOT SET UP TO SOLVE THE MOST CRITICAL BUSINESS PROBLEMS

As noted above, most organizations have pockets of AIA capabilities that have arisen organically rather than as part of a strategic plan. This results in several related challenges because groups representing AIA resources are typically not set up to address a company's most pressing, enterprisewide business issues. Very often, the issues an individual group or business unit experiences are not representative of broader, firmwide concerns. This section discusses the specific challenges we've observed most frequently in this area.

Investments in AIA Capabilities Are Not Aligned with Enterprisewide Business Objectives

It's a natural process: a business unit with its own P&L decides to invest in AIA to solve a key business problem or a set of these.

While that's an understandable development, the difficulty is that many business problems simply don't align with how business units or P&Ls are organized, causing disconnects and tensions around deploying AIA more broadly. We saw a good example of this in the introductory chapter, in the hotel and casino business. Harrah's P&Ls were established by geographic location (i.e., properties), which created incentives for each property to maximize its own profits. But to support a firmwide initiative that encouraged cross-market play required data from all properties, and there wasn't much incentive to share data or collaborate to this end.

A second version of the problem is that data systems don't align with the bigger-picture business problem that needs to be solved, again because these have evolved organically or historically, rather than strategically. For example, companies that grow largely through acquisitions will often have legacy systems that are not integrated—or poorly integrated—even if they are part of the same business. We illustrated this in the introductory chapter's example of the US cable company that wished to analyze "cord-cutting" trends among customers. They were hampered in the effort because the company used multiple, unintegrated billing systems—partly the result of past acquisitions—making it impossible to track customer behavior effectively across platforms and time.

Notice that these problems arise because traditional business decision-making in existing P&Ls or departments leads to a lack of an enterprisewide investment in and organization of the AIA capabilities required to solve key business problems. It's a very common problem, as the executives we work with confirm every year.

Missing or Poor Integration of Specialized AIA Skills

A second challenge in this area involves AIA skills. Specifically, data science encompasses multiple divergent skills, and many data scientists are so highly siloed that they may not even realize that there are complementary skill sets in the organization, or they may not be able to work easily across existing boundaries between specialized areas.

We often hear things like: "Okay, you've convinced me that data scientists are critical. So, do we have any of them? If so, what do they look like?" To answer this question, we tell leaders to think of four broad types of data scientists:

- *AIA technology* (data systems, distributed computing systems, analytics languages, cloud)
- *Exploratory/descriptive analytics* (reporting, visualization, web analytics)
- *Predictive analytics* (statistical methods, machine learning, AI)
- *Causal analytics* (causal inference methods, experimentation methods, AI)

That's because we believe it is far more helpful to create categories around *what* data scientists do (the tasks they perform, as in the list above) versus how they do it (the method by which they get the task done).

The challenge is that the skill sets required in each category are very different. The people who specialize in AIA technology, for instance, are closest to the IT side of the company, and often have an engineering bent as they build and support systems. Those that focus on exploratory analytics are closest to what we typically refer to as "business analysts," and often create reports or support data displayed in dashboards. Specialists in predictive analytics are usually trained as computer scientists or hard-core statisticians—these are the folks who are experts in machine learning, artificial intelligence, or statistical forecasting models. Finally, those dealing with causal analytics are typically trained as social scientists—economists, statisticians, political scientists, biostatisticians, epidemiologists, and others. They specialize in causal inference methods—or example, experiments, planned quasi-experiments, natural experiments, and causal model building.

But aside from the different backgrounds and skill sets is one very important issue: people from the different groups above often don't like each other! Even worse, they may not understand, respect, or value the work of other data scientists. Universities, as you may know, are highly siloed by academic area, and as a result each academic and professional field develops its own intellectual traditions and emphasizes different things than others do. For example, computer scientists who use machine learning to solve pure prediction problems don't need to think much about causality for their models to work well. Many economists, in contrast, are obsessed with causality—asking "why" questions is their bread and butter. Whether a causal model predicts well may be of secondary concern to these folks, and they may not be skilled at predictive modeling.

This sometimes spills over into how different people value different types of AIA. Early in our careers, we had a well-known economist tell us that data mining was the "work of the devil"! Today, this is obviously an extreme and naive perspective.

Specialization also creates communication problems. If you take a group of computer scientists and ask them to listen to an economist discuss a detailed causal model, many will be totally lost. Similarly, ask economists to sit through a technical discussion of a sophisticated neural network, and their eyes may quickly glaze over.

As a business leader, you need to recognize that data scientists may not work well together or even appreciate the knowledge, perspective, and skills others bring to the table. This is important, because data science is ultimately a *portfolio* problem when it comes to organizational skills: you need lots of specialized people under one roof, and subgroups need to be aware of one another and not so siloed that they can't work together. Very few organizations are able to get this right.

Part of the problem in many companies is that the top data science leader is not broad enough to serve as a helpful, integrating "umbrella" for that function within the organization. To illustrate this point, a while ago we helped interview candidates for a Fortune 500 firm's head of AIA position, which was a high-profile role with large expectations (and compensation!). One of the interviewees was trained as a machine learning expert and, like most of the other candidates, he had already run a data science team of 100 to 200 people for his current employer. When we asked him how important he thought experimentation was for the job, and whether he had experience with experiments, he replied, "It's really important to try things out."

Perhaps our question caught him off guard, but it suggested that he approached business problems largely from a computer science and engineering perspective, where A/B testing is not the norm. His expertise at machine learning was an asset for tackling prediction problems, but this specialization created a narrow aperture that ultimately was a handicap for a top role reporting to the CEO. In that capacity, a leader needs a broad lens—the ability to understand the purpose and potential of multiple data science areas, and how these could help address firmwide business problems. Most experts are specialists and are not trained this way.

The bottom line is that simply looking at someone's background or their PhD research focus isn't sufficient to understand the breadth of their data science perspective. To manage a broad portfolio of highly trained specialists and translate their efforts into business value requires a very unique leader. Search firms often get this wrong: they approach the problem by listing most of the skills from all four categories that we previously described. No single person can specialize in all these skills—it's simply not realistic. The takeaway is that as a leader you should look for data scientists who are specialists in one area but have a high DSIQ and deep appreciation of other areas. This type of professional knows what approaches are best for the problem at hand and are more likely to harness, hire, or allocate the right skills to get things done.

In large, siloed organizations, specialization of data scientists can also lead to an inefficient deployment of scarce talent. Imagine that your marketing group hires a talented data scientist who is particularly good at making sample size calculations, to ensure that marketing experiments are designed properly. While this is clearly helpful for the marketing team, the store operations team may also conduct experiments—but doesn't have funding to hire a specialist with deep understanding of sample size calculations. Worse yet, the marketing team is running only a few experiments each month, requiring only occasional use of their data scientist's skills. In this case, the specialist could potentially create more value for the organization, but the siloed structure makes it difficult to deploy his or her skills across the enterprise.

The flip side of this example, which is also bad, is that business units hire data science generalists rather than deep specialists. This results in business units avoiding problems that require more advanced data science skills—they stick to the basics. Unfortunately, many of the highest-priority, highest-impact problems require deep expertise. When firms choose this path, data science becomes a low value-added activity because business units lack true experts.

Failure to Retain Best People

Finally, many AIA groups struggle to attract and retain the best, most capable data scientists. Part of the problem is that many data scientists are "closet academics," which means they place a great premium on having some degree of intellectual freedom, such as enjoying dedicated time to work on the problems they find most interesting, rather than what business leadership necessarily wants them to work on. Similarly, they may be eager to hear about other projects within or outside the firm—not because they're looking to learn and apply something specific from them but because they're just interested in the issues and challenges these represent.

This is a very different mindset than a typical business manager may have. The challenge, as you might expect, is about how to manage and motivate employees of this type. It takes significant management skill to create an environment in which data scientists will stay engaged and thrive, rather than one that stifles their creative instincts and interests, which can result in low morale and high turnover. Creating this environment has to start at the top, with a data science leader and others who instill the right work policies and cultural elements for this particular workforce. Many firms stumble with this imperative. Try not to be one of them.

When it comes to data science talent, the big message is that you have to work hard to align the data and analytics skills in your organization. There is a multitude of pitfalls that can derail you. As we mentioned in the introductory chapter, many executives we work with say, "We have all this data but don't know what to do with it." The barriers described above suggest that even if you do know what to do with the available data, you may still struggle due to the misalignment of data, skills, and business objectives within the organization. The next chapter helps you take practical steps to address this large challenge.

AIA AND BUSINESS GROUPS DON'T KNOW HOW TO COLLABORATE

The previous section focused on the barrier posed by a lack of alignment of data and analytics skills with business objectives. This section considers the large challenge of getting AIA and business teams to collaborate effectively, which is a Sisyphean task. As described in the subsections below, facets of this challenge include communication, knowledge of capabilities, roles, and follow-through.

Data Scientists Can't Communicate What They Do

A little while ago, the new CMO of a major hospitality company flew to Florida to meet her firm's 50-person analytics team in person. Soon after that experience, we met to chat about AIA within her company. Even after spending a few days on site, the CMO told us, "I really have no idea what these folks are doing!" We all laughed, but this is a typical challenge for nearly every manager we work with; communication among data scientists and business leaders is difficult.

Why is this the case? Most data scientists' training, as you would guess, focuses on technical skills, with little emphasis on business communication. The best ones learn how to convey complex concepts and recommendations to businesspeople over time, which ultimately elevates them in an organization. But we find that the majority of data scientists struggle in this area.

To make matters worse, some AIA people don't care about whether a business leader understands what they are doing. For these folks, it is sufficient that their data science peers understand and trust their work—in some cases it's all that matters to them. When this mentality evolves to become your culture, business leaders are pushed even further away.

Finally, the vast majority of businesses have no formalized training programs to help data scientists more effectively share what they do and communicate the business implications of their work. In our own training workshops, we typically have a mix of data scientists and managers working side by side for multiple days. In terms of technical training, our workshops rarely advance the core skills of a data science specialist. But, by watching us talk about technical material to managers, data scientists often rave about the workshops. Their "aha!" moment is that they finally see how to communicate in a way that takes both the science and the business question seriously.

Business Managers Lack Knowledge of AIA Team Capabilities and Deliverables

Businesspeople, in many cases, don't know what AIA groups can and can't do. Our conversations with business executives and AIA leaders reveal a consistent mismatch between what managers think AIA groups should be able to do and what they can actually do. The business managers err on both sides: over- and underestimating AIA team capabilities. For example, we've heard of cases in which managers were really surprised that seemingly simple analytical problems were, in reality, very challenging—such as determining the ROI of an online digital marketing campaign. They assumed that because Google provides so much data, it should be fairly easy to calculate the ROI: "If we spend X dollars on a search campaign or display ad campaign, we should expect Y dollars back." But it turns out it's not so simple, as the digital car ads example we discussed in Chapter 4 showed. Because Google ads target only consumers who have indicated some interest in a product, comparing those consumers who received the ad and those who did not is subject to a major confound, namely interest in the product in the first place! Most leaders we interact with don't immediately see this.

Worse, managers are sometimes overconfident and brush off the car ads example, saying, "Oh, we would never do this!" In one workshop we shared the car ads example with a group of senior managers in a morning session. At lunch, the managers took us on a tour where we visited scrum teams who were working on the latest and greatest data science problems. The handful of teams we met shared big success stories. Sure enough, one of these success stories was a mirror-image of the car ads example—and none of the managers recognized this!

A related challenge here is that managers simply can't distinguish good from bad AIA, and this has several implications. Executives routinely tell us that when they hear pitches for AIA services from vendors, they can't effectively judge the quality of the work or offerings. Similarly, when models move beyond the basics and become very technical, many managers are unsure they can trust the results. Whether it's evaluating a vendor or interpreting results, managers are often afraid that vendors or teams use technical and scientific jargon to obscure low-value services or poor work. The sobering reality is that the world is filled with both low- and high-quality vendors. Thus your organization will likely generate both high-quality data science outputs and clunkers. Knowing this possibility and lacking the ability to sort it out, managers often "pump the brakes" and underinvest in vendors who may offer high-quality services. They may also unintentionally cast doubt on the work of data science teams, even when they believe they are supporting them. Again, when managers are unable to judge AIA, this leads to uncertainty that can be crippling to an organization.

Managers Don't Understand the Role They Must Play to Make AIA Successful

Many business leaders have a dangerous misconception: that they can work largely independently from AIA while still leveraging AIA to full effect. One version of this is "Hey, AIA team, we executed a business initiative, now can you figure out if it worked?" Another is "We just invested in collecting all this data—when are you going to start using it to deliver business results?"

Regrettably, it rarely works that way. Most of the time, the data needed to solve a business problem with AIA must be *planned carefully* ahead of time, as we discussed earlier in the book, especially in Chapter 7. Moreover, most AIA approaches require incorporation of *business assumptions* to deliver a meaningful result, as discussed in Chapter 10. Many businesspeople fail to recognize this and don't provide AIA with key assumptions. Managers also need to play a role in determining the correct *interpretation* of analytics results, since they are the ones who know the business best. It's very difficult to interpret the implications of AIA findings without a deep understanding of the business context.

All of this highlights the need for better alignment of business and analytics groups and individuals. "Align early and often" is the best motto here. On one hand, we've urged you to stay in your lane: businesspeople should be trusted to understand the business—including making business-related assumptions and interpretations—and AIA people shouldn't be questioned on the data and analytics side of things. But of course, these things all link together: good analytics depend on clear, valid business assumptions, and business-related interpretation of analytics results depends partly on the mechanics of those analytics. It's critical for people to talk to each other throughout the process, ideally as early as possible, to foster alignment—as underscored in Chapter 11. If you don't have that alignment, there will be lots of fallout from disconnects because business managers don't understand the best role to play for the AIA teams, and AIA groups won't understand how to help address key business objectives.

Poor Follow-Through on AIA Work

Finally, it's often the case that business managers make AIA requests with no clear path to action—that is, they haven't thought about how to turn the results of requested analytics into real business initiatives or tactics, or don't feel strongly enough about the business challenge to take action. This understandably causes great frustration for AIA teams, as they work hard to implement requested analytics, deliver results they are proud of and that point to actionable solutions, and then watch as business teams never implement the solution. This is not only inefficient, as it wastes AIA time and other resources—with large opportunity cost—but it is highly demotivating for AIA teams and creates further disconnects and tension between them and business groups, contributing to deeper organizational challenges.

THERE IS NO SHARED VIEW OF THE TRUTH

Another area of disconnects and misalignment has to do with data—what data is used, how it is used, and whether it is trusted.

Managers Don't Use the Same Data Elements

In too many cases, managers across the firm fail to use the same data elements to understand business performance and opportunity. For example, managers from different areas are often looking at data from different systems; that means that when they sit down together to discuss a business problem, they likely have divergent views of it and will reach different conclusions because they're literally using different data, with no integration.

The problem is especially severe when a business problem spans verticals and involves managers from multiple business units. Consider a narrative example of a retailer that recently shifted from an emphasis on product-based profits to customer profit, and data analytics was central to this initiative. When CFO James Chandler took on the task of leading this transformation, he immediately uncovered numerous problems related to how different business units used data. Chandler said, "When we pulled together the teams, what we discovered is that everyone was looking at the same data in a slightly different way. We all had access to the same systems, but there was a lack of standardization and data harmonization. This led groups to have inconsistent views of common metrics like gross margin or dead net cost." The enterprisewide mandate to move to a customer perspective surfaced a systemic problem that cut across business units but was also pervasive within business units. "We could have easily plowed ahead and constructed customer-level cost metrics," Chandler said. "But this would have been a meaningless exercise since everyone was looking at the same data differently. Instead, we paused and agreed on a set of enterprisewide standards; then we tackled the customer-level reports."

Data Isn't Just Data—It Contains Business Rules

We recently worked on a project with a major travel business that believed its data infrastructure was suboptimal. The company had several different enterprise data warehouses, each capturing different sets of data from more than 20 source systems: point of sale, reservations, call-center operations, and others. Over time, the organization's heavier data users had essentially jerry-rigged one of the warehouses to create customized databases that served their needs. In this way the business ended up with people in different analytics "pockets" using overlapping datasets that came from the same sources but were combined differently in multiple data warehouses. Each pocket included slightly different business rules, but the system, such as it was, worked well enough for their purposes and enabled them to drive business improvements and value.

Things changed when the corporation hired a new chief data officer. The incoming executive surveyed the data landscape and said, "This is a mess. We have no way of knowing what the ground truth is." As a solution, the CDO proposed simply getting rid of all the disparate data sources and putting everything online—specifically, a cloud environment into which all the data could be fed from the point of sale, reservations, and other systems. The leader felt strongly that this was the best way forward, rather than continuing to rely on the informal "pockets of analytics" structure that had emerged in the organization. The CDO also insisted that the new centralized data warehouse would be populated directly from the source systems to ensure consistent data quality. The implication meant that the new system didn't use the business rules that had been painstakingly formulated for existing databases.

What happened? First, the proposed system was a large undertaking, to say the least, requiring something like two years to implement. Second, and more problematically, the heavy data users in the firm weren't involved in putting the new system together. Not surprisingly, then, the move elicited significant vitriol, with data users saying things like, "I have a lot of business rules in my system, and it took me six years to get the whole thing where I want it. I'm not going to trust the centralized system over mine."

The result: a wholesale rejection of the centralized data system, with people retrenching into using the old warehouse-based approach they knew best. The point here is that analytics has to be useful for businesspeople, and the CDO failed to recognize this. The executive assumed that "data is data" and failed to appreciate that business rules and other features are essential parts of the system. So strive to take a more holistic view of the data in your organization to understand how to make systems most useful and accessible for the people who need them.

"I Don't Believe Your Data"

This is one of the simplest but most damaging barriers to using AIA effectively in organizations. When business leaders we work with don't like the recommendations generated by analytics, we often hear statements like "I don't believe the data," or "I don't trust the data because there are always errors," or "The numbers don't match mine, so something must be wrong with the data." Managers like to use these "nuclear bombs" when they want to discredit AIA results that do not align with what they believe is true—or what they want to be true. When managers express a lack of faith in the data, they chop AIA off at its knees. Data is at the core of every AIA initiative, and if you don't trust the data, you won't trust AIA.

THERE IS NO CULTURE OF EVIDENCE-BASED DECISION-MAKING

Last but far from least, we consider the absence of a culture built on evidence-based decision-making. In organizations with such cultures, data alone is mistaken for "evidence," little thought is put into data measurement and design, and analytics is used after the fact, rather than to inform key decisions up front. Let's explore each of these.

Data-Driven Versus Evidence-Based

Many companies consider themselves data-driven. For example, one large technology firm we work with explicitly places being data-driven at the core of its identity. In practice, this means that every decision managers make or propose is usually backed up with 20 or more pages of slides with impressive numerical analysis. The problem is that about 18 of those slides, when carefully considered, don't actually provide meaningful evidence that speaks to the decision in question. This highlights the reality that most decision-makers and those who have to review the decisions can't distinguish between analyses that provide real evidence for decision support and those that just look like they do.

No Forethought in Measurement

Earlier in the book we devoted two whole chapters (Chapters 8 and 9) to using opportunistic data, or data that you happen to have on hand or will collect in the normal course of business. But to provide sufficient evidence for important business decisions, such data often isn't enough. Good decision-making requires designing data (see Chapter 7), and that requires forethought at the time of execution to ensure that you secure the data you'll eventually need. Too many businesses fail to think ahead in this way. Indeed, many of the AIA leaders we interact with recognize this challenge in their organizations. They're aware of the need for a strategic measurement plan but say their hands are tied because there's simply no process for involving AIA team input up front, before business initiatives are launched. Having no plan in place usually means you lack the right data for AIA.

Analytics Used After the Fact

Finally, another common complaint we hear is that analytics is not used to generate better decisions. Instead decisions are made first, and then business managers seek to use analytics to justify the decision after the fact. This is the classic "shoot first" approach, which doesn't take into account how effective analytics can be when used up front. In many organizations, decision-makers haven't bought in to one of the primary roles of AIA: to improve decision-making. Embracing that function of AIA can help your business take a much more strategic, proactive approach to getting the most out of analytics.

Taken together, the barriers highlighted in this chapter often prevent the creation and development of an evidence-based decision-making culture. The next chapter discusses how to take practical steps to build such a culture, as part of a general effort to harness analytics most effectively in your organization.

CHAPTER 13

ORGANIZING FOR SUCCESS

In the last chapter we described the common barriers to effectively harnessing AI and analytics (AIA). These were:

- AIA groups are not set up to solve the most critical business problems.
- AIA and business groups don't know how to collaborate.
- There is no shared view of the truth.
- There is no culture of evidence-based decision-making.

Here, we present recommendations for overcoming those barriers, to get the most out of AIA in your organization. It is our obligation as data scientists to let you know that our evidence is largely anecdotal: it is not based on a large-scale, scientific study. Instead, our views have emerged from recurring patterns in our conversations with the thousands of leaders we have trained and consulted with over the past five years, and from our observations of what works and what doesn't.

Overall, we believe that organizing for success with AIA means taking strategic actions and making mutually reinforcing investments in the following areas:

- People
- Data and systems
- Organizational structure
- Culture

In the following sections, we will illustrate how your investments in these areas can address the barriers to scaling AIA discussed in the previous chapter.

PEOPLE

Many of the barriers we presented in the last chapter focus on the poor alignment of AIA teams and their priorities with key business objectives. AIA groups are often not set up to solve the most important business problems, and AIA and business teams struggle to communicate and collaborate. To resolve this challenge, it is critical to take the right approach to people.

Strategy, practices, and culture typically start at the top. So, we strongly advocate hiring the *right data science leader*: someone who understands business problems well and is genuinely passionate about solving them. Moreover, the best data science leaders can hold their own in the C-suite, which also speaks to our recommendation in the "Organizational Structure" section below about ensuring that AIA is well-represented in organizational leadership. Hiring data science leaders and team members who represent sufficient breadth of specialized AIA skills is also paramount, as too many businesses have gaps or deficits in key areas, such as causal analytics or machine learning, which diminishes their overall AIA strength.

Moreover, having the right AIA leader and team in place will help to improve retention. In the previous chapter we described how AIA people are often "closet academics" who want time to pursue their own projects and learn about areas of interest. The right data science leader will understand the unique requirements of data scientists and will be able to manage and motivate them effectively. This person will need to earn the respect of data scientists, which is often based on their appreciation for and skill on the technical side, and the respect of business leaders for delivering business value with AIA.

But before you mount a search for that person—and other AIA team members—be sure you understand the core nature of the business problems you want them to help solve. This way you can align the skills they bring with your firm's top priorities. If your primary focus is on problems that simply anticipate future outcomes, such as revenue forecasting or machine failures or fraudulent purchases, then you will want to focus on data scientists with skills in predictive analytics. In contrast, if you are focused on business problems that require you to test new initiatives and learn what is best—in order to influence outcomes—then you need causal analytics expertise. As we have discussed, these two priorities require different data scientists. Don't let your people strategy drive the business problems you work on; aim for the reverse.

Next on the people front, take steps to ensure your business leaders, managers, and decision-makers all have a working knowledge of data science, or a *high DSIQ*. As you know, that's the purpose of this book: to help readers gain that working knowledge. A strong firmwide DSIQ ensures a true culture of evidence-based decision-making, and enables business and AIA groups to work together most effectively. Recall from the introductory chapter our example of a leadership team that erroneously concluded that exposure to digital ads for cars increased likelihood of vehicle purchase dramatically. They overlooked that people already interested in buying a car were more likely to be exposed to digital ads for vehicles in the first place, rendering the conclusion invalid. A higher collective DSIQ would have helped the team recognize that flaw much earlier, saving precious time and resources.

To underscore this point, we believe there are four important benefits of having a strong DSIQ among people of all levels:

- Managers and decision-makers can distinguish good from bad analytics, which leaves everyone—leaders, peers, AIA teams—more accountable for AIA throughout your company and leads to an evidence-based culture.
- Operating units can leverage AIA for higher-value projects: managers can better estimate where AIA adds value, and avoid pitfalls.
- Operating units plan for both execution and measurement, which leads to better long-term decisions as managers focus continuously on both earning and learning.

- AIA groups work on the problems that have greatest business impact, which leads to lower turnover and attracts the best AIA talent.

As we discussed in the introduction to this book, developing a high DSIQ doesn't require you, a business leader, to become a data scientist. It means learning to use your critical thinking skills to understand what constitutes good analytics (and what doesn't), to recognize where AIA can add value in your organization, and to lead analytical efforts with greater skill and confidence. As you can see, a strong DSIQ will help you overcome the key barriers to harnessing AIA most effectively.

Finally, we advise investing in *business-to-AIA translators*, or people who are steeped in business problems but know enough about analytics to communicate easily with AIA groups. In fact, we think that such translators are among the most valuable employees for scaling AIA in any business. As a chief analytics officer for a global insurer told us, such translators are "very strong at pattern recognition. They connect the dots in new ways, provide insight, and are incredibly talented and experienced moderators."

Again, these professionals don't have to be data science experts, but they have to be fluent with AIA. Think of them as akin to project managers, or AIA-focused "account managers," similar to account managers in advertising agencies, who can talk effectively to their creative colleagues and business clients alike. Similarly, the translators we're talking about can communicate with both business and AIA teams with ease. We've found that these employees are most effective when sitting in the data science organization itself. Some companies even have what they call an *analytics enablement team* that includes translators; the group's entire job is to create a bridge between the business and analytics sides of the firm to deploy AIA most effectively.

DATA AND SYSTEMS

We advocate approaching data and systems on several interrelated fronts, as described in the subsections below.

Make "Truth in Data" Part of Your Data Governance

Recall from the previous chapter that a major barrier for AIA success is the lack of a shared view of "truth in data" across the organization. That is, managers in different areas may not be using the same data for decision-making; people are likely overlooking the reality that the context of data matters (including as related to embedded business rules); and there may be a tendency for business managers to simply say, "I don't believe your data" if the implications of AIA initiatives conflict with their agenda or view of the truth. All of this suggests a need to define "truth in data" by establishing a process that is both transparent and endorsed vocally by those at the organization's top: "We're all going to agree this is the truth, and we're going to work with this truth." A shared belief that the available and to-be-captured data, typically imperfect data, represents the truth is critical for AIA.

It is important not to confuse data quality with the concept of truth in data. For AIA to succeed in your firm, you need to agree on a standard for truth in data, right now. Does everyone agree that your data is good enough for making decisions with AIA? Truth in data establishes a standard of "good enough." In contrast, an important part of data governance is data quality, and over time you should always strive to improve the quality of your data, while recognizing that true perfection is unattainable.

Moreover, we advise you to make "truth in data" part of your overall approach to data governance. First, you need to establish a common benchmark of what is good enough. Then you should regularly seek to improve this benchmark as data quality improves, making your approach to "truth in data" a managed, thoughtful process.

Align Your View of Data Quality with AIA

Data quality is critical for AIA. In the past, your firm probably viewed data quality through the lens of supporting business functions. To support your AIA initiatives, you may need to review how you manage data quality—you'll likely find potentially large gaps to close. Maintaining and improving data quality is a central pillar of most data governance programs. As this is a broad topic, we want to highlight four data-quality issues you should consider, because they can have a meaningful effect on AIA-enabled initiatives. The sections below provide details on each.

Data Granularity

If data is represented by grains of sand coming into the company, you need to know exactly what those grains are and how they enter the company. At some point in the history of your company, somebody knew this and designed your IT systems with that critical piece of knowledge. The challenge is that most IT systems were *not* designed for AIA—they exist to manage accounts payable and receivable, create a P&L, and gather data to support operations. Thus, the data captured typically reflects different objectives than those of the analytics you have in mind.

   Consider an anonymized example from a financial services firm. Kim, an executive there, wanted to understand how a recently launched initiative impacted clients' financial portfolios. Specifically, she knew each client received a monthly statement summarizing their assets and financial return metrics. As such, Kim wanted to gather historical return metrics for a sample of customers so that she could measure the impact of her business initiative. Simple enough, right? It turned out this wasn't as straightforward as Kim had hoped.

   She called the head of analytics about her data requirements, who then contacted the head of IT to see how historical portfolio returns for clients could be extracted into a report. The IT head said they create monthly reports and these are saved as PDF files that are delivered electronically to clients. But the metrics in the reports were calculated in real time and not saved in a database. That meant the only way Kim could get the data she needed would have been to load the PDF files, scan each for the relevant metrics, and collect the data. While all of this was feasible, a business unit would have to pay for it, and the process would need to be prioritized in the IT queue.

Sound familiar? The reality is that much of the data you seek may not be stored because no one paid for it and no one thought it was valuable for business decisions. So understanding where data comes from and how it is captured is critical. In the end, nobody works with the grains of sand themselves; they work with items derived from the grains of sand.

Data Aggregation

Since most people in your organization don't work with raw data, you have to understand how this data is aggregated, organized, and turned into something useful. In the marketing world, for example, data is usually aggregated based on four main factors:

- *Time:* Hour, day, week, quarter, year
- *Product:* Multiple products within a brand may be analyzed as a single product
- *Geography:* Neighborhoods, cities, regions, countries
- *Household:* Purchases by multiple family members

Understanding how data has been aggregated enables you to make the right decisions with the data. But a further challenge is that some things aggregate nicely, while others don't. Dollars, ounces of liquid laundry detergent, and pounds of chicken aggregate well. That's because they're "count" metrics that can be converted to a common unit. But there may be other things you care about that don't aggregate so well. Prices, for example, don't naturally aggregate because the sum of prices paid for many transactions is simply revenue. So when we want a price for a brand, time period, geographic region, or business unit, we typically think of some type of average. This sounds simple enough, but is tricky in reality.

As an example, suppose a firm sells a single brand in multiple sizes, as might be the case for dish detergent or breakfast cereal. To make our illustration easier, let's consider a product available in large- and small-sized versions. Further, imagine a manager wants to use a dashboard to track brand-level metrics, one of which is "brand price." The analytics team that produces the data for the dashboard calculates the average weekly brand price, as shown in Figure 13.1.

Figure 13.1 Average Brand Price Increases over 20 Weeks

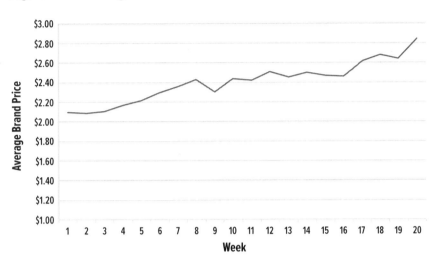

To users, this appears as "brand price," but the exact calculation is a weekly weighted average price, which is essentially the average price paid. Each week we compute the price times volume for each size, add these up, and then divide by total units sold.

Our graph shows that the average brand price trends upward. Users of the dashboard who don't dig into the formula would easily believe that managers have been gradually raising prices for the brand over the 20-week period. In reality, the price of both large and small products didn't change at all. What happened?

Say that the large size was priced at $2.99 and the small size was priced at $1.99, and that these remained unchanged during the 20 weeks. The average price increase observed, then, was driven entirely by changes in *unit volume* of the two products. The business had launched the larger size recently, and its sales had been growing, in part because the smaller-size product had become less popular. But the figure reflects none of this. In this case, aggregation of prices introduced variation that isn't really there.

Sticking with this example, a different kind of problem arises when a data scientist who doesn't know how the data above was aggregated creates a demand curve from the data and calculates a price elasticity that is used to assess and optimize prices. Because you now recognize how average price is computed for the brand, you realize that this would be a crazy idea—because there is no price variation! Hence, it is actually impossible to relate price changes to volume changes in this data. Yet, we have seen multiple attempts at this exact analysis in real life.

Going back to the general case, here is your big challenge: nearly all data is aggregated. Many people in your organization will make decisions about how and why to aggregate data. What guided their choices were most likely reporting on the past, financial disclosures, or other business objectives. Now, business leaders and data scientists are using the same data to address new business questions. Worse, nobody has kept a detailed record of how data was aggregated, or this knowledge is buried deep inside computer code. All of this means that before you start using data for analytics, it is critical to understand how the data in question was aggregated so that you can assess whether you can use it effectively to answer your new business question.

Consider an anonymized example of a financial services firm that wanted to understand the impact of a new initiative on revenue generated by brokers who sold stocks, bonds, and mutual funds. Every broker was affiliated with a local office; the offices differed by number of brokers and volume of overall business. Each quarter, the firm calculated the average revenue per broker and tracked this metric for reporting purposes. A natural assumption was that this would represent the sum of all broker revenue divided by the number of brokers. Unfortunately, that wasn't the case. To calculate this metric, each local office reported their revenue per broker, then the local office metrics were averaged among all the locations. It took some time for the project team to discover this fact; once they did, they had to collect new data to support the analytics project. Again, data that is useful for some original business purpose may not be appropriate for subsequent analytics—how data is aggregated is often the culprit.

Data Merging

How many separate data systems does your company have? Many businesses are dealing with multiple legacy systems for data—5, 10,

15, or even more systems—that don't talk to one another easily. This is frequently the result of past mergers and acquisitions; integrating data systems can be complex and costly, so it's often just not done. The result: data silos organization-wide.

As an example, we worked with a beverage company to follow a beer bottle's "journey" from the manufacturer to the retail shelf to a consumer's home. By now you probably won't be surprised to hear that wasn't as simple as it sounds. That's because it involved data from multiple disparate sources: the company sells beer through a two-step distribution process including wholesalers and retailers. The business captures manufacturing and wholesale data with internal systems, but the retail data is collected by syndicated data providers like IRI and Nielsen. So connecting the dots to understand beer-bottle journey factors such as price pass-through (manufacturing cost, wholesale price, retail price, consumer price) required securing large datasets from multiple sources and merging these accurately. A further complication is that data providers IRI and Nielsen track products using UPC codes (universal product codes), retailers often use SKU codes (stock keeping units), and the manufacturing plant in question used proprietary product codes! In the end, it took about six months just to integrate all the data for a single product category, due to the manually intensive process required. That's a lot of time—and money.

So it's important to think about the configuration of data systems in your organization. Are they separate, integrated, or some combination? And you must also consider how to merge data as needed for key analytics initiatives, recognizing this will likely be a large, costly undertaking. Just because you have a large set of data doesn't mean that it is synthesized and normalized!

Missing Data

We all know that every dataset will inevitably have missing data. But the more complicated part is understanding whether the data in question is real or imputed. Truth be told, it's actually much easier for data scientists to work with missing data than to work with some inferred number that's been entered into a missing data field. Thus it's a huge problem not to know what data is actual and what has been imputed—it all looks the same in the dataset. Let's look at an example where this has significant consequences.

One of the most important things to food companies that sell their products in grocery stores is what's called "in-store displays." These are the special displays of products, such as those at the end of an aisle, that can drive much larger purchase volume than typical shelf placement does. Consumers seem naturally programmed to give special consideration to products placed at the front of a store or the end of an aisle, which is why manufacturers pay grocery chains boatloads to display their products in these locations. But how do manufacturers know their products were actually placed correctly? Was compliance by the retailer 100 percent of the time or just 80 percent?

Answering this question is quite difficult and labor-intensive. Each week, representatives will walk through stores and manually scan in this information using a handheld device. They will record which products are displayed at the store's front, end of an aisle, and other locations. This is a time-consuming, expensive process, so manufacturers audit only about 5 percent of all stores.

From these audits, we have a dataset that indicates where all the products in question were placed in the stores visited—that focal 5 percent of all stores. What can we do about the other 95 percent, the stores that weren't visited? Extrapolate. Say we look at our 5 percent sample and find that sales went up by a factor of three in stores that had an in-store display, but stayed roughly flat at stores without a display. One can use this information to impute values for display for the 95 percent of stores that weren't sampled. In a store that was not visited, if sales went up by a factor of three, it is natural to assume there was an in-store display; if sales were flat, one could assume no display.

This approach works perfectly well if the only business question is something like "Did 100 percent of stores properly display my product this week?" Looking at this type of data, we might find that only 86 percent of stores are predicted to have an in-store display. Again, our data is well designed to answer this question—even though we visited only 5 percent of stores.

But suppose we want to answer a different question: "What's the return on investment for the in-store marketing?" In-store displays are expensive, so manufacturers should be interested in the financial return for their costly investment. A business's analytics team could build a model to relate weekly volumes sold to weekly in-store marketing for the products in question, using the complete dataset created earlier, including imputed values. Say they come back with an ROI of 352 percent. Sounds great, right? So what's the problem?

The missing data for the 95 percent of stores that weren't visited was filled in with an assumption that a significant bump in sales indicates the presence of in-store display. If you then assess whether there's a correlation between such in-store display and sales, surprise, surprise, you're going to find a large one!

To see what's going on through the lens of our Causality Checklist, think of our two groups as "no display" versus "display" and our outcome as average units sold, which we later translate into ROI. Among the 5 percent of stores that were audited, we know whether an item was displayed or not—so this determines which group they are in. But what determines which group the other 95 percent of observations appeared in? Not actual data. Instead, they were determined by our algorithm, which filled in missing data. And the algorithm uses units sold to assign the observations to "no-display" versus "display." Since units sold is our outcome of interest, we have a problem of reverse causality.

The implication is very important: the way in which the missing data is filled in can artificially inflate the measured ROI, dramatically. Think of it this way. Suppose in-store displays at a few locations are not very effective and the change in sales doesn't meet our threshold. When this happens, the algorithm classifies this observation as "no display" because volume is low. Moreover, only observations with a sufficient change in volume are classified as "display," which places all the high-volume observations into the "display" group. Because of how the missing data is filled in, high ROI becomes a self-fulfilling prophecy.

Unfortunately, this kind of issue comes up all the time. Missing data is filled in using some algorithm, which is often aligned with a valid business issue—like tracking and reporting. But a process that works for one business problem can result in seriously flawed analytics results down the line. You have to understand exactly how missing data is treated to ensure you're making the right evidence-based decisions.

Overall, our discussion of the four elements of data governance suggests that poor governance effectively dooms analytics in your organization. Consider a worst-case scenario where business units extract data from a centralized system and process the data on their local systems; then analysts within those units fill in missing data based on what they believe is correct in their business. That means the reports generated by a given unit can't be replicated by others, and different units will reach different conclusions while all claiming to use the same data, a sadly common situation!

Develop Data Governance Practices to Support AIA

In addition to reviewing data quality, you may need to review practices that are part of your overall data governance strategy, and create or adjust these as needed to best support AIA. Below are four important practices to consider:

- *Establish a data "library system":* Think of available data as being like a library book, and build a system around that concept. For example, a given dataset can be "checked out" for a given period of time, after which it must be renewed. But eventually the borrower must return the data to the source. That means all parties will know how the data was extracted, so there's no mystery around that, and the process can be re-created easily for others, yielding the same data to be checked out organization-wide and preventing inconsistency. The system will also make clear who has a specific set of data at any given time. The requirement that people return data also prevents data from being siloed in their unit or group. Well-known companies like Teradata have developed and advocated for such processes.
- *Establish a reproducible process for analytics:* Spreadsheets, while we still love them, are analytics applications of the past when it comes to AIA. That's a stark reality many businesses must

face. In today's business world, to generate reproducible results, you should move to code-based processing, as carried out by R, SQL, and Python. That's why data scientists giving presentations these days commonly share a URL where audience members can go to find the exact code and data they used in their analysis. By running the code, you can re-create exactly what's in the presentation—including slides, tables, and figures—at the push of a button. It looks like magic, but it's just data science with a little help from technology. Have you ever wanted to re-create a chart from a presentation? Often it's impossible. In our Kellogg MBA courses, for example, we use "R Markdown," which enables us to create these reproducible documents. Every leader needs to understand how results and findings from AIA can be quickly and consistently reproduced. At most companies, this requires new processes.

▪ *Develop data aggregation principles to support analytics:* Data aggregation is inevitable. So don't just let the IT group fly solo in making decisions about it. Instead, collaborate with IT on how aggregation should be carried out to support AIA initiatives, with ongoing input from the business side. In this way you can develop an evolving set of aggregation principles in line with analytical goals and initiatives.

▪ *Mandate consistent hierarchies and definitions:* Consistency is critical. Many data problems happen due to a lack of process and control over data system hierarchies and definitions, yielding inconsistency. Ensure everyone is on board with system features that will support AIA; then keep these consistent. Otherwise you'll almost definitely face problems down the line.

More generally, as you move to an evidence-based, data-driven culture you should carefully review your approach to data governance, because more than likely it was not designed to support AIA initiatives. How best to unearth the biggest issues? Our advice: get to know the IT folks in charge of your data and systems, and get to know your data scientists. Talk to them over coffee. Take them to lunch. In many companies, the people in charge of technology don't get the most glamorous office locations and are often physically separated from business units. This significant barrier to good communication can be easily overcome with a cup of coffee or a casual lunch. If you want to learn about how to improve data governance, you probably need to increase your communication with these folks. Show genuine interest, pick their brains for how data systems currently operate, and try to learn how they could operate better through the lens of supporting AIA.

ORGANIZATIONAL STRUCTURE

How you organize plays a critical role in the effectiveness of AIA in your business. The advice we offer here centers on ensuring that AIA is well-represented, structured strategically, and supported by strong connection and communication between the business and AIA sides of the organization.

Executives often ask us whether AIA must be represented in the top leadership group or can be led from some levels down. We believe the answer depends on the role of AIA in your company. One scenario is that AIA is *not* strategic for the future of the business. If so, the C-suite's three- to five-year plan probably needs no direct input from an AIA leader. The role of AIA in this case will be to help execute the plan while looking continuously for ways to increase revenues ("Which customers are most likely to buy?" or "Which combination of features maximizes customer willingness to pay?") or reduce cost ("What functions could be automated?" or "What manufacturing parameters minimize material waste?").

An alternate possibility is that AIA is central to the business strategy and plays an integral role in the C-suite's three- to five-year plan. An increasing number of companies see AIA in this way. For example, Honeywell Aerospace has made the "connected aircraft" the core of its corporate strategy: "For aircraft operators, connectivity presents a new set of operational, efficiency and comfort benefits that were previously unavailable."[1] All this is powered through AIA.

Another example is Accenture, the giant consulting and services company. Accenture has transformed itself around AIA by undertaking the "goal of transforming into an insights-driven enterprise that embeds analytics into the core of its operating model."[2] In these cases, where AIA plays an explicit, integral role in the C-suite's intermediate-term plan, it is our view that AIA must be represented in the top leadership group, such as through a chief analytics officer or another senior executive with this general focus.

The person in this role can identify and weigh in on the role AIA can play in the broad business strategy. Also, because enterprisewide commitments to AIA often create incentives-related and organizational challenges, having an AIA representative at the top leadership level can help resolve these issues. Finally, having AIA at the topmost level also ensures that complementary investments in IT, training, and data governance are aligned with the C-suite's vision for AIA in the three- to five-year horizon.

What happens when AIA becomes central to the company but doesn't have a seat at the senior leadership table? This was the example we provided in the introduction: a major North American cable company whose new CEO could not obtain insights on strategic customer retention issues because IT investment had been made without coordination with AIA.

As far as broader organization, in a steady state, we believe that in most companies AIA is best organized in a *hybrid* way. Specifically, we advise establishing a centralized, analytics-focused Center of Excellence (CoE) that enables you to:

- House specialists who may not be needed "everywhere all the time"
- Create a diverse community of data scientists with a wide range of complementary specialized skills
- Ensure that AIA is well-represented in leadership
- Develop expertise and resources to help AIA people communicate with others in the organization

Such a center addresses many of the barriers discussed in the previous chapter, including through coverage of the full range of necessary AIA skills, retention of the best AIA team members, alignment of

AIA investments with top business objectives, and improved align-ment and communication between business and AIA teams.

As part of the hybrid approach, we also recommend embedding AIA groups in business units but having them dual-report to the CoE. This again helps forge a strong, ongoing, two-way link between business and AIA groups to foster better collaboration. As discussed in the previous chapter, it's about ensuring business and AIA teams "align early and often," because good analytics depend on clear, valid business assumptions, and business-related interpretation of analyt-ics results requires understanding the mechanics of those analytics. A lack of alignment between these areas leads to disconnects and tension, with poor awareness of how each can help the other and, worse, potential suspicion about motives and agendas. So the goal is to ensure that AIA groups are surrounded by relevant business prob-lems, to help them understand the business context of the work they do and thus contribute analytics that address key business challenges and priorities.

While this is our general advice for organizing AIA optimally, the hybrid strategy may not be the right prescription for every orga-nization. For example, if you're building an AIA organization from scratch, it may make sense to focus mainly on the CoE, without nec-essarily embedding AIA groups in business units. Similarly, if large business units already contain very strong AIA teams, then there may be less need for the CoE. The idea is to find the organization that works best for you where you are now, and to evolve this with your business.

CULTURE

Having an organizational culture that supports and promotes AIA is critical, as we've suggested in this chapter and others. Culture is simply the spoken and unspoken norms, values, and practices that influence thinking and behavior within your business. In Chapter 12, we noted that a missing culture of evidence-based decision-making is a major roadblock to harnessing AIA. Here, we present several prac-tical steps to take to establish and make the most of such a culture.

Make Measurement Plans Routine

First, it's critical to make measurement plans routine. This addresses the challenges of missing forethought in measurement and using AIA to justify rather than to make decisions, as presented in the previous chapter. The goal is to complement a culture of execution with a culture of measurement. Many companies have evolved to excel in execution, with well-thought-out tactics and operations. But measurement of success often remains an afterthought: the business plan contains a goal but no measurement plan for how to determine whether the goal was achieved. As should be clear to you from reading this book, a goal is not a measurement plan. Thus, we suggest requiring that every proposed initiative be accompanied with a measurement plan that spells out how the initiative can be evaluated after implementation. This should not only result in better planning for necessary data and analytics, but will also force people to think about the value of their initiative more thoroughly up front, as it will eventually have to pass a more rigorous analytics test due to the new measurement policy.

Institute New Ways of Working

Second, institute new ways of working. Creating business value with AIA requires a highly collaborative back-and-forth among a diverse set of people. Some companies we work with have implemented this process though Agile methodology using scrum teams. Some businesses complement this approach with weekly meetings of an "AIA Council" consisting of business and AIA group stakeholders across different business units. One distinguishing feature of these ways of working is that the groups are peer-centric, not hierarchical.

Regardless of the exact implementation, the purpose of these new ways of working is threefold. First, to hold everyone to a high standard when it comes to linking AIA with business objectives. Regrettably, we have seen our share of proposed analytics projects where the "so what" was not clear. Second, a collaborative back-and-forth keeps everyone intellectually honest about whether the planned AIA-based initiative is of high quality (e.g., "Does it pass the Causality Checklist?" and "Can we use data on hand, or does it have to be designed?"). Peer feedback encourages evidence-based decision-making and discourages people from using AIA after the fact rather than up front for decision-making. We think peer feedback is preferable to that generated by a typical hierarchical system, which carries more politics, instances of "pulling rank," and fear of failure. That's the reason feedback from peers is the norm in academia, where the standards of evidence-based decision-making are strongest. Third, these new ways of working can lessen duplication of effort around data and AIA, and therefore increase the speed of execution and/or lower the cost. We have heard numerous stories where instituting an AIA Council led to the realization that several teams were doing the same data preparation work, ultimately resulting in consolidation of the efforts. Similarly, one business unit might already have deployed an AIA model that could easily be repurposed for a different problem. Finally, improved communication across the enterprise can consolidate usage of multiple vendors.

Celebrate Failure

Finally, it's important to celebrate failure as an integral part of AIA efforts, again to support a true culture of evidence-based decision-making. After all, "experiments" wouldn't be called that, or needed, if they yielded success every time! The idea is to ensure that the message from the top and throughout the organization is one that encourages experimentation, learning, and flexibility. There's a reason Google, W.L. Gore, Tata, and other well-known global companies all celebrate or even reward failure[3]—it takes the stigma out of taking calculated risks and promotes a more open culture of sharing and learning from (thoughtful) mistakes. So think about how to celebrate AIA failures as part of your organization's culture.

* * *

In summary, in Chapter 11, we discussed how your DSIQ enables you to plan effectively for AIA. In Chapter 12, we highlighted common barriers that impede the scaling of AIA across the organization. In this chapter we have presented recommendations for overcoming those barriers so that you can get the most from AIA in your organization.

Your high DSIQ, together with an understanding of what actions you need to take in the domains of people, data and systems, organizational structure, and culture will enable you to leverage AIA most effectively to drive business value.

Success Stories with AIA

n this final section we present real-life stories of several companies that have harnessed AIA effectively to create value.

Allstate Builds Firmwide DSIQ

Insurance icon Allstate always had AIA capabilities, especially as part of the firm's claims and pricing strategy and operations. But in the new millennium's second decade, the business recognized how central and important analytics was to functions and objectives firmwide—and how AIA aligned with Allstate's strategic position as a leading technology-driven company.

In line with this, leaders sought to redefine the firm through the strategic growth and application of technology, data, and analytics. Starting in 2017, Allstate carried out this effort through a major investment in a three-pronged, enterprisewide AIA initiative focused on people, structure, and culture. Here, Maureen Kalas, Allstate's director of data, discovery, and decision sciences, describes the business's transformational AIA journey.

AN AMBITIOUS SHIFT

"Allstate has a long history of—what I will put in air-quotes— 'analytics,' but mostly in the pricing function," Kalas says. "So our product pricing using actuarial science has been very much part of our DNA. In the early 2010s we recognized that there was greater opportunity to use analytics at a more sophisticated level, and to invest in different, more advanced analytics techniques and capabilities."

At ground level, dealing with data was part and parcel of Allstate's business. "We've always been a data company because that's how insurance works," Kalas says. "You're measuring data and analyzing it to achieve your goals." But now leadership wanted to bring an AIA-focused mindset to every level, function, unit, and team in the organization.

In 2017, Allstate launched a strategic, enterprisewide plan for analytics. This would require additional investments in Allstate's centralized analytics group (known as D3), leveraging the numerous, deep levels of analytics expertise within existing business units, and boosting the overall DSIQ of more than 4,000 managers across the enterprise.

BOOSTING DSIQ

People had always been the heart of Allstate's success. But the AIA initiative meant shifting people's perspective as related to analytics, while boosting collective and individual DSIQ. This started at the top. "We wanted to strengthen analytics talent across the enterprise," Kalas says, "and not just our doers of analytics but our decision-makers. This became the impetus for a more focused effort to really build awareness and what we began to call 'analytics fluency' across the leadership group."

Beyond the top decision-makers, the business sought to shift many employees' focus and sense of professional identity more toward AIA. Kalas says, "We had to awaken all the data scientists who live in other areas and don't necessarily come to work as data analysts; but they're wrapping that into their daily work now." The firm also invested in "translators," or "people who can cross that line of understanding business but also analytics," as Kalas says.

To quickly boost organizational DSIQ, leaders worked with the Kellogg School of Management to build an online analytics training course, then followed this up with in-person workshops to help people connect AIA better to their business-unit-based work. "We originally expected to focus the training on senior-most leaders," Kalas says. "But our CEO ultimately felt strongly that we should also be reaching out to midlevel leaders, to have broader impact and reach the people who would be influencing decisions at many levels of the organization."

The online course, which took participants through a comprehensive AIA Framework (the same one presented in this book), became the largest-scale corporate culture training effort Allstate had ever undertaken. "We invest quite a bit in creating opportunities for people, and have had tons of individual learning opportunities," Kalas says. "But to hit 4,000 people within 15 months was unprecedented, and signaled the degree to which our CEO and our operating committee valued this as part of our effort to truly become a technology company."

The follow-up "train the trainer" workshops focused on helping people throughout the organization—most weren't data scientists—apply analytics to their business using the AIA Framework. Kalas says, "The idea is to have them come up with their business problem, identify their business initiative, and then go through the exercise of figuring out how to address the problem using data and analytics." The hardest part for participants was conceptualizing the business problem as a question that could be addressed with AIA, but they became more capable with this over time.

The workshops were led by co-trainers including both technical and nontechnical managers from across the company. "The business leaders involved had expressed some interest or passion or aptitude for analytics," Kalas says, "and then we had the technical person there co-facilitating." People from different functions and business units participated in a given workshop to promote cross-area collaboration and synergies: "We had a claims person and an attorney and an operations leader and a technology leader sitting side by side, so that different questions and use-case ideas would come from different business areas and hopefully spark some ideas for them as well." Each workshop group also included people from all levels of seniority. "Our more senior folks were very careful to set aside their mantle of authority and just be somebody else at the table generating ideas on sticky notes, working alongside people from the front line," Kalas says.

As hoped, the training and workshops helped to foster analytics champions organization-wide, from both technical and nontechnical backgrounds. "It made people resources for their business unit," Kalas says. "If you're from the sales organization and you see a sales leader up there giving [AIA-driven] presentations, you're more likely to go to that person if you have questions."

A CULTURE OF AIA

Allstate's AIA-focused investment paid off in a culture embracing analytics more fully and an organization much more capable of delivering value with AIA, as Kalas notes: "In the past, the research team would identify some actionable items and the business would say, 'That's cool, we should do that.' Now it's often the other way around, where the business will identify opportunities in a collaborative manner. It needs to be driven by the business to have traction."

For example, the HR team was able to apply AIA more deliberately to their largest challenges. "They could identify the burning issues that need to be addressed," Kalas says. "And think of those as specific questions to resolve, like the Top 10, and then begin to narrow them and restate them in ways that could be answered using data or analytics."

The cultural shift was also evident in pervasive use of AIA ideas and terms firmwide. "The language is becoming more consistent across the organization," Kalas says. "'Quasi-experiment' has suddenly become part of our language! 'Confound' is another word we use regularly." Having a new language and vocabulary of AIA translated directly into taking steps to implement analytics techniques, such as experimenting with large and small initiatives, and testing more routinely for confounding factors. Kalas acknowledged the organizational shift sometimes resulted in slower speed: "Just asking the question [such as about confounds] conflicts with our culture of action. This remains a challenge for us."

AN ONGOING JOURNEY

Overall, Allstate continues to reap many tangible and intangible rewards of its efforts to integrate AIA more deeply into organizational thinking, skill, and culture. As a sign of how far the business has come, the D3 group has been working to quantify the value of analytics itself, to improve ROI. Of course, leaders, including Kalas, recognize that harnessing the power of AIA is a continuous process: "We are a company with 80 years' worth of legacy systems and technology built up around a product-based approach, rather than a consumer-based view of the world, which makes it difficult to quickly execute large A/B tests [and other AIA initiatives]. We've taken some great steps in working to address that, but we still have a long way to go."

Vanguard Builds an Ecosystem of Analytics Excellence

For investment management giant Vanguard, success came at a price.

The low-cost mutual funds the firm offers were once considered underdogs in the retail investing game. But over several decades, they became wildly popular with consumers, catapulting Vanguard to the world's largest provider of mutual funds.[1] Not surprisingly, by the new millennium's second decade, many other firms offered similar investment options, and Vanguard had to reconsider its approach to customer acquisition and service.

In 2015, Jing Wang, now Vanguard's head of the Center of Analytics and Insights, faced this challenge head-on when senior management asked her to enhance and integrate the firm's consumer analytics capabilities. Working strategically, she was ultimately able to structure a high-performing center of analytics that proved its value to the firm many times over as part of a growing, broader culture and community of AIA at the business. But none of it came easy, as the story of how Wang made it happen suggests.

FROM OPERATIONS TO ANALYTICS

"The client-experience factor plays such a huge role in a digital environment," Wang says.[2] "Clients have been trained by the Amazons and Apples of the world, and have much higher expectations about their interactions with Vanguard. This led us to believe that we need to become better at using analytics to provide a much more individualized experience for our clients." The firm served millions of investor customers directly, and had data reflecting many dimensions of customer behavior. But leadership now wanted to use such information to create unprecedented insights on how to engage customers and deliver greater financial and emotional value to them. "Our data system was built for operation, not analytics," Wang says.

While building an "ecosystem of analytics," as Wang labeled it, would not be easy, Vanguard's senior leaders provided her high-level, visible support: "I had a very strong sponsor: Chris McIsaac, the head of planning and development, who reports directly to the CEO. Him being personally interested in investing in the business area has been helpful, because it has a lot of signaling value."

FINDING THE RIGHT TALENT

Among Wang's early efforts was finding the right people to enhance the firm's AIA capability. "When we started, we had a small, uniform analytics team," she says. "Most of them were skilled practitioners in the marketing-analytics area." She recognized the need to broaden the team's training and expertise, and hired senior- and junior-level data scientists, data engineers, engagement leads—or those who can translate analytics into practical business applications—and machine learning engineers. Even within those groups, creating diversity was key. Among data scientists, for example, Wang looked to hire experts in statistics, natural language processing, and deep learning.

More broadly, she sought out hires with PhDs across areas ranging from physics to math to social science. "People start to have different flavors of expertise," Wang says. "Different perspectives help to open people's eyes to different ideas and create innovative solutions much faster than before." Having a dedicated HR person for her area and maintaining relationships with local universities and training programs like the Insight Data Science Fellows program helped her find the right talent. In fact, Wang herself is not a data scientist by training—she holds a PhD in physics—but she was able to hire a skilled data science manager to work alongside her.

THE CHALLENGE OF ALIGNMENT

Beyond hiring data scientists, Wang worked to engage people across Vanguard around a more comprehensive, cohesive analytics effort.

Specifically, she sought to create a shared structure, language, and understanding around data science and analytics in a company that already had multiple existing pockets of analytics capability firmwide. "Vanguard has traditionally had very strong analytics capabilities in the investment area," she says. "But they don't call themselves 'data scientists.' They call themselves 'investment analysts' or 'financial analysts.' When you say 'data science' it's very generic and can be anybody who can manipulate data."

As a result, she had to work to align people on what analytics skill sets and competencies were associated with a given job level and grade: "I wanted people to be able to say, 'Hey, I'm working in this division. I'm doing all these things at a level two. So here's what I need to do to get to level three in another division, another group.'" To tackle this challenge, Wang created opportunities to share best practices and post jobs in data science.

Better internal alignment around analytics enabled more fluidity with responsibilities and career paths at Vanguard, as well, which improved engagement and retention. "It's critical to retain analytics talent," Wang says of the change. "It's also a win-win. We realize that we can help to transform the company culture by playing an active role in bringing in new talent, incubating them here, doing things that encourage them to stay here, and looking for the right opportunities to send them to other business divisions. We become like their alma mater."

PROMOTING COLLABORATION BETWEEN BUSINESS AND AIA

Building a more analytics-focused culture also meant educating business managers on how to work with data scientists and others handling AIA. "At the beginning," Wang says, "people thought that we're a reporting function, that we can manipulate data. We would have to step back and say, 'What are the business questions that we're trying to solve? What are our objectives and goals?'" Answering those questions revealed that in many cases the AIA solution required was larger or smaller than the business manager originally had in mind. "Sometimes we had to show the business that their hypothesis is not the right hypothesis," Wang adds.

As people across the company understood the applications of AIA better, the value of the organization Wang was building became more clear. "Now people know we're here," she says. "We have this reputation for solving the most complex questions for the business." This was especially the case for the frontline business-to-consumer (B2C) side of the business: "If you tell people that using this [AIA-driven] tool can allow them to have a really great conversation with the client when they call in, that's great. It makes their job easier." Convincing those on the business-to-business (B2B) side was harder in some cases, especially when people—such as relationship managers—had been successful for decades without help from AIA. Wang says, "It can be harder to encourage them to change their process."

Ultimately, Wang built Vanguard's Center of Analytics and Insights to carry out three primary functions: market research (which existed in the previous organization), data science and machine learning, and analytics enablement. The last area is about implementing analytics training and education across levels of the firm and "pulling together analytics practitioners from different functions to build a community promoting real analytics muscle," as Wang says. "Our analytics community is very broad. Anyone is welcome."

LESSONS LEARNED

One of Wang's largest overarching lessons has to do with implementation. "Implementation is key," she says. "You can build a beautiful model, but if it is not implemented, it's useless. When I think of implementation, I start to think about automation. So, for instance, instead of feeding [salespeople] raw data to digest, what if we just suggest three potential clients every day and say, 'Go talk to them.' But that takes technology, that takes behavioral change, that takes a mindset shift. It takes, to be honest, a lot of leaders starting to think differently and manage differently as well."

Looking back, Wang recognizes how easy it is to underestimate the challenge of building organizational AIA capability. "I could not have prepared myself for the amount of change management that we did," she says. "Senior leadership cannot magically snap their fingers and everything will happen. We really have to work with all the layers of the organization, including the IT team that actually built the application." She tackled that challenge in part by aiming for early, focused wins that would help people see the value of consumer analytics: "You have to show people how it's done. Because it has never been done before."

Canadian Tire Creates an Enterprisewide Analytics System

For Canadian Tire Corporation (CTC), the analytics journey started with training.

"The Tire," as the Canada-based company is known, sells more than just tires, with product offerings in categories including automotive, hardware, home and pet, and sports and recreation, among others. In August 2017, the company created a centralized analytics system to integrate formerly disparate analytics efforts and share capabilities and insights firmwide. Critical components of the system include a strategic, rigorous approach to experiments related to marketing, discounts, and store labor, and a central Data Analytics Council that brings internal analytics groups together to coordinate efforts and reduce redundancy. But it all started with a concerted training effort for leaders firmwide.

Here, CEO Greg Hicks, VP of data analytics Scott Dowding,[3] and retail banner Sport Chek president TJ Flood discuss CTC's process for building strong enterprisewide analytics practices, along with some of the challenges they've encountered along the way.

TRAINING AND DATA

To create a foundation of shared purpose and understanding around analytics, CTC started with training. "Our former CEO Stephen Wetmore sent 400 of our senior team through several days of analytics training at Kellogg in 2017 and 2018," Hicks says. "It was a big investment for us, but one that we believed would be worth it. We always had pockets of analytics expertise, but this was the start of our enterprisewide transformation."

Alongside the training effort, in mid-2018 the company launched Triangle Rewards, a loyalty program that would generate large volumes of data for analysis, with customers earning rewards for purchases at multiple CTC brands—"banners," as the company calls them—including Canadian Tire itself, Sport Chek, and the firm's gas stations. "It was critical for our one-company, data-driven approach," Dowding says. The investment paid off: by late 2019, Triangle Rewards had 9 million active loyalty members, representing about 70 percent penetration of all Canadian households.[4]

"WE KNOW VERSUS WE THINK"

Central to CTC's larger analytics focus has been an emphasis on experimentation, as overseen by a central experimentation team. "Our experimentation team provides the business with a structured environment for A/B testing, providing factual support for business decisions," Hicks says. "Ongoing testing creates a culture of 'we know' rather than 'we think'—business leaders have a platform to prove out theories grounded in their experience and intuition."

CTC aims for true experiments, requiring test and control conditions to create data to draw a causal relationship between actions taken and desired outcomes, such as positive impact on sales or margin. For example, the experimentation team designs high-volume A/B testing by splitting web traffic randomly between alternative landing pages to compare engagement.

"We aim for a 'test-and-learn' process that's cyclical in nature," Flood says. That is, the results of a given experiment often spark ideas for refinement or a new test. As such, CTC breaks the experimentation process into three main components:

- Planning and prioritization
- Design and execution
- Results and impact

Figure 14.1 depicts the comprehensive experimentation process CTC follows. The subsequent sections discuss the three main components noted above.

Planning and Prioritization

CTC centralizes management of testing—across all banners—through the experimentation team. "This ensures tests don't overlap or conflict and provides the opportunity to use learnings from one banner to inspire testing in other parts of the company," Flood says. Monthly experimentation steering committees (including the banner president, lead marketer, VP analytics Dowding, and others) facilitate planning and prioritization of testing. "The business identifies testing ideas and hypotheses and the experimentation team designs the test—including size, scope, and duration," Dowding says.

The senior executives agree that business leaders sometimes push for faster results or more limited scope (to lower the cost to their business), but that the centralized structure helps to prevent test design from being compromised by organizational hierarchy. They provide a paraphrased example of an email exchange illustrating one such conversation:

EXPERIMENTATION LEAD: You asked to add an additional test group of stores to our marketing-promotion test, which reduced test and control group sizes. We will have to double the test duration to eight weeks to accommodate that.
BUSINESS LEAD: Not sure why. Let's stick to the original duration.
EXPERIMENTATION LEAD: To have conclusive results, we need to listen to the data scientists who are experts at designing experiments.

Figure 14.1 Canadian Tire's Experimentation Process

A structured approach to A/B testing provides factual support for business decisions across all banners and functions

Hypothesis / Theory → **Test Design** → **Steering Committee** → **Test Execution** → **Analyze Results** → **Steering Committee** → **Plan Rollout**

Testing is anchored on a specific **hypothesis** from the business

Formulate a specific hypothesis
i.e., Alternative distribution can drive +2% lift in POS

Define success
Breakeven POS growth to offset cost ~+2%

Discuss test limitations
Available budget, distribution constraints, etc.

# of stores/markets, test duration
Statistical power calculations/simulations

Ensures alignment on testing objectives and a design balancing operational limitations with statistical significance

Steering Committee ensures alignment on testing priorities and approach plus visibility across functions

Committee Members
Banner President
Lead Merchant
Lead Marketer
Store Lead
VP Analytics

Coordination/Support
Analytics AVP
Experimentation Mgr

Rotating Guests
Business Owners of recently completed tests

Test designs reviewed to gain alignment on objective, success criteria, and execution. Approved tests move forward to execution and analysis.

Steering Committee provides platform for immediate action based on test results

Determine whether results are conclusive
Were the differences in test vs. control statistically significant?

Results vs. success criteria
Sales growth may have been positive, but did it offset the cost of the CP distribution?

Study store/product attributes
Is the sales lift consistent across urban/rural markets/influence the rollout plan?

Test results and recommendations reviewed to get alignment on actions/rollout plan. Opportunities for additional testing identified.

BUSINESS LEAD: But you don't let an aeronautical engineer fly a plane, do you?

EXPERIMENTATION LEAD: No, but you let them design the plane, or it would be a very short flight!

"The strongest consideration in prioritizing testing is current business priorities," Dowding says. "For example, if the focus is on increasing efficiency, testing will lean toward opportunities to test changes that will reduce costs." Other considerations include magnitude of impact and operational feasibility.

Design and Execution

Once prioritized, a potential test moves to the design phase, including identification of a hypothesis, selection of test and control groups, and estimation of expected sensitivity. Flood says, "The experimentation team works closely with the business sponsor to ensure the test is answering the right question and operationally feasible." Dowding adds, "There's often a gap between an idea to be tested and the actual hypothesis—going from one to the other helps to filter out ideas that haven't been fully thought through. We need to listen to the data scientists who design the experiments."

The team takes great care with sampling and measurement approaches, weighing pros and cons. Most tests use multiple types of measures to validate findings. The two main options are store-level testing—random selection of stores to be in test or control group—and loyalty-level testing, where individual customers are assigned to test or control groups. Nonloyalty customers may still experience test conditions, but only loyalty customer responses can be recorded—not an ideal situation, as the executives acknowledge, as it assumes the loyalty customers are representative of all consumers.

For execution, again the experimentation team and business work closely. A relatively simple experiment might be a promotion tested in a set of stores Canada-wide, with coordination of email, website, and flyer messaging related to the promotion, and avoidance of contradictory offers in adjacent stores. "We need to make sure that only the people near the test stores receive the promotion email," Flood says.

Results and Impact

Upon completion of an experiment, results are reviewed with relevant business partners, followed by presentation to the steering committee leadership team. "Results from one banner can influence testing across others," Dowding says. "But each banner requires its own testing, as we've found the effectiveness of marketing, discounting, and other tactics to vary significantly across banners."

Overall, CTC applies its experimental approach to three areas of investment: marketing (format, content, timing), discounting (such as messaging timing and discount amounts for "spend and get" offers), and store labor (e.g., relationship between total associate in-store hours and sales). Outcomes of interest include quantified sales efficiency, ROI, and others. "We compare the marginal return of varying tactics and invest in the tactic with the highest return," Dowding says.

THE DATA ANALYTICS COUNCIL

A core part of CTC's analytics effort is the Data Analytics Council (DAC), a group of analytics professionals that meets every two to three weeks. "It's a venue and vehicle for information-sharing and collaboration," Flood says. "The idea is to promote regular communications and structured discussion across the multiple data and analytics groups within the company." Among those groups are Merchandising Analytics, Supply Chain, Store Operations Analytics, Marketing/Promotion Analytics, Experimentation and Analytics, and several others.

The DAC aligns firmwide analytics efforts in three ways:

- Driving and influencing data and analytics strategy and road map, including applicability across the enterprise, trade-offs, and investment decisions

- Creating awareness of other teams' analytics, including methodologies, data sources, tools, and requirements
- Fostering a CTC analytics community that spans internal organizations

As such, the DAC works to align and coordinate analytics efforts across CTC (including for the analytics road map and data governance), centralize specialty support functions and leverage their scale (recruiting, education, community building), and share, reuse, and expand analytics capabilities to increase value to CTC (weather-impact modeling, for example).

Early in the year, each group within the DAC presents their objectives for the year, identifying areas for possible collaboration. On an ongoing basis, the council reviews work done by specific groups, including as related to experiments, new data processes, new tools, and others. Concrete examples of value the DAC has created include identification of redundant efforts at web-scraping (it was being performed by three different groups using three separate vendors and was aggregated into one joint effort) and centralization of weather-data sourcing for use in financial planning and analysis, assortment planning, marketing, and other efforts. "We were able to source free government weather data, place it in a centralized data lake, and provide all teams access to it," Dowding says.

Flood highlights another benefit of the DAC: "It provides a forum for support groups to address our analytics community." For example, HR worked with the DAC to standardize analyst levels and naming conventions across the firm, along with benchmarking compensation for comparable roles and coordinating recruiting efforts functional teams had handled separately.

A SUCCESSFUL ANALYTICS SYSTEM

CTC's effort to create a centralized, systematic approach to analytics continues to pay off, with ongoing integration of efforts across the firm and sharing of learning. "We're happy with how the system works," Dowding says, "but recognize it's always a work in progress."

Hicks agrees: "We're continuously looking for new ways to refine and expand. It's important to maintain a culture of learning in analytics, and our system has helped to create that."

All signs suggest CTC's effort will continue delivering value through analytics, while growing that capability firmwide.

Royal Caribbean Sets Sail for Continuous Analytics Improvement

It was a different kind of journey for Royal Caribbean Cruise Lines (RCCL), a leading operator of global cruise lines: one focused on the business's analytics and AI capabilities.

In 2018, Richard Fain, CEO of Miami-based RCCL, was eager to overhaul the firm's approach to driving value with analytics. "We'd been on a journey to better analytics for a while, starting at a fairly low level," he says. "But now we wanted our decision-making to be more methodical, more data-driven."

A key starting point for that journey was a collective belief in the power of analytics, as Fain describes: "We've realized that data-driven decision-making is *better* decision-making, and want ever more accuracy and availability of data; our mantra has been 'continuous improvement'—we're always culturally dissatisfied with what we're doing now, and believe we can always do things better."

Fain and his team had to draw on that mindset continually as they built the right structure and systems for getting the most out of AIA. A critical point was the decision to hire Matt Denesuk as SVP of data analytics and AI in mid-2019. Denesuk had worked previously in analytics for IBM and GE before cofounding Noodle.ai, which delivers enterprise AI services to client businesses. He left Noodle to join RCCL.

Here, Fain and Denesuk describe the voyage they've helped the firm take, including challenges faced and lessons learned along the way.

LEARNING FROM EXCALIBUR

One source of motivation—and data—for RCCL was the Excalibur Project, which the business launched in 2017. The idea of Excalibur was to harness digital technology to facilitate the guest and employee experience using smart devices. For example, Excalibur allowed guests to take a selfie on their phones and then automatically check in using facial recognition technology and board the ship much faster. "It was a digital way of connecting with our customers, a tool to make their lives easier," Fain says. "That led to a cornucopia of new data about what our guests wanted—and we wanted to take advantage of that for better decision-making." Before that, many business decisions were made without a complete view of customer needs. Leadership wanted a more comprehensive, integrated approach.

"We had more data on more things than ever before," Fain continues. "But it was still a by-product as opposed to a target. People were doing amazing things with the tools and the data that they had, but we weren't seeing an orchestrated attempt to accomplish that on a corporate-wide basis." For example, managers in business units were modifying enterprise data for their needs, but not doing this in an integrated way. "So we asked, 'How do we do this better?' The idea was to develop talent in-house and bring in some people from the outside to understand what data to collect and how to make best use of it."

RCCL's board was highly supportive of the push for better analytics. "We devoted half of one full board meeting just to Excalibur," Fain says, as an example. "There was very strong support to take that to the next level. Indeed, the board pressured us to be more, not less aggressive in this quest." Board-member connections also helped RCCL leaders meet with the head of automaker Ford's analytics to gain insights. Similarly, the board helped Fain advocate strongly for analytics: "One board member pulled me aside and said, 'You're going to have a quarter where things are a little weaker and somebody's going to suggest cutting investment in analytics and AI. So be prepared to resist that.' And, sure enough, that is exactly what happened."

With executive and board support in place, the team thought about where to focus the broad analytics initiative. They decided revenue management was a key target, for example—for forecasting bookings. "Most of our revenue management has been based on looking at historical patterns," Fain says. "But historical patterns aren't terribly relevant today [due to COVID], for example, so how do you manage revenue in a world where there's no history? We think data analytics and AI will enable us to use current facts for our decision-making."

FINDING THE RIGHT STRUCTURE

Organizational structure has played a large role in RCCL's approach. Critically, Fain proposed creating a top analytics position—RCCL had never had a top data science and AI role—and having it report directly to him. "It's a fact in corporate America that what reports to the CEO gets the most attention," he says. "And it was an area that most people didn't understand when we started. So having the head of data science report to me was a way of emphasizing to the organization that this is important, that this area would be a key driver of success going forward." Creating the position was part of a broader overall investment in analytics capabilities.

Even with a more analytics-friendly structure and investment in place, organizational resistance is inevitable. In RCCL's case, it came largely from budget pressure. Fain says, "When budgetary time came and everybody wanted to spend more than they had been spending and they saw we were spending all this money on data analytics and AI, it was a very human response to say, 'If you gave me that money I could improve my area more.'"

A MULTIFRONT EFFORT

A pivotal moment in RCCL's journey was hiring Matt Denesuk for the top analytics role. The SVP of data analytics and AI joined in mid-2019.

As communication was central to Fain's vision, he hired Denesuk partly for this skill set: "We had to have the department prove itself to the other senior leaders in the organization. So Matt had to be able to explain to them what he was doing and why it was beneficial. Being able to communicate was a key requirement. He spoke English, rather than technical speak. And he had the technical skills."

While Fain was eager to hire a data analytics and AI leader, Denesuk was initially hesitant: "I'd never been on a cruise or even to Miami. My family was well-settled in California. But the recruiter suggested I just meet the people there. And I was impressed with Richard [Fain]. He asked good questions and had done his homework on me and my last company. I could tell they were really committed to having analytics be a potent strategic function for the company. You often hear people say they want to do something with analytics or AI but they're not really committed to it; there's always resistance at different layers of the organization. But Richard was fully committed, and the board as well."

As he became more interested in the role, Denesuk began to see many potential applications for analytics in the cruise industry. "It's like a city on the water," he says. "But you have total control over almost all the data, even better than hotels and airlines because you have the whole life cycle of the customer—in a hotel, they may not go to your restaurant. So I thought it was a great environment to do cutting-edge analytics and AI." He took the job.

With Denesuk on board, he and Fain thought about next steps. "I didn't give him a lot of guardrails to begin with," Fain says. "I gave him an office, a pad of legal paper, and suggested he develop a plan. I told him we needed sufficient scale that his organization would create a measurable outcome—we didn't want to go to all the effort to have it be inconsequential. We wanted this to fundamentally improve our profitability. He came back with an organization plan and project plans and we were off to the races."

To develop the plan, Denesuk first took the time to learn about the business and its leaders. "I was just a sponge for a bit," he says. That included spending many days early on with the revenue management team, for example. "When people asked about my vision I told them I first just want to learn," he continues. "People think as an analytics expert you can tell them how to do things right out of the box. I tell them it doesn't work like that. So a lot of my early time was spent just identifying the high-value areas, and understanding the data that's there and the analytics capability." As expected, he found a disorganized data structure: "pseudo-data warehouses everywhere," as he said.

Part of Denesuk's charter was also to build a centralized AI and analytics organization in the form of a center of excellence: "In some cases it's just supposed to be a small handful of people who catalyze things around the company. But I think you have to be able to *build* solutions and do things in a rigorous and proper way, with peer review and best practices. That means hiring really good data scientists and data engineers and data analysts. I wanted to work toward this idea of enterprise AI. So we started recruiting right away—partly by giving talks locally and at conferences about how great the cruise industry is to work for." He also worked to develop data dictionaries and other resources to support the effort.

Broadly, Denesuk and Fain sought to reinvent key organizational areas such as revenue management and marketing, starting small-scale. "We wanted positive proof points early on," Denesuk says, "through projects that could show a real dollar impact quickly in these areas." Fain characterized these as "quick early wins": "To give the new effort credibility in the organization we wanted to show people that there were some things we had always been doing a certain way and now we're doing them this way and we've generated more revenue, reduced costs, helped the environment, whatever the standard is." For example, RCCL used improved analytics to look at revenue management and "titrate" pricing decisions, as Fain says— "We saw quick, tangible results." A project to help prioritize actions in the call center provided another quick win.

These efforts emerged from a broader view. Denesuk says, "You do a portfolio model where you inventory the potential business impact of a project and the resource level and risk involved. We did a quick version of that kind of analysis." The analysis and early results helped Denesuk and Fain focus analytics on three broad areas: revenue (demand), customer (experience), and operations (predictive maintenance, supply chain, others). They worked to hire VP-level leaders for each. "I had committed to not poaching top data scientists from elsewhere in the company," Denesuk says, "but realized we couldn't staff the AI and analytics community to the hoped-for level sufficiently quickly, so we aimed to create a 'soft' community across the company, with things like lunch and learns, guidance on best practices, and inviting people in for conferences—to build up our core capability first, then the community and longer-term structure."

Pivotal to the community would be what Denesuk called "data science strategists"—translators who could understand the business and choose and package the AIA projects to be delivered. "They help understand if it's doable and can have some measure of success," he says. "They can speak to the business side and the data analytics side and keep the business 'customer' engaged."

The wins have continued, and as RCCL has improved its use of analytics, it has integrated AI more deeply into operations. "We understand how people react to price changes, so instead of 1,000 price changes a week we may be doing 20,000 now," Fain says. "But it isn't as though we created a 'nerd squad' that does the calculation and sends it over. It was an integration between the IT department and digital department to develop a holistic system."

LESSONS LEARNED

Several lessons have emerged from RCCL's ongoing journey.

One key learning has been around placing the top analytics person in the C-suite, rather than one or two levels below. "The passion or excitement the CEO has for the function is key," Denesuk says. "People in various business units often are already using data and analytics in some way and they want to keep control of it. So they want lots of different analytics leaders—for revenue, supply chain, and others. It's a distributed model. They don't trust a centralized function, or even an outside vendor like IBM. But it's hard to retain good talent in that kind of model—you're going into a small group with a narrow function. Still, it takes a deliberate act to do something central; there are compelling reasons, but the business may not embrace it at first."

Denesuk also emphasizes the general importance of integrating AI and analytics capability with domain knowledge to drive value: "Before, you'd get data and apply mathematical modeling or machine learning to predict something like sales or consulting-engagement win rate. You can build a bunch of models, but it may not work well and not even be worth deploying. So over the years I understood it works when you bring domain knowledge into it, such as being able to know when the dataset is complete or if you need to put some constraints on what you can learn from it. Like when I worked at GE, we really had the knowledge of how they designed and maintained the equipment, so the models were so much better."

Importantly, even with strong analytics and AI capability and domain knowledge, efforts won't always deliver returns. That's where a strong focus helps. "Most things you try in this area fail," Denesuk says. "This is true in any kind of R&D function. This isn't engineering; it's kind of a hybrid within an engineering and an R&D function. What has helped us is a singular focus on a business KPI, rather than a business solution. So the business KPI, not a model, should be your lodestar. Like focusing on maintenance cost. Maybe I can predict statistically when certain classes of components will fail so I can preorder them or get the right labor ready, to reduce that cost. The key is to first focus on the business KPI and not commitment to any path of moving it. Then you can try 20 different ways of moving that KPI, and one of them will probably work eventually."

All lessons RCCL learned are rooted in the theme of continuous analytics improvement. Denesuk says, "It has to be part of the culture. Many companies just put a model in place and it's not a living entity—and it's not documented well, maybe even like a semi–black box." Fain trusted him to help build the right dynamic system for such ongoing improvement: "It was a leap of faith for him," Denesuk says. "And it was communicated to me by various board members how deeply committed they are to this effort." He, in turn, earned their trust through communication and delivery of results: "I've tried to communicate to keep everyone on board, especially about the pace of progress. There's this initial grace period when no one's expecting anything, but then they expect something, once you've been there long enough—like about how much revenue we're going to deliver next year. You have to balance saying the pace of progress is different and giving them some kind of numbers to think about, even if rough."

Ultimately, Fain and Denesuk have built an evolving structure and system that will enable them to continuously improve RCCL's use of analytics and AI to reach even higher-value shores in the future.

STORY 5

Accenture Builds Analytics Capability for Competitive Advantage

New data. New tools. New methods.

That became the mantra at Accenture in 2015, as the consulting giant sought to build and use AIA capability in an unprecedented way—to create large value for the firm and its clients across sectors.

Like its peers, Accenture had decades of experience with data-driven problem-solving, using analytics tools and frameworks to help clients create returns-generating strategies and tactics. In 2011, the firm had created its Accenture Digital unit to house data scientists and design thinkers, acquiring several outside firms to build specialized teams with valuable analytics capabilities.

When Mark Knickrehm was the group chief executive of Accenture Strategy he helped formulate the strategy that led to Accenture Digital. But subsequently, he and other leaders recognized the firm had to take a more *integrative* approach to analytics, for their benefit and that of clients. One of those leaders was Ketan Awalegaonkar, now global head of analytics strategy and advisory at Accenture Digital; he joined the firm in 2017.

The shift to taking a more integrative approach to analytics led to transformative change at Accenture, driven by the "new data, new tools, new methods" approach to client work and organizational structure and culture. Here, Knickrehm and Awalegaonkar explain how they and other leaders worked to bring the new analytics strategy to life, the large value it has helped the firm bring to clients, and the challenges of making the change. Along with the "new data, new tools, new methods" approach, they describe how applying these to client challenges helps businesses move up along three "horizons" of integration and capability as related to data, analytics, and AI.

"WHAT ARE THEY GETTING OUT OF IT?"

"Many of the companies we help have built armies of data scientists and tried to move to the cloud in one way or another," Knickrehm says. "So the question becomes 'What are they getting out it?'" He also points out that Accenture consultants already take an analytic, fact-based approach to their client work: "We don't change clients' minds—and managers don't change leaders' minds—without some set of facts to build a compelling case. We've always had to do that. We're building a case for them to do something different and put a million or billion dollars into an idea."

Doing that successfully, Knickrehm, Awalegaonkar, and other leaders realized, meant taking a hard look at how Accenture treated analytics internally. The firm had always recruited and trained analytical people able to use state-of-the-art data science. But by being more strategic about their own approach to analytics, the firm could ensure clients got the most out of their data, people, and other resources, following Accenture's three-pronged approach: new data, new tools, new methods.

NEW DATA, NEW TOOLS, NEW METHODS

"If you stick with the previous generation's simplified data and analytics, you're not going to be able to ask and answer better questions," Knickrehm says. "If you're not figuring out how to use unstructured data, such as in healthcare, or video and picture data, you won't be able to solve key problems. Strategists and managers may not be the ones hooking things [analytics systems] up, but they have to know the power that sits in them and how to use them to get answers. The data scientists may not know the questions to ask."

Accenture also ensures consultants keep up with the newest AIA tools. "The tools allow you to do things in real time and make changes in real time—and our strategists have to lead the way," Knickrehm says. Here, too, he emphasizes it's about keeping up with fast-changing tools and technologies: "The Excel-based world is moving away. The four big cloud providers—Microsoft, Amazon, Google, and Alibaba—are putting so much money, energy, and focus into their tool sets, like Amazon's Polly product for voice-recognition data, to utilize the power of speech and voice. If you don't know how to use them, you're not relevant anymore. Not just the data scientists, but strategists, too, and not just learning from a book but by working with someone. You don't just outsource it to the data scientists."

For example, R and Python have become go-to coding tools for businesses to create value with analytics. "You can't just relegate coding down to technology," Awalegaonkar says. "You need it for up-front experimentation. Even many of the MBAs we hire from top schools struggle with learning how to navigate this world. They may not need to know how to code, but they need to be able to interpret the outcomes of the code."

Knickrehm notes that those providing the tools are trying to make it easier for non–data scientists to use state-of-the-art analytics tools. "So data scientists need to keep up," he says. "If data scientists are using the same tools as last year, that's a problem. And managers need to step into that void, absorb some of that capability, and push data scientists into other areas. Many of our teams working with major clients don't need a data scientist. They can use the tools themselves."

By "new methods," the Accenture leaders mean new methodologies, or ways of working—everything from Agile approaches to design thinking to scrum teams, with a general focus on smaller, more multifunctional teams.

Over the past decade, Knickrehm, Awalegaonkar, and other leaders had led efforts to learn and combine in-house AIA skills and methods such as design thinking, to be able to bring these to client projects. "For a little over four years we did things mostly on our own," Knickrehm says. After that period, around 2015, the firm brought more data science-based approaches to clients, but soon recognized a problem, as Knickrehm notes: "We were shipping data scientists to clients to do what they wanted them to, but they were mostly just augmenting clients' data science skills; they weren't working collaboratively at the heart of a business problem clients were trying to solve. We had data science scale, but it just wasn't being applied to the right problems. For example, the data science health team presented all the cool things they could do—like solving a problem by combining genetic and other data—but I realized they had no idea what the world of health needs. And they wanted help to do that."

Awalegaonkar agrees: "Earlier, clients came to us and said, 'Give us data scientists and we'll throw them against problems and see what sticks.' Then, the next phase of maturity was about their asking us to use the new data, new tools, and new methods to solve previously unsolved business problems. They said, 'Help us unlock these mega-problems that unlock a couple billion dollars' worth of value.'"

That recognition led to Accenture's combining strategy, data science, and client teams to attack problems such as predicting Intensive Care Unit demand (using GPS-based mobility and other data) in Spain with unprecedented accuracy, to improve capacity planning and resource deployment including through home medical visits for severely ill patients.

"By bringing different skill sets together," Knickrehm says, "we brought data scientists closer to the problems that mattered, and their hypotheses improved, and the strategist now understood the state of the possible—like combining social, picture, and video data and doing similar things across industries." Awalegaonkar adds, "It's also about using machine learning to supplement hypothesis-driven thinking."

Such insights became the motivation to create Nexus—Accenture's program to formalize the integration of capabilities to solve client problems with data and analytics, while continuously building new skill and capacity. "We had to figure out how to differentiate against more established consulting peers," Awalegaonkar says. "The idea was to change the game using AI—to bring the concepts of AI and scaled data to strategy consulting to shift the nature of consulting, to use AI and ML to drive more impactful results." The effort started in earnest in 2017.

THREE HORIZONS OF DEVELOPMENT

Pushing the limits of analytics-driven strategy through Nexus and other Accenture groups and initiatives has helped leadership envision three horizons, or phases, of scaling and development for clients eager to apply AIA.

The first horizon is about companies simply trying to understand the data they have. "They may say, 'I have all this data in my technology stack—what do I do with it?'" Awalegaonkar says. That may result in working toward some level of personalization based on past customer purchase, for example, with the help of a data scientist; often an industry expert, strategist, and data scientist work together in this phase.

The second horizon is partly about using broader data—the "new data" Knickrehm refers to—such as third-party geospatial data, for example, to enhance a personalization strategy, or getting more granular in analyses, such as to understand demand signals more deeply. "The line between data scientist and strategist starts to blur here," Awalegaonkar says. But businesses in this stage often have data and models scattered organization-wide, much of it in Excel and other legacy tools and systems. They lack the structure and organization to scale business strategies without incurring proportionate costs.

That's where what Awalegaonkar calls Horizon 3 comes in. He points out: "We've found that you can't scale digital and AI data in the traditional way. Specifically, clients need a way to manage a world with millions of models and thousands of data elements. So it's about creating prewired assets and algorithms on a very complex digital platform that takes the cost of development way down. It has to be reusable, with very cleaned-up datasets, It's the holy grail, where client companies can scale their business strategy through digital platforms and break the 'scale curve' where your revenue scales way faster than your AI and analytics cost or asset structures. They essentially break the linearity between cost and revenue."

For most businesses, even thinking in terms of the third horizon, which involves much more powerful automation, began in earnest only in 2019. "In this phase," Awalegaonkar says, "the lines between an AI engineer, data engineer, and data scientist blur. It's a whole new world." By his estimate, only a very small percentage of the Global 1000 businesses operate at this horizon.

LARGE CLIENT IMPACT

Proof of Accenture's new strategy's value is in the large, growing client impact they've seen—and increased demand for their consulting work.

"Now we can help solve many previously unsolvable problems," Knickrehm says. "Clients' IT people aren't bringing this to them. In many cases the businesspeople haven't immersed themselves in these new capabilities. In fact, they're sometimes the ones pushing back on what's possible. We have to convince senior clients and do enough piloting to help them see the smoke if not the fire. Now clients are hearing what we can do and saying, 'Can you come back tomorrow?' They're not asking three firms to compete for the business. Our strategists have new tool sets on their laptops and can do much of this even with Amazon tools. Accenture's strategy analyst is like a 'mini data scientist' now."

Consider examples of clients Accenture has helped to reach Horizon 2 and 3 of development. A giant hotel chain, for example, wished to better understand how to convert a prospective customer entering its website with dynamic offers. Again Accenture helped leaders rethink the problem, as Awalegaonkar explains: "Most hospitality businesses don't think about people who don't even hit the consideration set [those who don't come to the site]. It's about looking at external datasets and marrying them in real time to say, 'Why not go launch a banner or display ad to promote to someone based on their search words?' It was a very different way of thinking about it."

In a different domain, a well-known digital video site partnered with Accenture to optimize its personalization algorithms. "You have only microseconds to come up with the next video and ads to offer, based on what they're viewing," Awalegaonkar says. "We created a set of algorithms to guide the process, refreshed multiple times a day. It had to account for millions of permutation combinations per person. We had them think through their logic and helped develop all the analytics behind it. They can handle the product engineering, but we help with the nonengineering functions."

In yet another industry, an energy icon made progress on Horizon 2 with Accenture's help. "They have hundreds of thousands of wells they have to dig and drill, and they're leaving managers to make their own decisions," Knickrehm says. "They're not taking full advantage of all the data, such as 'This well should be drilled this way with these propellants.' They might be able to get 3 to 5 percent more efficiency out of the wells, which would be massive for them."

Accenture has helped the business understand the best conditions for drilling, along with supporting other key decisions with data, as Knickrehm suggests: "It's not just about drilling when the pressure is high enough, but injecting different things in different orders based on the geology. They're combining data into huge databases, putting in more data sensors in the well, and learning. They haven't taken decisions away from the field manager but are making that person a much more intelligent decision-maker."

Similarly, a global fast-food chain has ascended to Horizon 2 and 3 while partnering with Accenture. The business initially wished to understand the impact of store features such as larger drive-through menu boards to highlight new choices. "It worked well for four or five years," Knickrehm says, "then got too complicated for customers and even clogged up the back-end, for their structured cooking process. That caused delays. People didn't like waiting and went somewhere else."

Accenture worked to help the client understand the large volumes of real-time data they were collecting at the drive-through point-of-sale, including by combining video data (who is in the car) with advertising trends, weather conditions, cooking speeds, and other information. The work has led to large-scale investment in a new, more strategic menu system customized to both customer and environment, using predictive analytics to improve the customer experience. "This was a great example of new data, but also new tools and things like scrum design methods, to get the work done fast," Knickrehm says. "We brought strategists and scientists together to figure out how to give customers more of what they want efficiently—a classic business problem."

The food business reached Accenture's Horizon 3 with investment in a highly sophisticated data and analytics platform. "It's a new operating model," Awalegaonkar says. "They're industrializing analytics. It can help them scale initiatives globally across the entire chain at one-tenth or one-twentieth the cost. And it can help them have one store cover a larger area, especially as in-store dining declines and delivery rises." That approach has enabled the business to boost profits—and share price—in recent years, even while annual revenue has remained steady and foot traffic has actually fallen. "You can think of them as more like a tech company now because they want to start to trade on loyalty and platforms," he adds.

Horizon 3 businesses tend to have many times the market capitalization of their peers, as is the case for a major overseas automaker client of Accenture. "They're way ahead with their scaling on digital, AI, and data," Awalegaonkar says. "They invested in their digital infrastructure to scale AI. They use AI on everything from automation in factories all the way through personalization, such as being able to tell customers if they're braking too hard and thus paying higher maintenance costs. They think of themselves as being in the mobility business now." He suggests their new AIA-driven approach will help them survive in an industry increasingly disrupted by "CASE" factors: connected, autonomous, shared, electric.

Any such collaborations, across sectors, require the understanding and buy-in of top management. "We have to help clients' senior management understand why we can use new data, new tools, new methods to solve this problem they've never been able to solve before," Knickrehm says. "We have to be able to articulate it, and help them understand the upside, in terms that matter to them—such as increase in customers coming through or dollars per customer order. The senior Accenture strategist has to be able to do this. And then we need to be able to orchestrate the project." He estimates that over 50 percent of the work Accenture does is helping client leaders construct effective programs, or "putting the pieces together."

Moreover, Accenture works with clients to improve their own analytics capabilities through skills and culture and deploy Accenture solutions. "We need client teams to look different," Knickrehm says. "For example, we often need IT people embedded at the very beginning of projects with the business folks, to do these things faster because they had the needed skill set to put our ideas into practice."

LESSONS LEARNED

Knickrehm acknowledges that driving the internal changes required to transform Accenture's approach wasn't easy: "It's difficult to change people who think they're expert at something. Our data scientists thought they had these problems well-defined and didn't need any of this strategy stuff. And strategists felt they'd been doing analytics since college and asked, 'Why do I need this?' It was the socially engineered magic of bringing them together that made the difference."

One successful change tactic was sending specific groups of strategists and data scientists for analytics training at the Kellogg School of Management, as Knickrehm notes: "It wouldn't work if we just let people randomly go. It was getting the energy data scientists and energy strategists to commit to going at scale. It was about collective learning. We sent them in teams and they kept working in teams."

Knickrehm and Awalegaonkar also helped the firm focus on what senior leaders needed to do differently. "The partners had to sit in those client meetings and articulate a different vision," he says. "That's where it all starts. The demand is so huge for this sort of analytics skill set, but you need senior people with teams backing them up who can actually do it. And changing our most senior leaders' capability is the hardest to do; leaders in different [internal] organizations want their metrics to be sacrosanct. So group leaders had to go to Kellogg, too."

Overall, the large-scale effort has led to a sea change at Accenture, with formerly separate strategy and data science teams coming together to create an "ecosystem" with unprecedented analytics capability to drive client and firm value. "It's a living thing," Knickrehm says. "It has informed our structure and where we want to go in the future." Awalegaonkar simply concludes, "We've changed the game—for ourselves and our clients."

ACKNOWLEDGMENTS

We dedicate this book to our families

The tireless dedication and assistance of many colleagues, friends, and family made this book possible.

We thank all the participants in our executive education programs for their contributions to this book. Many of the examples, cases, and fictional narratives are due to extensive conversations with these senior leaders. We are grateful to the Kellogg students who took our Retail and Customer Analytics courses. They challenged us to make complicated data science accessible and relevant to executives. We thank our colleagues on the Kellogg faculty, especially Eric Leininger for his numerous years of support and mentorship.

Our programs at Kellogg would not have succeeded without the fantastic leadership of Will Garrett, Paul Christensen, Tom O'Toole, Sally Blount, and Francesca Cornelli, or without the support of the entire Kellogg executive education team. We particularly thank Nancy Cacioppo, Carolyn McHugh, Susan Hardy, Dan Chow, and Melissa Passalacqua. The dedicated efforts of Alicia Healy, Barbara Lanebrown, Anne France, Allie Kunkler, and the film crew made our online programs possible.

We thank Sachin Waiker for his extensive effort, mentorship, and guidance in the writing of this book. Our agent, Sheree Bykofsky, and Amy Li from McGraw Hill helped us navigate the unknowns of the publishing world.

Finally, we thank MIT and our mutual advisor Birger Werner-felt—the greatest PhD advisor ever!—for launching our careers.

Eric would like to thank the many coauthors and PhD students who have shaped his research and academic career. He would also like to thank family and friends for their love and support. A special thank you to Quentin, Mary, Pam, Joe, Anne, CC, Judy, Mark, Laura, Mikael, Emi, John, Jennifer, Chris, Diane, and the entire Anderson gang.

Eric's wife, Liz, was always available as a sounding board for ideas and feedback. She spent countless hours editing and proofreading the final versions of the manuscript. He could not have done this without her. Thank you! He also thanks his children, Grace and David, for their patience and encouragement during the COVID-19 summer as he spent hours working on the book rather than going to Nauset beach.

Finally, Eric would like to thank his colleagues on the board of directors and management at Canadian Tire.

Florian thanks his family for enabling his academic career and laying the groundwork for writing this book. He owes much of his success (in life and career) to his parents' love and support (despite not becoming an archaeologist!). His brother, Jeromin, inspired him to apply for a PhD at MIT and has been an unwavering supporter all his life. Florian's wife, Meghan Busse, has taught him much of what he knows about drawing conclusions from data, and she made a writer out of him. She also gave Florian the time—often at great personal cost—to pursue the AI and analytics journey that led to this book. Words cannot express enough thanks. Finally, Florian thanks his children, Jasper and Nicholas, for patiently learning more about "probabilistic equivalence" than any kid should have to!

Florian would also like to thank his mentors and coauthors who have greatly influenced how he thinks about the link between theory, data, and inference.

NOTES

CHAPTER 1

1. The CMO Survey, www.cmosurvey.org (accessed March 23, 2018).
2. Matt Asay, "85% of Big Data Projects Fail, But Your Developers Can Help Yours Succeed, *Tech Republic*, October 10, 2017, https://www.techrepublic.com/article/85-of-big-data-projects-fail-but-your-developers-can-help-yours-succeed/ (accessed March 23, 2018).
3. For example, see Reema Bhatia, "AI Is Here: Is Your Company Ready?," *Forbes*, May 17, 2018, https://www.forbes.com/sites/forbestechcouncil/2018/05/17/ai-is-here-is-your-company-ready/#1ebfcf732776 (accessed December 15, 2018).
4. Michael Lewis, *Moneyball: The Art of Winning an Unfair Game*, Norton, 2003.
5. For proof of how long baseball data has been around, look no further than www.baseball-almanac.com, which includes data for players and teams dating back to 1876.
6. Average ultrasound lifespan information from European Society of Radiology, "Renewal of Radiological Equipment," *Insights Imaging*, October 2014, 5(5): 543–546, https://www.ncbi.nlm.nih.gov/pmc/articles/PMC4195838/ (accessed March 9, 2020).
7. Rajiv Lal and Patricia Carrolo, "Harrah's Entertainment Inc.," HBS Case Number 9-502-011, 2001, p. 6.
8. Harvard Business School, "Teaching Note: Harrah's Entertainment Inc.," 5-502-091, page 9.

CHAPTER 2

1. Jacob Roberts, "Thinking Machines: The Search for Artificial Intelligence," July 14, 2016, https://www.sciencehistory.org/distillations/magazine/thinking-machines-the-search-for-artificial-intelligence (accessed March 31, 2020).

2. Kris Hammond, personal communication. We thank Kris for many conversations that inspired our views on AI.
3. See for example, Andrew Strong, "The Cost of Reliable Wind Energy," Cambridge Consultants, https://www.cambridgeconsultants.com/insights/the-cost-of-reliable-wind-energy (accessed March 10, 2020).
4. Andrew Strong, "The Cost of Reliable Wind Energy," Cambridge Consultants, https://www.cambridgeconsultants.com/insights/the-cost-of-reliable-wind-energy (accessed March 10, 2020); Jack Wallace, "Wind Turbine Downtime and the O&M Team," *Renewable Energy Focus*, January 1, 2009, http://www.renewableenergyfocus.com/view/1397/wind-turbine-downtime-and-the-o-m-team/ (accessed March 10, 2020).

CHAPTER 3

1. We performed this informal analysis using Indeed.com listings (https://www.kaggle.com/elroyggj/indeed-dataset-data-scientistanalyst engineer, accessed on March 13, 2020).
2. Danyel Fisher and Miriah Meyer, *Making Data Visual*, O'Reilly Media, 2018.

CHAPTER 4

1. For example, in Q3 of 2019, GM spent approximately $3,843,000,000 on incentives, which, annualized, corresponds to more than $15 billion in incentive spend. See Cox Automotive, "General Motors: Pushing Sales Aggressively Throughout the Strike," October 28, 2019, https://www.coxautoinc.com/market-insights/general-motors-pushing-sales-aggressively-throughout-the-strike/ (accessed March 15, 2020). For GM's advertising spending see Statista, "General Motors Company's Advertising Spending in the United States from 2007 to 2018," https://www.statista.com/statistics/261531/general-motors-advertising-spending-in-the-us/ (accessed March 15, 2020).
2. "December Sales Will Fall as Auto Industry Sets Record for Transaction Prices, Incentive Spending," Business Wire, December 23, 2019, https://www.businesswire.com/news/home/20191223005125/en/December-Sales-Fall-Auto-Industry-Sets-Record (accessed March 12, 2020).
3. This example is inspired by the paper "1000 Cash Back: The Pass-Through of Auto Manufacturer Promotions." (2006), *American Economic Review*, Vol 96 (4), pp. 1253-1270, by Meghan Busse, Jorge Silva-Risso, and Florian Zettelmeyer

4. Chris Barry, Rob Markey, Eric Almquist, and Chris Brahm, "Putting Social Media to Work," *Bain Insights*, September 12, 2011, http://www .bain.com/publications/articles/putting-social-media-to-work.aspx (accessed March 13, 2020).

CHAPTER 5

1. For more on aircraft auxiliary power units, see "Auxiliary Power Units," Honeywell website, https://aerospace.honeywell.com/en/learn/products /auxiliary-power-units (accessed March 21, 2020).
2. For more on calculations used by digital map applications, see Richard Russell, "How Does Google Maps Calculate your ETA?," *Forbes*, July 31, 2013, https://www.forbes.com/sites/quora/2013/07/31/how-does -google-maps-calculate-your-eta/#1b6a2905466e (accessed March 21, 2020).
3. Telecommunications industry net promoter score average from Sophia Bernazzani, "Net Promoter Score Benchmarks to Help You Understand Customer Loyalty," *Hubspot*, https://blog.hubspot.com/service/net -promoter-score-benchmarks (accessed March 21, 2020).
4. For more on call-center workforce forecasting, see "A Guide to Workforce Forecasting in the Contact Centre," CallCentreHelper.com, https://www.callcentrehelper.com/workforce-forecasting-57254.htm (accessed March 21, 2020).
5. Readers who have a data science background may have noticed that AUC is usually defined under the receiver operating characteristic (ROC) curve. We have found that it is much easier to explain the idea of AUC under the cumulative gains curve. Moreover, the AUC under the cumulative gains curve is just a linear transformation of the AUC under the ROC curve.

CHAPTER 6

1. Dawn Chawn, "The AI That Has Nothing to Learn from Humans," *The Atlantic*, October 20, 2017, https://www.theatlantic.com/technology /archive/2017/10/alphago-zero-the-ai-that-taught-itself-go/543450/ (accessed March 25, 2020).

CHAPTER 9

1. Trygve Haavelmo, "The Probability Approach in Econometrics," *Econometrica* 12, Supplement (July 1944), pp. iii–vi, 1–115, (quote from p. 14).

2. Eric T. Anderson, Nathan M. Fong, Duncan I. Simester, and Catherine E. Tucker, "How Sales Taxes Affect Customer and Firm Behavior: The Role of Search on the Internet," *Journal of Marketing Research*, 47(2), 2010, pp. 229–239.
3. Zack Bhan and Eric T. Anderson, "The Long-Term Cost of Backorder Delays: A Quasi-Experimental Approach," working paper, Kellogg School of Management, 2020.
4. This example is based on a study that one of us coauthored. If you want to see a full-scale implementation of using regression discontinuity and DiD on opportunistic data, see "1000 Cash Back: The Pass-Through of Auto Manufacturer Promotions," *American Economic Review* 96 (4), 2006, pp. 1253–1270, NSF funded (with Meghan Busse and Jorge Silva-Risso).

CHAPTER 10

1. See "Biometrics," U.S. Customs and Border Protection, https://www .cbp.gov/travel/biometrics, and Laura Hautala, "Facial Recognition Can Speed You Through Airport Security, But There's a Cost," CNET, March 21, 2019, https://www.cnet.com/news/facial-recognition-can-speed-you -through-airport-security-but-theres-a-cost/ (accessed March 28, 2020).
2. The name of the CMO in this real example is disguised for privacy reasons.

CHAPTER 11

1. Ron Kohavi, "Online Controlled Experiments: Lessons from Running A/B/n Tests for 12 Years," KDD2015 Keynote Presentation, https://exp -platform.com/kdd2015keynotekohavi/ (accessed March 31, 2020).

CHAPTER 13

1. Honeywell, "The Connected Aircraft," Honeywell.com, https://aerospace .honeywell.com/en/pages/honeywell-connected-aircraft (accessed March 29, 2020).
2. Accenture, "Transforming Accenture into an Insights-Driven Enterprise," Accenture.com, https://www.accenture.com/us-en/success -transforming-accenture-intelligent-enterprise (accessed March 29, 2020).

3. Henry Stewart, "8 Companies That Celebrate Mistakes," Happy Co, June 8, 2015, https://www.happy.co.uk/blogs/8-companies-that -celebrate-mistakes/ (accessed March 29, 2020).

SECTION 5

1. See for example, Landon Thomas Jr., "Vanguard Is Growing Faster Than Everyone Else," *New York Times*, April 14, 2017, https://www.nytimes .com/2017/04/14/business/mutfund/vanguard-mutual-index-funds -growth.html (accessed March 29, 2020).
2. A version of the interview with Jing Wang was published in an eBook, *The Marketing Leader's Guide to Analytics and AI*, Kellogg School of Management, 2020.
3. Dowding is also CFO of the retail banners Sport Chek and Mark's.
4. Jamie Grill-Goodman, "How Canadian Tire Is Turning Customer Data and Personalization into ROI," RIS News, November 13, 2019, https://risnews.com/how-canadian-tire-turning-customer-data-and -personalization-efforts-roi (accessed April 10, 2020).

INDEX

Page numbers followed by *f* refer to figures.

ABOUT THE AUTHORS

Eric T. Anderson is the Hartmarx Professor and Director of the Kellogg-McCormick MBAi program at Northwestern University, Kellogg School of Management. Professor Anderson is the marketing department editor of *Management Science* and was formerly Chair of the Kellogg Marketing Department. He held previous academic appointments at the Booth School of Business and W.E. Simon Graduate School of Business. He holds a bachelor's in electrical engineering from Northwestern University, a master's in engineering economic systems from Stanford University, and a PhD in management science from MIT.

His articles have appeared in such scholarly journals as *Journal of Marketing Research, Marketing Science, Management Science, Journal of Economic Theory,* and *Quarterly Journal of Economics.* He has also published articles in *Harvard Business Review* and *Sloan Management Review.* His papers have received numerous awards for their impact on both practitioners and academics. He has received several awards for teaching excellence at Kellogg.

Florian Zettelmeyer is the Nancy L. Ertle Professor of Marketing and a Research Associate of the National Bureau of Economic Research (NBER). He is the former Chair of the Marketing Department at the Kellogg School of Management at Northwestern University. He founded and directs the Program on Data Analytics at Kellogg, the school's analytics and AI initiative. He was a coeditor of *Quantitative Marketing and Economics* and an associate editor at *Management Science.* He held academic appointments at UC Berkeley and the University of Rochester. He holds a Vordiplom in business engineering from the University of Karlsruhe (Germany), a MSc in economics from the University of Warwick (UK), and a PhD in management science from MIT.

His papers have appeared in the *American Economic Review, Journal of Marketing Research, Marketing Science, Management Science, Quantitative Marketing and Economics,* and *Journal of Consumer Research.* His papers have received several awards for their impact on both practitioners and academics. He has also received many awards for teaching excellence.